THE
SEA
CHANGE

H. Stuart Hughes

THE
SEA
CHANGE

THE MIGRATION OF
SOCIAL THOUGHT, 1930–1965

1817

Harper & Row, Publishers
New York, Evanston, San Francisco, London

Portions of this work appeared in *American Scholar*.

FIRST EDITION

LIBRARY OF CONGRESS CATALOG CARD NUMBER: 74–2989
ISBN: 0–06–011998–5

To the memory of
Hans Meyerhoff

Contents

Preface

THIS study concludes the investigation which I began with *Consciousness and Society* and which subsequently, as I explained in the preface to the second volume of the series, *The Obstructed Path*, developed into a trilogy. Like its predecessors, it is a free-standing work that can be read independently of the others. And as with them, I have followed my by now habitual procedure of writing throughout in the past tense and dispensing with a bibliography.

Two portions of Chapter 3 have earlier figured as follows: the section on Salvemini was given as a Lauro De Bosis Memorial Lecture at Harvard University in October 1971 and was repeated the following May (in Italian) before the Circolo Italiano di Boston; the section on Neumann (in slightly different form) was published in 1969 in *The Intellectual Migration*, edited by Donald Fleming and Bernard Bailyn.

My work on this book confronted me with a new and perplexing problem: here, as opposed to the earlier volumes of the trilogy, I was personally and sometimes even closely acquainted with a number of the protagonists. I hope that the survivors among the cast of characters—and they are lamentably few—will not be too grievously wounded by my critical comments.

During my last year of writing, death carried off three people whose reading of the book would have been particularly important to me: George Lichtheim, who so notably enriched my knowledge of Marxism in all its guises; Karl Loewenstein, the last direct link to Max Weber's circle, who first introduced me as a senior at Amherst College to the universe of German social thought; and

Inge Werner Neumann Marcuse, the widow of one and the wife of another leading figure in this study, who never allowed friendship to stand in the way of expressing the full vigor of her beliefs.

My gratitude goes first to Dorothy Skelley, who typed the successive installments of the manuscript with meticulousness and unfailing good humor; second, to two of my Ph.D. students, Martin Jay and Paul A. Robinson, whose books *The Dialectical Imagination* and *The Freudian Left* I have tried to acknowledge amply in the footnotes to Chapters 4 and 5; and third, to those whose conversation sustained my spirits and contributed to my thoughts in ways of which I suspect they were mostly unaware—Lewis A. Coser, Henry Hatfield, Gerald N. Izenberg, David S. Luft, and John E. Toews.

My wife, Judy, besides giving me constant intellectual companionship, added to her customary and indispensable critique of my reasoning a more specific contribution to my understanding of ego psychology without which the latter part of Chapter 5 would have come out in a far weaker and more tentative form.

THE
SEA
CHANGE

CHAPTER

I

The Great Migration

IN THE PERSPECTIVE of the 1970's, the migration to the United States of European intellectuals fleeing fascist tyranny has finally become visible as the most important cultural event—or series of events—of the second quarter of the twentieth century. Why it took until then to recognize so obvious a phenomenon is something of a mystery. Perhaps it was that the presence of émigrés on the American scene was so much a part of our daily lives that we were unable to see it as "history." Perhaps it required a certain time for the individual aspects of the great migration to sort themselves out: after the passage of three decades and the restoration of European culture, it became apparent that the older generation of the émigrés had died, that those who had returned to their lands of origin had been re-Europeanized, and that the majority who had chosen to remain in their adopted country had been absorbed into American society—in short, that the emigration experience was over.

Some such recognition prompted the almost simultaneous publication of three works on the subject at the end of the 1960's.[1]

1. Laura Fermi, *Illustrious Immigrants: The Intellectual Migration from Europe 1930–41* (Chicago, 1968); Donald Fleming and Bernard Bailyn, eds., *The Intellectual Migration: Europe and America, 1930–1960* (Cambridge, Mass., 1969); *The Legacy of the German Refugee Intellectuals* (special number of the review *Salmagundi*) (Fall 1969–Winter 1970). For an assessment of these studies, see my review article "La grande emigrazione intellettuale," *Rivista storica italiana*, LXXXII (Fasc. IV, 1970), 951–959. One should fur-

From them we have learned a great deal about the scope of the emigration and the activities of its leading personalities. We now have a clear idea of the approximate number and national distribution of the intellectuals who left Europe for the United States. We know that nearly half of them were Germans (or, if one adds the Austrians, two-thirds) and that a corresponding (and overlapping) two-thirds were of Jewish origin. We have had our earlier impression confirmed that French émigrés were comparatively few and that still fewer of them chose to remain in America. And we have discovered—rather more surprisingly—that Italians accounted for only a small percentage of the emigration, their eminence and their success in their new country compensating for the thinness of their ranks.[2]

Beyond the matter of numbers, we have repeated evidence of the intellectual stimulus that emigration provided, of how the experience of living suspended between two cultures fostered rather than confined the flowering of talent. This "creative force of an interstitial situation" was not without precedent.[3] We may think of such illustrious exiles as Thucydides and Dante, or Joseph de Maistre meditating the fate of postrevolutionary Europe in the snows of St. Petersburg. A geographical and emotional displacement has often provided the shock that has set the mind off its familiar course and turned it toward introspection and social or psychological probing. Yet the emigration of the 1930's went beyond any previous cultural experience: in its range of talent and achievement it was indeed something new in the modern history of Western man. The émigrés themselves were "astounded at how much they accomplished" and were "the first to assert that they would not have accomplished as much had they remained in their

---

ther note two earlier, briefer works, Franz Neumann et al., *The Cultural Migration: The European Scholar in America* (Philadelphia, 1953), and Helge Pross, *Die Deutsche Akademische Emigration nach den Vereinigten Staaten 1933–1941* (Berlin, 1955), and the sociological and psychological study by Donald Peterson Kent: *The Refugee Intellectual: The Americanization of the Immigrants of 1933–1941* (New York, 1953).

2. Fermi, *Illustrious Immigrants*, pp. 13, 95, 122. The usefulness of Fermi's statistical analysis of some 1,900 émigrés is limited by the fact that she has cast her net very wide, including, for example, Poles and Russians in addition to her main category of victims of fascism.

3. Editors' introduction to *The Intellectual Migration*, p. 8.

homelands."[4] Of course there were exceptions: older men too weary and disillusioned to adjust to American life, those so wedded to their native languages as to be unable to recast their work in English, the proud and the inflexible who refused to accept positions they thought unworthy of them. Yet the predominant impression they made was one of triumphant achievement in a new land.

How are we to account for this success—and in an America where economic depression and a scarcely concealed anti-Semitism all too often set limits to the welcome the émigrés received? No single explanation or combination of explanations suffices; we have only to recall an Einstein or a Schönberg to realize that the quota of genius among the émigrés was once again unprecedented. Yet there were in addition certain characteristics of America in the 1930's and 1940's that made it receptive of foreign talent to an extraordinary degree. The society was open—far more inclined than that of Germany or Austria or Italy to the recognition of individual merit irrespective of birth or class. Beyond that, it was a pluralist society in which an alien accent occasioned little comment and in which the majority of the citizenry that was not of Anglo-Saxon origin was in these very decades breaking through to positions of leadership. Quite specifically, the institutions of higher learning were more varied and less rigid than the European: in a situation in which individual professors enjoyed little power or prestige, it was comparatively easy to add the foreign-born to their number. And when the Second World War broke out, the government itself proved willing to put into positions of trust men whom it might well have considered enemy aliens. Finally, the very anti-intellectualism of so many Americans challenged the newly arrived Europeans to put their thoughts in a form that the wider public could understand: the theologian Paul Tillich has spoken of this experience as having "deprovincialized" him, to which the philosopher Theodor W. Adorno adds that he became "inclined . . . toward critical self-scrutiny" when he saw that "in America . . . no reverential silence in the presence of everything intellectual prevailed."[5]

4. Fermi, *Illustrious Immigrants*, p. 16.
5. "Scientific Experiences of a European Scholar in America," *The Intellectual Migration*, p. 367.

More particularly, those branches of American activity that were on the verge of making a great leap forward could profit to the full from the arrival of the refugees from Europe. Atomic physics and psychoanalysis offer the two major examples of fields of endeavor in which the émigrés came just at the critical moment—when the native-born, already professionally prepared, were eager for the advanced training and direction that Europeans could give them. These two disciplines, in which the center of gravity definitively crossed the Atlantic during the war years, suggest the extent of a shift in intellectual weight that made the former pattern of deference toward the Old World no longer necessary or appropriate.

This much we now know about the great migration. Its general outlines have been established, and its contributions to American culture have been fully recognized. But the other side of the process is less well understood. It is here that the difficulties begin—and specifically in the sphere of the social thought that underlay and buttressed so much of the work of the emigration. We know that the arrival of the émigrés enriched American intellectual life; we know that it meant a loss for Europe from which the Continent took decades to recover. But what of the refugees themselves? If it is true that they accomplished more than they would have if they had remained at home, did this mean an increase in their own understanding or simply a diffusion of that thought to the larger audience their hosts provided? In widening its influence, did Central European sociology or psychology become shallower? Or did its "sea change" give it a bite and specificity that it had lacked before? In short, how did the experience in America alter the character of thought itself? We can approach this range of questions by going beyond chronicle or external biography to a psychosocial analysis of that experience as a major intellectual drama in its own right.

I. *Lands of Origin*

At the end of the 1920's, Benito Mussolini had already governed Italy for seven years. For the last three of them, his power had stood virtually unchallenged. Italian Fascism had won acceptance at home and abroad as a new form of rule, despotic to be sure, but one which seemed suited to the presumed political immaturity of its subjects. Through his agreement with the Vatican in 1929, the Duce had settled to the satisfaction of the vast majority of his countrymen the quarrel of Church and state that had bewildered the Italians and divided their loyalties for two full generations. So popular indeed was this accord that by 1931 the opposition to the regime was growing weary and demoralized. And in that same year, when an oath of Fascist allegiance was demanded of Italy's 1,250 university professors, only a dozen refused.

These latter, however, were almost all scholars of distinction. And among those who took the oath it was an open secret that hundreds had settled their struggles of conscience by putting ahead of abstract principle their duty to support their families. Such behavior was thoroughly in accord with Italian practice. Most of what Mussolini had done was not. "None of the principal concepts and aspects of Fascism was in harmony with Italian traditions and predilections."[6] Its ruthless application of police power threatened ancient habits of indiscipline and tenacious local pride. Its efforts at ideological indoctrination flew in the face of an age-old skepticism about political formulas of all descriptions. Its self-centered national assertiveness vulgarized and perverted the Italians' proudest claim—that they exemplified the values of a universal humanist culture. With so much to his discredit, it is curious that Mussolini succeeded in winning over to his side the greater part of Italy's intellectuals.

The tradition of skepticism itself prompted a disabused acceptance of the latest political novelty that the turn of fortune had brought to a much-tried people. Beyond that, Fascism both profited by and intensified a drawing inward of Italian culture that was already becoming manifest in the immediate postwar years. Italy's participation in the First World War had brought to a halt the effort at "deprovincialization" associated with the work of Benedetto Croce; for Croce and his like, the rupture with Germany marked a cruel hiatus in their closest philosophical affilia-

6. Leonardo Olschki, *The Genius of Italy* (New York, 1949), p. 455.

tions.[7] Similarly in the arts such experimental movements as Futurism and Surrealism by the mid-1920's had spent their force or been diverted into ideological channels. Meanwhile the country's younger poets were turning to a "hermetic" cultivation of an intensely private aesthetic sphere. Even before Fascism had fastened its grip on Italian cultural life, there was becoming perceptible a separation of that culture from wider European currents of thought and expression.

During the first decade and a half of Mussolini's rule Italy's aging culture hero, Gabriele D'Annunzio, lived impotent and pampered in a fantastically decorated villa on Lake Garda. His gorgeous rhetoric now dried up and outmoded, the self-styled Nietzschean superman accepted with princely dignity the bounty of a regime which by plagiarizing his style had cast him into irrelevance. D'Annunzio's brief moment of triumph had come with his seizure of Fiume in 1919. Two years later the challenger had appeared who was to usurp his place as Italy's foremost creative writer.

In just over a month's time in the year 1921 Luigi Pirandello had written the plays that established his international fame—*Six Characters in Search of an Author* and *Henry* IV. By the time of Mussolini's March on Rome Pirandello had emerged from obscurity to the position of his country's most passionately discussed man of letters. It was quite natural that the recently installed Duce should have been eager to make the new luminary's acquaintance and should have proposed a meeting. What is harder to explain is that Pirandello accepted, wrote of Mussolini in laudatory terms, and even became a member of the Fascist party.

The question of Pirandello's relations with Fascism has both pained and perplexed Italy's intellectuals. The course of those relations in itself suggests the ambiguous reaction of most Italian writers to the Fascist regime and the impossibility of making any simple statements about it. Initially Pirandello shared the widespread sentiment that Mussolini had given his country the order it desperately required, along with the illusion that his rule would be milder than it in fact proved to be. Subsequently the dramatist's

7. Benedetto Croce, "La Germania che abbiamo amata," *Propositi e speranze* (1925–1942): *scritti varî* (Bari, 1943), pp. 33–45.

ardor cooled, he insisted more sharply on his own independence, and in the early 1930's he spent much of his time abroad, assuming when at home an attitude of "absent-minded compromise, which relapsed every so often into insincerity and adulation of the Duce," until his death in 1936.[8] In Pirandello's case, self-seeking prompted to only a minor extent his conformist behavior; the official subsidies his theater received were modest and unreliable. It was rather that Fascism had struck a chord in his nature which his public never suspected and which was apparently in radical opposition to the implicit ideology of his own writings.

Ostensibly there was nothing Fascist about Pirandello's plays. Quite the contrary: the emotional universe they depicted—atomistic, dissociated, relativist—seemed to undercut or dissolve the rhetoric of solidarity that the regime propagated. Below the surface, however, Pirandello's behavior suggested fright at what he himself had revealed about his fellow men—and at the success that had greeted it. His victory had preceded Mussolini's by only one year: the two events had become linked in his mind, as he tried to exorcise by a punctilious loyalty to his chief the scandalous act of dissection he had performed on his own class. After the vertiginous period in which he had led his characters to the brink of madness, he appreciated the "normalization" that Fascist rule provided. Of solid bourgeois stock, catapulted to fame in his mid-fifties, Pirandello never lost the ideological timidity, the distrust of democracy and socialism, that betrayed his origins.[9] Nor could he shake off the sense of injury at the hands of better-known writers which his long years of obscurity had left with him. It was symptomatic of his spirit of contradiction and distaste for his peers that he chose precisely the wrong moment to announce his adherence to the Fascist party—the aftermath of the assassination of the Socialist deputy Giacomo Matteotti, when the regime itself was in danger of collapse and when a number of the prominent intellectuals who had at first endorsed it began to have second thoughts.

Chief among those who withdrew their support and against whom Pirandello nursed a particular grievance was Benedetto

---

8. Gaspare Giudice, *Luigi Pirandello* (Turin, 1963), p. 455.
9. *Ibid.*, pp. 441–448.

Croce. If the former had become Italy's most debated writer, the latter remained its most influential. Paradoxically enough, Croce's conversion to anti-Fascism strengthened rather than diminished his intellectual dominance. For the Neapolitan philosopher— serene, self-confident, and respected by Mussolini as untouchable—had license to say the things his countrymen dared not utter, in part because he did so in a lofty philosophical form that held no active threat for the regime. (And being a private scholar of ample means, he was not obliged to confront the moral dilemma of the oath that vexed the university professors.) With Croce in charge of the literary opposition, intellectual competition lapsed. Younger social thinkers failed to appear; the older ones disappeared or fell silent. In 1930 Vilfredo Pareto had been dead for seven years, carrying with him to the grave the secret of what he really thought of his country's new regime; Antonio Gramsci was wasting away in one of Mussolini's prisons, patiently composing the fragmentary writings that were to lie unpublished for another two decades; Gaetano Mosca had ceased to speak out on political matters, after delivering at the end of 1925 his last address in the Italian Senate—a dignified refusal to vote for the basic law establishing the Fascist dictatorship. Croce had likewise opposed the law; after another half-decade he too decided that it was no longer worth his while to exercise his rights as a senator.[10]

Secure in his Neapolitan *palazzo* or his villa at Sorrento, Croce maintained his hegemony over Italian cultural life. And the character of his influence changed markedly during the interwar years. Before 1914, Croce had raised the level and enlarged the range of Italian thought; even his hostility to social science had acted as a force of liberation, since his target had been a dogmatic "scientism" or positivism in the study of human affairs. After the war, Croce's example had the reverse effect: with a nonpositivist social theory now in the field (as in the case of Weber) or one whose implications extended far beyond its positivist origins (as with Freud) Croce's continued refusal to countenance sociology or psychology, his unrelenting denigration of them as confused and merely practical in aim, discouraged younger men from venturing

10. For a comparative analysis of the work of these four social thinkers, see my *Consciousness and Society* (New York, 1958), Chapters 3, 6, and 7.

into territory which was both philosophically suspect and ideologically dangerous.

Croce disliked social science for his own abstract reasons; Mussolini feared it as potentially subversive. Their double condemnation made its pursuit almost impossible during the Fascist years. The quite accidental convergence of Croce's distaste and the hostility of the regime is apparent in the vicissitudes of psychoanalysis in Italy from a promising start to near-extinction.

As early as 1910 the Florentine literary review *La Voce* had published a special issue devoted to "the sexual question" in which the work of Freud had been discussed with respect. Here and there Italians with inquiring minds were beginning to look into the new theories emanating from Vienna. But it was as philosophy rather than as therapy that psychoanalysis first impinged on the Italian mind—a philosophy loosely associated with the antipositivist views of Henri Bergson or William James. Italy's participation in the First World War ended this phase of tentative inquiry: with Austria the nation's enemy, the intellectual products of the Hapsburg capital were automatically quarantined. And by the time that scientific ties were reestablished with Vienna, the Fascist regime was already on the horizon.

Mussolini and his ideological associates could not fail to distrust a theory of the emotions that at the very least relativized and reduced to human proportions their own ethic of strenuous endeavor. And in this one respect the official verdict echoed the popular attitude: Freudianism struck the average Italian as morbid and foreign to his country's "Mediterranean" health of mind. Such was also the view of the Catholic Church—which had its theological reasons for objecting to the atheist, pansexual, and determinist implications of psychoanalytic theory. As a predominantly Catholic country, Italy proved even more reluctant than France to accept the teachings of Freud. This resistance found sanction in the opposed but mutually reinforcing objections of philosophers and men of science, most of whom were unbelievers in matters of religion.

The medical men and the psychologists remained true to the tradition of Cesare Lombroso, the physician and speculative anthropologist who had figured as one of the most influential

European positivists of the late nineteenth century. To the disciples of Lombroso, a physiological or organic explanation sufficed for the disturbances that psychoanalysis delineated in terms of unconscious emotional conflict; hence, Lombroso had made Freud superfluous. To the idealist philosophers and literary critics, Freud's work smacked of the positivism they loathed; hence, they were inclined to assimilate Freud to the familiar and detested Lombroso. (Croce's attitude was more nuanced, but he too misunderstood psychoanalysis and linked it with a miscellany of intellectual tendencies he scorned.) "On the pretext that there had already been Lombroso, the Italian scientists rejected Freud. . . . On the same pretext, and encouraged by the attitude of the scientists, the men of letters and the critics likewise rejected Freud. With the former, the pretext was disguised as love for Lombroso, with the latter as hatred" for the very same man.[11]

Under these circumstances, it is remarkable that psychoanalysis made any headway at all during the interwar years. Yet in 1925 the Italian Psychoanalytic Society was founded; Trieste and Rome became the centers of modest clinical progress; and in 1931 Freud's most authentic Italian follower, Edoardo Weiss, published a series of lectures that for the first time gave his countrymen a clear idea of psychoanalytic theory. One explanation for this slow but cumulative advance was that the movement was too obscure to attract much unfavorable attention. Another was the relative tolerance of Mussolini himself, who in the spring of 1938, at the time of the Nazi annexation of Austria, received Weiss in person and offered either to intervene with Hitler on Freud's behalf or to give him refuge in Italy. The master chose to go to England instead. And later in that same year a misfortune descended upon the psychoanalytic movement that scattered its adherents or drove them underground for the next seven years.

Mussolini's imposition of anti-Semitic laws on the German model had nothing to do with hostility to psychoanalysis. But since the greater part of its adepts, in Italy as elsewhere, were of Jewish origin, its diffusion and practice necessarily suffered. Weiss and most of his colleagues went into exile, where they played only

11. Michel David, *La psicoanalisi nella cultura italiana* (Turin, 1966), pp. 7–8, 18–24.

a minor role in the post-Freudian evolution of psychoanalysis in the Anglo-American world. A few stayed on in Italy, temporarily diverting their professional endeavors into more acceptable channels. Until the mid-1940's, in Italy as throughout Central Europe, psychoanalysis virtually ceased to exist.

Before disappearing from the Italian scene, it had left behind a literary monument that showed a greater familiarity with its theory than any comparable work in French. Some found Pirandello's plays Freudian in inspiration; this the dramatist vigorously denied, alleging quite correctly that he had made his psychological observations on his own. It was Italo Svevo, rather, the Triestino author of *The Conscience of Zeno*, published in 1923, who came closest to being Italy's psychoanalytic man of letters. Living in a city of mixed population and cultural affinities that had only recently passed from Austrian to Italian rule, well acquainted with both James Joyce and Edoardo Weiss, Svevo was attracted to psychoanalysis without ever fully assimilating it. Alternately respectful and rebellious, eventually taking refuge in an ironic detachment from Freudian influence, even Svevo shared the multiple hesitations with which Italy's avant-garde intellectuals approached the psychoanalytic universe.[12]

And on a wider scale, the same hesitancy marked Italian social thought as a whole. After its triumphs of the early twentieth century, it had become conventional; Croce and his followers had drawn its sting. Hence the greater part of its practitioners found themselves able to bypass the Fascist experience. They treated it as little worse than an encumbrance. "In other countries subjected" to such a regime "most writers chose between scornful rejection and fiery involvement: the intellectuals of Italy were more often cautiously and politely indifferent."[13]

In retrospect their timidity has not passed unquestioned. One of the most sensitive and scrupulous of the young professors who took the oath, recalling the incident nearly four decades later, has concluded that he made the wrong choice:

12. *Ibid.*, pp. 58, 66, 371–372, 374–375, 379–380, 385.
13. P. Vita-Finzi, "Italian Fascism and the Intellectuals," *The Nature of Fascism*, ed. by S. J. Woolf (New York, 1968), p. 244. See also Emiliana P. Noether, "Italian Intellectuals under Fascism," *The Journal of Modern History*, XLIII (Dec. 1971), 630–648.

For us professors who . . . did not refuse the oath . . . people later tried mercifully to find a justification: we saved the possibility of educating young people, of maintaining the university at a cultural level that subsequently permitted a cohort of anti-Fascists to emerge from those indoctrinated by the regime. . . . One should recognize that the university climate during the Fascist period was not entirely suffocating. . . . The most implacable Fascists, the toughest ones, were unrefined and of limited intelligence, incapable of catching on to the "poison" in a line of reasoning that did not seem actually to offend the regime. . . . In educated spheres the tone was set by "converts" who wanted to persuade themselves and others that they had not changed, that they had not abjured the values of their youth, . . . [and who] . . . left uncensored an analysis that might stimulate in the young a judgment on the regime, a historical allusion that invited a comparison. . . .

While risking scarcely anything, we were able to educate the alert minority among the young . . . to reason and to compare. . . .

But having recalled all that, I must add that the justification found for us is worth very little.

Those who chose the right road were those who . . . outside Italy, among the exiles, renounced their university chairs and bore witness.[14]

In fact, only a small minority emigrated. And these left Italy in two waves. The first departed in the mid or late 1920's, when the despotic character of the regime had become clear. The second—and much larger—exodus came in 1938 and 1939 after the inauguration of Mussolini's anti-Semitic campaign. Parenthetically we should note that this series of actions once again violated the traditions of a people which nourished little hostility against the Jews. Italy's twentieth-century fall into anti-Semitism was to be only a brief hiatus in its dominant experience of tolerance and assimilation.

14. Arturo Carlo Jemolo, *Anni di prova* (Vicenza, 1969), pp. 145–146.

Aside from those of Jewish origin—and Italy's Jews were far less numerous than those of Germany—few among the emigration could be counted as primarily intellectuals. Most of the more prominent figures were political activists, intent on overthrowing the regime which governed their country. And at first the militant among them preferred to live in France rather than in Britain or America, since it bordered directly on Italy and was culturally more familiar to them. This activist emphasis, this tarrying on the European Continent as long as possible, distinguished the Italian emigration from the German or Austrian. It meant that among the Italians there occurred no such wholesale transplantation of Old World culture to the New as was effected by the refugees from Central Europe.[15]

Hence it is not surprising that the achievement of the Italian emigration in the field of social thought was largely confined to a critique of Fascism itself. When a prominent literary critic such as Giuseppe Antonio Borgese or a historian like Gaetano Salvemini came to the United States, it was as an analyst of Fascism that he made his mark. The polemical task of passing judgment on Mussolini crowded out his more abstract concerns and gave his writings a severely practical purpose.

North of the Alps fascism had failed in its initial bid for power. The postwar discontents that in Italy had swept Mussolini into office, in Germany had spent themselves in a many-sided struggle that in the end left bourgeois democracy in control. After the collapse of his Munich *Putsch* in 1923, Adolf Hitler required another decade to fight and cajole his way to the chancellorship of the Reich. The years in which Italian Fascism was steadily consolidating its control were the years of Weimar Germany's reprieve—the second half of the 1920's, when contemporaries were lulled into the illusion that economic prosperity and a conciliatory foreign policy had together exorcised the "demonic" in German politics and ideology.

15. On this whole subject, besides Fermi, *Illustrious Immigrants*, pp. 48–51, 116–123, see Aldo Garosci, *Storia dei fuorusciti* (Bari, 1953), and Charles F. Delzell, *Mussolini's Enemies: The Italian Anti-Fascist Resistance* (Princeton, N.J., 1961), Chapters 2–4.

The fact that the advent of fascism in Italy and its progress in Germany were out of phase meant that Europe's intellectuals awoke to the reality of life under such a regime only when it was too late to do anything about it. While the Italians were making their personal adjustments and concessions with little sympathy from abroad, their German counterparts were at the height of their international cultural prestige. The fortuitous circumstance that the Weimar Republic's last years coincided with the zenith of its intellectual achievement made all the more bitter the succeeding experience of barbarism.

Already the turn of the decade had a precarious atmosphere that gave a special intensity to the life of the mind. With anxious clairvoyance Karl Mannheim peered into the future in the series of essays entitled *Ideology and Utopia* with which in 1929 he assessed his predecessors' struggle to define the ideal bases of society. A similar mixture of assurance and trepidation characterized Berlin's new status as the most stimulating metropolis in the Western world. While Paris might be more beautiful and London more urbane, there was in Berlin an appreciation of aesthetic novelty, a sharpness of tone, a quickness of mind, a juxtaposition of contrasting styles, that persuaded men of talent to put up with its lack of outward charm and the abrasiveness of its personal encounters. In the late 1920's Berlin finally became the unquestioned cultural capital of the German-speaking world. Munich, Frankfurt, and the rest kept their former eminence, but the city on the Spree was the place where the young and the gifted preferred to go.[16] Even Vienna found itself outclassed. With the Hapsburg Empire shattered and Austria shrunk to an exclusively German state, its capital was no longer as self-confident or as cosmopolitan as it had been before. Vienna lived on its aesthetic memories and cultivated a distaste for modern technology. It too had to defer to Berlin.

The Austrians in 1919 had expressed a decided preference for union with the Reich. This the victorious Allies had prevented, and the *Anschluss* of the two nations was not to be achieved until

16. For an evocation of Berlin's cultural life in the late Weimar years, see Peter Gay, *Weimar Culture: The Outsider as Insider* (New York, 1968), pp. 128–132.

1938 under the very different circumstances of Nazi rule. Meantime Central Europe had found unity in the cultural sphere. The distinction between Germans and Austrians had become blurred, as large numbers of the latter, discouraged by the depressed economic circumstances and the lack of opportunities in their own country, sought careers in the Reich. With the creation of the Slavic successor states to the Austrian Empire, German-speaking professional men no longer had access to positions they had once nearly monopolized throughout the former Hapsburg domains.[17]

Hungarians encountered comparable difficulties. Hungary's intellectuals, mostly Jewish and leftist, had already begun to suffer from discrimination in the early 1920's—even before the consolidation of Fascism in Italy. Since they generally spoke German with ease, they could readily move to Vienna or Berlin, where they became absorbed in the local intellectual milieu. Hence when they were forced to make a second move—this time across the Atlantic —they were scarcely distinguishable from Germans and Austrians. In the great migration, as in the culture of the 1920's, the Central Europeans shared a common experience. The chief difference was that those in Berlin or Munich were obliged to leave after 1933, while the Viennese could wait another half-decade.

For independent-minded German-speaking intellectuals, the course so many Italians pursued of pretending to ignore their country's new regime was not a realistic option. For one thing, the imposition of the Nazi *Gleichschaltung* was too rapid and rigorous to permit such evasions. For another, the high percentage of Jews among the German and Austrian intelligentsia meant that many who were not ideologically suspect were threatened on "racial" grounds. Yet for the most part Jewish origin and anti-Nazi sympathies paralleled and reinforced each other: those who manifested either or both found themselves automatically barred from the German "folk" community. The decisive reason why German-speaking writers and professors confronted a sterner ethical choice

17. Karl Mannheim, *Man and Society in an Age of Reconstruction*, trans. from the German by Edward Shils (London, 1940), p. 99 n. For a characterization of the Viennese intellectual milieu in the 1920's, see William M. Johnston, *The Austrian Mind: An Intellectual and Social History, 1848–1938* (Berkeley and Los Angeles, 1972), pp. 73–75, 391–396.

than their Italian counterparts was that the predominant definition of Germanism was harsher and more exclusive than that of
italianità.

During the 1920's a split in German culture had become evident
which in fact went far back into the preceding century. In the
ebullient, multiform intellectual life of the Weimar Republic the
basic cleavage ran between those who adhered to a *völkisch* ideal
and those of cosmopolitan sympathies. In retrospect the latter
were to seem more typical of Weimar culture—the former, if less
eminent and original, were always numerically stronger and surer
of their popular backing.

In its simplest form there was nothing particularly sinister about
the *völkisch* ideal. Its celebration of rootedness in the soil did not
differ notably from the nationalist doctrine propagated by Maurice
Barrès in France; the Germanic theorists shared with the French a
spuriously naïve admiration for peasants and the rural life. Yet the
German notion of harmony between man and nature had racial
and metaphysical connotations that were lacking elsewhere:

> The nature of the soul of a Volk is determined by the native
> landscape. Thus the Jews, being a desert people, are . . .
> shallow, arid, "dry" . . ., devoid of profundity and totally
> lacking in creativity. Because of the barrenness of the desert
> landscape, the Jews are a spiritually barren people. They thus
> contrast markedly with the Germans, who, living in the dark,
> mist-shrouded forests, are deep, mysterious, profound. Be-
> cause they are so constantly shrouded in darkness, they strive
> toward the sun, and are truly *Lichtmenschen*.[18]

Few leading German intellectuals of the 1920's would have
subscribed without qualification to such a set of propositions. But
the style of thought was congenial to a majority among them.
Moreover, certain ideological corollaries of "Germanic" thinking
were embraced by a great many who would not have characterized
themselves as *völkisch*. Among these associated ideas was the old
distinction—which Oswald Spengler had popularized and to
which even Thomas Mann had succumbed in his wartime writ-

18. George L. Mosse, *The Crisis of German Ideology: Intellectual Origins
of the Third Reich* (New York, 1964), pp. 4–5.

ings—between Germany as the dwelling place of authentic "culture" and France as the epitome of a "civilization" that was superficial, charming, and merely clever. Along with it went a conviction that what bothered foreigners about the Germans was in reality the source of their superiority: their country's troubled, erratic behavior betokened its spiritual depth, and the outbreaks of ferocity to which it was intermittently subject were signs of a "demonic" force that could be in turn creative and destructive. In short, the Germanic wing of professors and writers were quite happy to recognize and to extol the elements in the national tradition which marked it off from the "civilized" West—for example, its apparent unfitness for parliamentary democracy. They took pride in the very same manifestations of national uniqueness that were a cause of anguish to those of cosmopolitan leanings.

That the Germanic—or *völkisch*-minded—welcomed the advent of National Socialism is a matter of historical record. It is also relevant to add that they got rather more than they anticipated. Here lay the fundamental ambiguity of the Nazi ideological experience. Initially Hitler appeared to be doing no more than what the Germanic theorists had long aspired to: giving strong leadership to a healthy and united people and bringing into the fold those beyond the national borders who shared its speech and its cultural traditions. Few suspected that this was only his minimum program, that hidden within the literal meaning of the Führer's rhetoric lurked a project without precedent in history. The peasant and warrior mentality which the *völkisch* had preached ended in war—this was to be expected. What only a handful of Germans ever fully grasped was that the conflict in question was eventually to lose all semblance of a struggle for recognizable national ends, that it was to become an endless, insatiable succession of acts of pillage and annihilation, with "racial" victory the final and unattainable goal.[19]

As this macabre scenario unrolled, more and more German intellectuals took refuge in what they called "inner emigration." They quietly dropped out of the National Socialist consensus. At

19. This is in substance the line of reasoning in Ernst Nolte's *Der Faschismus in seiner Epoche* (Munich, 1963), trans. by Leila Vennewitz as *Three Faces of Fascism* (New York, 1966), pp. 407–414.

its lowest level, inner emigration meant little more than prudent silence; it was thoroughly familiar to writers and professors who had regarded as another mark of their countrymen's superiority their ability to stand "above" the political battle. An aloof neutrality which in practice meant conformism had in the past been the normal stance of German men of letters. In this cautious guise, inner emigration meant merely reverting to type. There were a few, however, for whom it signified a proud and conscious secession from the national community. After a harrowing stay in a concentration camp, which he was subsequently to narrate in *Der Totenwald*—the forest of the dead—the novelist Ernst Wiechert found no recourse but silence. Similarly, in the stillness of his Munich lodging the Catholic essayist Theodor Haecker composed the *Tag- und Nachtbücher*—the diaries by day and night—in which he set down his anxious musings on the evil he saw around him.

Thus in its various guises the experience of inner emigration bridged the gap between the Germanic and the cosmopolitan intellectuals. Yet for the most part only the more conservative among the latter were able to fall back on such a course. The rest found the atmosphere of Nazi Germany stifling; they could not bear to witness its brutalities and lies and the indignities it inflicted on their Jewish acquaintances. Besides, they were already marked down as potential dissidents. Some lost their jobs; others departed after receiving official threats or warnings from their friends. In the early years of Hitler's rule, nearly 1,700 scholars and scientists were dismissed from their posts, including more than 300 professors; something over three-quarters of these were of Jewish or partly Jewish origin. And a correspondingly high percentage emigrated. The absorption of Central European thought by Britain and America from the 1930's to the 1950's was to be facilitated by the fact that that thought was transmitted by the heterodox wing of the German-speaking intelligentsia whose vocabulary and conceptual frame were closer than were those of the orthodox majority to the rational-empirical tradition of the West.

Cosmopolitanism, pacifism, left-wing sympathies—or perhaps a merely generic *esprit frondeur*—these were the marks of a dissidence that dated from the Wilhelminian era and that under the Republic had for a brief period come close to setting the dominant tone. Its foothold in the universities was never extensive or secure. Although there were influential professors such as the historian Friedrich Meinecke who supported the Republic and its democratic institutions, they tended to be sober-minded scholars with few links to the life of active politics; there seem to have been only four academics of any prominence who took a Marxist line—among them Karl Mannheim (whose ancestors were both Jewish and Hungarian!). The real home of the dissident and cosmopolitan-minded was the world of journalism and the arts. Here wit and scorn could range untrammeled by professorial inhibitions.

It has frequently struck foreign observers that the land of the murky Germanic ideology was also the nation that produced Heinrich Heine and Karl Marx and Friedrich Nietzsche—that "so many of the great debunking analysts of modern culture" were "German or Austrian, not English or French." It was as though the arrogance and self-assurance of the majority made fury or irony their opponents' only recourse. "The result was that mild criticisms of conventional notions were very hard to express. To challenge the orthodox at all, the critic almost had to make a leap into a new vocabulary."[20]

The chief of the new vocabularies was that of psychoanalysis—as the greatest of the German-speaking "unmaskers" was Sigmund Freud himself. In the cosmopolitan milieu where Anglophilia or Francophilia or Semitophilia (or combinations of them) reigned, the single clearest sign of membership in the fraternity of dissidence was an acceptance of the psychoanalytic way of thinking. Right up to the Nazi takeover, Central Europe remained the stronghold of psychoanalysis. Vienna, as Freud's home city, was of course its capital. But Berlin had become a close rival: alone among the Psychoanalytic Institutes that of Berlin could hold its own alongside the Viennese. It was here that in 1922 Freud had delivered his last public theoretical utterance. The city where he found his most faithful immediate disciples—Karl Abraham and

20. Fritz K. Ringer, *The Decline of the German Mandarins: The German Academic Community, 1890–1933* (Cambridge, Mass., 1969), pp. 201, 240–241, 440–441.

Max Eitingon and Hanns Sachs—was also the place where some of the most imaginative analysts in the emigration received their training.

While Germany's intellectual dissenters frequently tried to be classless or "bohemian" in their style of life, its leading social thinkers remained "bourgeois." This was certainly true of practicing psychoanalysts, whose personal habits—however permissive their theoretical beliefs—were for the most part conventional. The same was true of the few but eminent figures who held university chairs. And it was even the case with a major creative writer such as Thomas Mann. Yet the dissident intellectuals' adherence to bourgeois values and a bourgeois life style did not pass unquestioned: it was a constant source of perplexity to men who could not help asking themselves whether the lack of congruence between the boldness of their ideas and the cautious way in which they conducted their lives betokened some hidden inauthenticity. The question of the viability of "bourgeois humanism" in an apocalyptic era was the first of two nagging and related problems that such humanists carried with them into exile.

The second was that of *Geist*—of intellect or mind or spirit (depending on how one chooses to translate a German term heavily laden with favorable implications). In this respect the difference between the Germanic majority of the intellectuals and the cosmopolitan-minded minority was not so great as might be imagined. Most of the latter spoke of *Geist* in very nearly as awestruck tones as did the conventionally educated among their countrymen. And the notion of their own roles was correspondingly exalted. As the purveyors of *Geist*, German writers and professors had claimed the status of "a priestly caste" legislating "ultimate values to a peasant population." In the 1930's, despite the buffeting it had received in the world of reality, this claim was still confidently advanced: even some of those who regarded themselves as cultural revolutionaries—men like Theodor W. Adorno, Max Horkheimer, and Herbert Marcuse—remained sufficiently close to the teachings of Hegel to find no inconsistency in such a stance. The "abstract language of cultivation" was the common coin of German men of letters.[21] It was bound to clash

21. *Ibid.*, p. 268.

with the vocabularies current in the Anglo-American world—and in so doing to reinforce the doubts that the more self-questioning of the émigrés already entertained about it.

II. *The Literary Precursors: Hesse and Mann*

The émigrés' John the Baptist was Hermann Hesse. When Hitler came to power Hesse had already been living in the wilderness for two decades—if one can refer in such terms to the idyllic village in Italian Switzerland where he had eventually settled. In 1933 his reputation as a novelist rested primarily on the two works in which he had addressed himself to his countrymen's characteristic intellectual vices: *Demian,* of 1919, with its torrential assault on hypocrisy and conformism; and *Steppenwolf,* of 1927, in which he had chronicled his own unavailing efforts to come to terms with bourgeois society and in the process had attempted the infinitely more difficult feat of subjecting to the play of a relativizing irony the values of pacifist-minded intellectuals like himself.

Thus there was something disconcerting about Hesse's role as Germany's literary exile of longest standing. Regarded from afar, his credentials appeared impeccable: those who took flight after 1933 might well have admired the foresight of a man who even before the First World War had sensed where his nation was heading. More closely regarded, however, Hesse had little to teach his countrymen that could be of use during the twelve years of Nazi rule. It was not only that *Steppenwolf* had suggested a withdrawal from daily struggle to the crystal spheres where the laughter of the immortals—Goethe, Mozart, and the rest—echoed in mockery of human self-righteousness. Beyond that, the two novels with which Hesse followed it were still more detached and allegorical. And by 1934, when he published the introduction to what was to be his most ambitious work, *The Glass Bead Game,* Hesse's evolution into a proponent of pure aesthetics and intellectualism seemed complete.

The game that this introduction outlined epitomized the loftiest ideal of *Geist.* "A . . . virtuoso flight through the realms of the mind," it embodied in imaginative form a synthesis of the cultural creations of the Western world:

> The Glass Bead Game is thus a mode of playing with the total contents and values of our culture. . . . All the insights, noble thoughts, and works of art that the human race has produced in its creative eras, all that subsequent periods of scholarly study have reduced to concepts and converted into intellectual property—on all this immense body of intellectual values the Glass Bead Game player plays like the organist on an organ. . . . Theoretically this instrument is capable of reproducing in the Game the entire intellectual content of the universe.[22]

Music and mathematics provided the rules and precedents for its meticulous ritual. Indeed, the Glass Bead Game could most readily be thought of as a theme and variations—or as a series of themes drawn from disparate fields of cultural endeavor that were set in an elaborate contrapuntal relation to each other. Hesse's descriptions of the game were deliberately vague: he evidently wanted to present it "in terms so general that the reader" could "produce his own associations from almost any area of modern intellectual life." Yet it seemed to stand above all "for the tendency toward abstraction and synthesis characteristic of the years between the two world wars—in non-objective art, in atonal music, in symbolic logic."[23] Although Hesse's personal preferences were nostalgic, although he found himself most at home with strict classical music and in the magical world of German Romanticism, he was sufficiently aware of what was going on around him to be able to offer his contemporaries a foretaste of their intellectual future. The introduction to *The Glass Bead Game* delineated with a single complex metaphor the implications of his countrymen's cultivation of disembodied *Geist*.

This was the point that Hesse had reached in the early 1930's.

22. *Das Glasperlenspiel* (Zürich, 1943), trans. by Richard and Clara Winston as *The Glass Bead Game* (New York, 1969), pp. 15, 38. Note that the translators use for *Geist* the word "intellect" rather than "spirit."

23. Theodore Ziolkowski, *The Novels of Hermann Hesse: A Study in Theme and Structure* (Princeton, N.J., 1965), p. 77.

The advent of Hitler could not fail to affect the character of the novel which was to detail the vicissitudes of the game through three centuries of imaginary future history. As Hesse labored over it during the first decade of Nazi rule, its outlines changed by imperceptible but cumulative stages: it gradually ceased to be an exercise in pure cerebration; it moved from the realm of aesthetics and intellectualism to a concern for the public arena and human solidarity. By 1943, when *The Glass Bead Game* was finally published, those who had read the introduction nine years earlier discovered to their surprise that Hesse's protagonist had in the end abandoned his position as a supreme virtuoso of the mind and thrown in his lot with struggling humanity.

Among those who welcomed *The Glass Bead Game* with gratitude was Hesse's closest counterpart among German novelists, Thomas Mann. There was "scarcely another work," Mann wrote, that inspired in him "such warm and respectful feelings of comradeship."[24] When Mann himself had gone into exile in 1933, he renewed with Hesse ties of mutual honor and affection that dated back for more than twenty years—just as the same separation from his national community threw him into closer contact with Freud and made him the spokesman for the German literary world in exile on the occasion of the master's eightieth birthday in 1936.

If Hesse was the original prophet of the emigration, Mann early became its most prominent and representative figure. Such a role would not have come naturally to him in his first years as a novelist, when he had been absorbed in finding his own aesthetic stance to the exclusion of political concerns. But as the 1920's had gone on—as Mann had accepted and defended the Weimar Republic and in his major novel *The Magic Mountain* (1924) and his short story "Mario and the Magician" (1930) had affirmed the power of "goodness and love" against the gathering forces of terror and obscurantism—he had attained almost in spite of himself the status of an enunciator of public values. During the Weimar years, Mann was crossing a double divide: he was passing over from

24. *Die Entstehung des Doktor Faustus* (Amsterdam, 1949), trans. by Richard and Clara Winston as *The Story of a Novel* (New York, 1961), p. 74.

German national to cosmopolitan sympathies, and he was shifting
the axis of his work from private sensibility to ideological commitment. Eventually "his old age was taken up with a ceaseless publicist struggle against fascism"—as his fictional characters traveled
"from isolation to human and social community." Thus Georg
Lukács wrote of the man he admired as the greatest of the
twentieth century's "critical realists."[25]

Mann's initial attitude toward his own emigration had been
more hesitant. Even when he had found a home that suited him
near Zürich in the autumn of 1933, he could derive little satisfaction from an exile which might last the rest of his life. His ties to
German culture were too close; he shrank from an irreparable
rupture; after toying with the idea of southern France, he chose a
city where the German language was spoken. Not until 1936, in
response to a Swiss critic's characterization of the writers in exile as
Jewish and un-German, did Mann unequivocally align himself
with his fellow men of letters who had also left their country. As
he wrote to Hesse in explanation, he had felt a need to clear up
the "ambiguous, half-and-half notions" that were current about
his relationship to the Third Reich.[26] Two years later, when with
the annexation of Austria Mann decided to settle permanently in
the United States, he had thrown off all doubt about his choice.
He now saw his exile as a kind of spiritual ambassadorship in
behalf of German culture: "What does it mean to be without a
homeland? My homeland lies in the works that I bear with me.
Sunk within them I experience all the cosiness of being at home.
They are my language, the German language and its form of
thought, a possession handed down by my country and people
which I have developed further. Where I am, there is Germany."[27]

In America, Thomas Mann the exile came into his own. At first
he lived in Princeton, attracted by the university's offer of a special
lectureship in the humanities. But two years of this variety of

25. *Thomas Mann*, 5th ed. (Berlin, 1957), trans. and abr. by Stanley
Mitchell as *Essays on Thomas Mann* (New York, 1965), pp. 49, 54.
26. February 9, 1936, *Letters of Thomas Mann 1889–1955*, sel. and trans.
by Richard and Clara Winston (New York, 1971), p. 249.
27. Quoted from an unpublished portion of Mann's "Tagebuchblätter,"
dating from early April 1938, in Herbert Lehnert, "Thomas Mann in Exile
1933–1938," *The Germanic Review*, XXXVIII (Nov. 1963), 291.

"jokes," as he put it, amply sufficed. He moved to southern California, where he found a plot of land and built a house in a lemon grove close to the sea. The climate and landscape appealed to him, as did the chance to devote himself to his writing free of academic commitments. Yet his time was never fully his own: he gave of his thought and energy to other refugees less fortunate than he, and he broadcast messages of hope to his countrymen who had remained in Germany. He was well aware of his special position and the responsibilities that went with it: the wealthy and the powerful made a great fuss over him; his fame brought him security and comfort in the form of lecture fees and royalties for his novels in translation. Nor did his public activities reduce his capacities for creative work as some of his friends had feared. The reverse may have been true: Mann's polemical efforts seemed to provide the outside stimulus which his continued artistic production required.[28]

Hence it was not surprising that he should eventually have come to speak of the experience of exile in terms of warm commendation. In a lecture delivered in Washington in November 1942, he characterized the current "diaspora of European culture" as "something very strange and unprecedented" which had assumed "an entirely different significance from that of any former emigration"—it meant nothing less than the possibility of creating a "new feeling of humanism" that might bring unity to the whole world.[29] Never had the hopes of humanity been higher. At the very moment when Mann was speaking, the tide of war was turning in North Africa and at Stalingrad: the defeat of Hitler now loomed as probable, perhaps even as certain. As the emigration's public spokesman, Mann gave voice to the delicious, transitory euphoria that lay between the early trials of adjustment to a new land and the moral perplexities of the cold war that were to follow.

The occasion for the lecture in Washington was the completion of Mann's tetralogy of novels on the biblical theme of Joseph and his brothers. By far the most extended of his works, it had ab-

28. Henry Hatfield, "Thomas Mann and America," special no. of *Salmagundi*, p. 174.
29. "The Joseph Novels," *The Atlantic Monthly*, CLXXI (Feb. 1943), 100.

sorbed the greater part of his energies for a full decade and a half. It had been his "steady companion," "insuring . . . the unity" of his life through all his changes of scene and fortune.[30] The first two novels—*The Tales of Jacob* and *Young Joseph*—had been written before his exile and could still be published in Germany during the initial period of Hitler's rule. The third, *Joseph in Egypt*, whose unfinished manuscript had been recovered by Mann's oldest daughter from his already confiscated house in Munich, was completed in Switzerland and appeared in Vienna in 1936. It remained for the concluding volume, *Joseph the Provider*, to ripen in its author's mind under the appropriately "Egyptian" sky of California.

The themes of the Joseph novels were as varied as the circumstances of their composition. An enormously expanded version of the spare account in Genesis, the books proceeded in leisurely fashion with interspersed digressions and loving attention to detail. Most obviously they suggested Mann's solidarity with the suffering Jewish people—as though when he had undertaken his task in the mid-1920's he had already suspected what was to come. A decade and a half later he granted that "there were hidden, defiantly polemic connections" between the novels and "the growing vulgar anti-Semitism" which he had "always found repulsive. . . . To write a novel of the Jewish spirit was timely just because it seemed untimely." More broadly, Mann hoped that his work would depict the triumph of "crafty goodness" over "stupid . . . slave drivers." His old theme of humanism was with him still, but it had now turned "away from the bourgeois toward the mythical aspect." And to carry these disparate elements, he had settled on an "indirect, a stylized and bantering language" whose humor frequently failed to penetrate the veil of translation.[31] Mann's readers might well be puzzled by a set of novels that were at once high comedy and a deeply felt affirmation of Western civilized values.

The key to such apparent contradictions lay with the contemporary leader who all unsuspecting had offered Mann the half-mythical type-figure he required. As the cycle of Joseph drew to its

30. *Ibid.*, p. 96; *Story of a Novel*, p. 14.
31. "The Joseph Novels," pp. 93–94, 96; to Agnes E. Meyer, July 26, 1941, *Letters of Thomas Mann*, p. 368.

close, its protagonist little by little took on the attributes of that other "provider," Franklin D. Roosevelt (and the novelist correspondingly began to give his ancient Egyptians the national peculiarities he both admired and mocked in the Americans among whom he dwelt). Mann had a respect for Roosevelt bordering on adulation. He had twice been entertained at the White House and had come away from these visits utterly bewitched. Like the legendary Joseph, the American president seemed to combine cunning and kindness in appropriate measure. While Mann found it "hard to characterize" Roosevelt's "mixture of craft, good nature, self-indulgence, desire to please, and sincere faith," he saw in him "something like a blessing" from on high that made him the "born opponent" to Adolf Hitler.[32]

Sixteen months after *Joseph the Provider* was published in Stockholm, Roosevelt lay dead. And in the meantime Mann's thoughts had turned more somber. The bourgeois humanist ideal that in Joseph himself and in the American president had found such reassuring incarnations had again become doubtful as the Second World War drew to its ambiguous end.[33] The completion of Mann's cycle of biblical novels marked a high point of confidence among the émigrés before the phase of self-questioning began.

III. *Wahlverwandtschaften*

Just as there was a curious affinity that kept Mann's American readers faithful to him even when his writing was most "difficult"—just as he held on to an audience that knew him only in translation and that eluded comparable writers in exile such as his older brother Heinrich—so we can detect in other realms of thought what the Germans call *Wahlverwandtschaften*. Some styles of thinking prospered, and others withered or barely held their own in the new American setting. And the most important

32. To Agnes E. Meyer, January 24, 1941, *ibid.*, p. 355. On Mann's relationship to Roosevelt see the article by his nephew Klaus H. Pringsheim, "Thomas Mann in Amerika," *Neue deutsche Hefte*, XIII (1966), 29–31.
33. See Chapter 6.

explanation for their success or lack thereof was the extent to which the German idiom in each case could be carried over into English relatively intact.

In this respect the creative writers and the social thinkers among the émigrés faced different problems. The former continued to use their own language and to depend on translators for their American public; the greater part of them, including men as eminent as the dramatist Carl Zuckmayer and the novelist Hermann Broch, passed their years in the United States in almost total obscurity.[34] This was the cruel price they paid for settling in a land where their native tongue was spoken by only a very few and read by no more than a small educated minority—a minority probably smaller than it had been a generation earlier, before the blight of anti-Germanism in the First World War had discredited the study of the German language in a fashion from which it never recovered. The social thinkers, with rare but distinguished exceptions, made the opposite choice: they did their best to write in English—awkwardly at first, then with growing confidence. Yet only the youngest or most adaptable of them fully mastered their new tongue: most were acutely conscious of what they had lost along the way. As a veteran of these linguistic struggles viewed them in retrospect:

> Working in a language which is not the language of one's dreams is to miss many over- and under-tones, ambiguities and poetic notions, the spontaneousness and even the silences. Dimensions of thought and feeling must be replaced by a technique of significations, using spoken words in prefabricated, studied sequences which threaten to impoverish that which they ought to enrich. . . .
>
> Uneducated people quickly learn to make small talk in canned phrases. Intellectuals learn slowly and tend to speak "translatese," painfully aware that it is one flight below the level they would like to inhabit intellectually.[35]

34. For Zuckmayer's experiences, see his *Als Wär's ein Stück von mir* (Frankfurt, 1966), trans. by Richard and Clara Winston as *A Part of Myself* (New York, 1970).
35. Henry Pachter, "On Being an Exile: An Old-Timer's Personal and Political Memoir," special no. of *Salmagundi*, p. 19.

Thus the émigrés found themselves using an English that the classically inclined could equate with what the ancient Greeks termed *koine*. Those whose native languages were German or Italian or Magyar were forced to write in an idiom that was ungracious, narrow in range, and merely serviceable. Yet the Americans were polite about it, far more polite than the British would have been. The editors at the publishing houses did what they could to turn Teutonic English into a passable imitation of the literary language, and the public, accustomed to the slipshod writing of so many American-born authors, did not protest. The result was to convert English into still more of a lingua franca than it had been before. As with Greek in the Hellenistic age, the widening of its sphere of influence was accompanied by the danger that it would lose its fine edge and its ability to convey nuances of thought and expression.

A rare optimist among the refugee intellectuals might find it of advantage to his thought to be obliged to translate it into a language which did not lend itself to verbal bedazzlement. Tillich used to recall with wry self-irony the mixture of pleasure and dismay he experienced at seeing Germanic profundities vanish when put into plain English. The more usual reaction was a sense of linguistic impoverishment. And this impoverishment worked both ways—on the émigrés themselves and on their hosts, whose own grasp of the literary idiom was frequently none too secure. Again and again in the postwar years British scholars would complain of the Teutonic-American jargon in which the social science from across the Atlantic was composed. A generation after the event—when the refugees who had become Americanized might be presumed to think more naturally in English than in their native languages—it was still difficult to weigh linguistic loss against intellectual gain.

So much for the matter of language in the literal sense. In the broader sense of conceptual idiom, one can detect a bifurcation in the intellectual influences that radiated out from Central Europe in the 1930's and 1940's. The more metaphysical current associated with the trio Hegel, Husserl, and Heidegger was welcomed in

France.[36] The more concrete and empirical styles of thought—
whether in philosophy or psychology, history or sociology—found
a home in Britain or the United States. Three in particular of such
Wahlverwandtschaften between the German- and the English-
speaking worlds deserve closer attention: the approaches deriving
from Max Weber, from Sigmund Freud, and from Ludwig Wittgenstein.

1. When Weber died in 1920, he left no organized school
behind him. His influence in his own country was in no sense
comparable to that of his contemporary Emile Durkheim, whose
students and whose methods continued to dominate French social
science during the entire interwar period. Even when alive, Weber
had been an isolated scholar; after his death, his precepts about a
"value-free" study of society were more frequently honored than
observed. It was not until it reached the United States that the
Weberian inheritance became a major force in social thought.

In part this delayed influence was due to the state of German
sociology itself. As much a product of quasi-priestly scholarship as
the older learned disciplines, it had in common with them a nostalgia for a simpler world of agrarian relationships. Yet it refused
to indulge such yearnings. It had no ideological ties to the landed
aristocracy—nor, we may add, to the capitalist middle class, nor
even to the proletariat, despite its concern for the "social question" and the fact that a large part of its conceptual apparatus
derived from Marx. Though far from being truly neutral in the
realm of values, it fostered a stance of detachment and discrimination. The work of the German sociologists was suffused with "a
sense of resignation. . . . They proposed . . . to accept some
facets of modern life as inevitable or even desirable, while seeking
to temper its more accidental and less tolerable aspects. This
attitude led them to control their emotional response to their new
environment, to uphold a heroic ideal of rational clarification in
the face of tragedy."[37]

Thus hovering above the ideological wars of the Weimar era,
the sociologists remained insulated from the harsher aspects of
their own milieu. Nor did they succeed in finding acceptance

36. See my analysis in *The Obstructed Path* (New York, 1968), Chapter 5.
37. Ringer, *Decline of the German Mandarins*, p. 163.

within the mainstream of German academic life. It was not true, as has frequently been asserted, that their labors were almost exclusively abstract or historical. Before the First World War they had inaugurated a series of quantitative surveys of conditions among the working class, and some of this interest had carried over into the postwar period. But such research lacked continuity and a secure organizational base.[38] It required the move to America to prod German sociology toward a more consistently empirical stance.

Moreover, the sociologists and the sociologically minded historians who emigrated to England or the United States tended to be the less conventional and the more experimentally inclined. Besides Mannheim and some of his students, they included a larger number who carried with them the methodology and style of thought that they had acquired either directly or by derivation from Weber. And of these many were only too happy to learn from their American counterparts the techniques whose development had been arrested in their own country.[39] The result was an initial example of transatlantic synthesis—a merging of sociological traditions in which the Germans characteristically supplied theory, the Americans a talent and enthusiasm for empirical research. Such was the origin of the international discipline of sociology as we know it today.

In the process the example of Weber made itself felt very gradually and sometimes imperceptibly—and this is a further explanation for his delayed influence. The Weberian attitude permeated social thought by slow capillary action, frequently through the work of scholars whose connection with Weber himself was either tenuous or not fully conscious. "Handicapped by . . . discontinuous and incomplete translations," the reception of his teaching "was bound to be fragmentary." In the end it achieved recognition through piecemeal appropriation by men facing "a particular theoretical need or research problem. The result might be called 'creative misinterpretation' "—a fate not

38. Anthony Oberschall, *Empirical Social Research in Germany 1848–1914* (Paris and The Hague, 1965), p. 137.
39. See Paul F. Lazarsfeld's engaging account, "An Episode in the History of Social Research: A Memoir," *The Intellectual Migration*, pp. 270–337.

necessarily damaging to a corpus as wide in range and as tentative in assertion as Weber's.[40] In America Weber, like some mythic deity, underwent a series of transformations whose consistency with one another was frequently hard to detect.

The émigrés who worked in the Weberian tradition illustrated what the implacable dissector of the Nazi system Franz Neumann was to characterize as the optimum solution to the problem of cultural adaptation. They did not abandon their "previous intellectual position and accept without qualification" a new one. Nor did they "retain completely" their "old thought structure" and take upon themselves "the mission of totally revamping the American pattern"—or perhaps withdrawing "with disdain and contempt into an island" of their own. They chose the far more difficult assignment of integrating "new experience with old tradition."[41]

2. In contrast to the legacy of Max Weber, which was subtle and diffused, the other comparable *Wahlverwandtschaften* can be readily documented. Freud and Wittgenstein lived on into the period of emigration, the one until 1939, the other until 1951. Both of them maintained regular contact with disciples and admirers scattered throughout the English-speaking world. And both settled in England rather than the United States—which is in itself a reminder that the British aspect of the emigration requires greater attention than it has usually received.

In the case of Freud, however, despite the fact that his daughter Anna remained in England and continued his work there, the bulk of his most influential heirs crossed the Atlantic. In practical terms, this decision made sense: psychoanalysis was already established on the American scene, and its practitioners who arrived after 1933 or 1938 could adjust rapidly to their new situation. The more important of them were familiar to their hosts through earlier encounters at international congresses; most of the others experienced little difficulty in launching themselves into clinical practice. Indeed, the American milieu was more welcoming than

40. Guenther Roth, " 'Value-Neutrality' in Germany and the United States," *Scholarship and Partisanship: Essays on Max Weber* (with Reinhard Bendix) (Berkeley and Los Angeles, 1971), p. 35.
41. "The Social Sciences," *The Cultural Migration*, p. 20.

the one they had left. In Europe the members of the psychoanalytic movement had lived the life of sectarians walled off by a hostile environment. "They had, as it were, experienced premature training in the psychological condition of being émigrés, and this must have stood them in good stead when they had to become émigrés in the full sense of the term." In the United States minds were less likely to be closed to them, and people were curious about the message they brought. They arrived at an auspicious moment, when with the widespread questioning of the secularized Protestant ethic that had followed the economic crash, the Americans were hungering for an alternative system of thought which would "explain man to himself."[42] In the emotional hesitations of the 1930's, psychoanalysis—at least on the more popular level—found its chance.

Such success also carried dangers. In the relatively benign American setting, Freudian theory ran the risk of being "revised" beyond recognition, of being watered down to the point of extinction. The psychoanalysts who settled in America were obliged to steer a careful course between stubborn fidelity to the lessons of the founder and wholesale acceptance of the blander outlook of their new compatriots. A large number went aground on one or the other shoal. Yet it was in the treacherously propitious atmosphere of the United States that psychoanalysis completed its decisive post-Freudian advance—the development of the ego psychology associated with the names of Heinz Hartmann and Erik H. Erikson. Here too we can find examples of a fortunate integration of new experience with established tradition.

3. Wittgenstein's arrival in Cambridge in 1929 and a visit of his friend Moritz Schlick to the United States in the same year marked the beginning of the major phase of interaction between the logical analysis of Vienna and the comparable philosophies that were already being formulated in Britain and the United States. This exchange antedated, then, by nearly a decade the wholesale flight of philosophers from Austria after the *Anschluss* of 1938. Wittgenstein chose Cambridge because he knew it already and thought it a good place to "do" his sort of philosophy.

42. Marie Jahoda, "The Migration of Psychoanalysis: Its Impact on American Psychology," *The Intellectual Migration*, pp. 429–430, 433.

Rudolf Carnap and other members of the Vienna Circle subsequently emigrated to the United States for similar reasons. The predominantly empirical tone of American philosophy promised a favorable reception; its pragmatic and instrumental approaches paralleled in less rigorous fashion the findings of the Viennese.[43] Precise in method, respectful toward natural science, prizing clarity above all else, the logicians from Central Europe were admirably equipped to address their new English-speaking students. Still more, since they cast their teaching so far as possible in the language of unambiguous symbols, the problems of translation that vexed the other émigrés were reduced to a minimum. Within less than a generation English almost effortlessly replaced German as the lingua franca of logical analysis.

Such was the situation in the United States. In Britain matters were more complex. Wittgenstein's arrival in Cambridge not only reinforced the position of that university as the philosophical capital of the West. It also encouraged a new direction in his own work which he had just begun to stake out. Living in England, teaching in English, but continuing to write in German, Wittgenstein was drawn by force of circumstance to pursue his speculations on the function and characteristics of what came to be called ordinary language. The new concerns that established him as the most influential Central European thinker at work in the Anglo-American world also provided the forum for the crucial intellectual drama immediately preceding the emigration itself. It is fitting to start the analysis of this primarily American experience with an account of the philosophical prologue played out on English soil.

43. Herbert Feigl, "The Wiener Kreis in America," *ibid.*, pp. 643–647.

CHAPTER
2

Philosophical Prologue in England

I. *The British Peculiarity*

S INCE THE LATE nineteenth century the sequences of British thought had been out of phase with those on the Continent. The English and the Scots had pursued their own course, borrowing from abroad only such concepts as fitted their characteristic and self-defined purposes. Just as in the early part of the century, the reverberations of the French Revolution had occasioned a less widespread questioning of the Enlightenment than had appeared in Germany or in its country of origin, just as the tradition of Bentham and the two Mills had descended in untroubled succession from the pre-1789 world of ideas, so the intellectual battles of the generations succeeding John Stuart Mill took place in a different order and had a different tone from their counterparts across the Channel. In Britain both liberalism and a plain, commonsense brand of positivism were home-grown products that had become second nature in philosophical discourse. Both could claim a legitimate ancestor in John Locke. And the positivist stance had been reinforced by the triumphs of natural science in the Darwinian age.

Against the dominance of this latter attitude, idealist thought could offer only a wavering or intermittent challenge. The full panoply of German idealism did not reach the British universities until a half-century after its best days on the Continent—and

when it did come it was in Hegelian guise. Britain's major encounter with the idealist way of thinking was out of date even in
its own time. At the turn of the century, when Continental
theorists—notably Durkheim and Weber—who had experienced
idealism and positivism alike in their pristine forms were beginning to define a new canon of social thought that would combine
and transcend what they had learned from both, in Britain such
philosophers as F. H. Bradley and Bernard Bosanquet were still
trying to introduce their recalcitrant countrymen to Hegel.[1]

Hegelian idealism—or Absolute Idealism, as it was sometimes
called—figured as "an alien import, . . . an exotic in the English
scene."[2] It was not surprising, then, that its brief preeminence
should have been easily and permanently overthrown. The demise
of the idealist style, and the concomitant definition of Britain's
most pervasive twentieth-century modes of thought, came at the
hands of two distinct sets of writers. The two had in common,
however, besides their distaste for high-flown abstraction, the fact
that they reached back across the period of Hegelian aberration to
a robust and authentically British philosophical past.

The first in time was the pragmatic, nominalist social science
primarily exemplified by Alfred Marshall in economics and
Graham Wallas in sociology. Renouncing nineteenth-century aspirations toward universal theory, men like Marshall and Wallas
concerned themselves with the discrete and the particular. They
were also deeply involved in social reform and in the practical
application of their ideas. More modest in aim than their Continental contemporaries, they refused to worry about the epistemological problems that seemed so urgent to Germans and French-
men and Italians around 1900. The British social thinkers preferred measurement to speculation, and solid fact to theories of
knowledge.[3] Their most influential achievement was to come in

1. For a fuller account of this contrast, see my *Consciousness and Society*
(New York, 1958), Chapter 2, and Noel Annan, *The Curious Strength of
Positivism in English Political Thought* (L. T. Hobhouse Memorial Trust Lec-
ture No. 28) (London, 1959).

2. G. J. Warnock, *English Philosophy since 1900* (London, 1958), p. 9.

3. Reba N. Soffer, "The Revolution in English Social Thought, 1880–
1914," *The American Historical Review*, LXXV (Dec. 1970), 1938–1941,
1963; Martin J. Wiener, *Between Two Worlds: The Political Thought of
Graham Wallas* (Oxford, 1971).

the next generation with the new economics of John Maynard Keynes.

The second set of thinkers who overthrew Absolute Idealism were the Cambridge philosophers G. E. Moore and Bertrand Russell. In his *Principia Ethica*, published shortly after the turn of the century, Moore undertook to refute both positivist and Hegelian teaching with his contention that what was "good in itself" was "quite unique in kind"—that it could not "be reduced to any assertion about reality." This separation of the realm of value from the realm of fact (or science) paralleled the almost simultaneous methodological pronouncements of Max Weber: the Englishman and the German had in common their precarious situation of conducting a battle on two fronts. On the one hand they found it necessary to challenge the easy-going positivist practice of moving back and forth between scientific and ethical assertions without giving warning to the reader. On the other hand they assaulted the Hegelian notion that in some realm of the spirit the two types of statement could arrive at a majestic synthesis. As Moore put it, "to search for 'unity' and 'system,' at the expense of truth," was not "the proper business of philosophy."[4]

It is curious that the parallelism between Moore's and Weber's efforts has seldom been observed. Their vocabularies and the subjects they discussed were so different that their underlying intellectual compatibility has remained unrecognized. Yet both were concerned with asking the right questions—that is, those that philosophers had not asked before—and with finding out the meaning of those questions once they had been proposed. In Weber's case, such procedures figured as the preliminaries to an investigation of human society; in the case of Moore and his associates, these initial clarifications became the main business at hand. In the early, quasi-mathematical work of Moore's Cambridge contemporary Bertrand Russell, philosophy found itself reduced and refined to the narrow scope of the logical analysis of language; and this it remained in the practice of Russell's stricter successors. Moore's legacy was more open: his simple, candid, direct style of argument and his respect for "common sense" in no

4. *Principia Ethica* (Cambridge, 1903), pp. 114, 222.

way debarred the two generations of students who fell under his influence from pursuing whatever attracted them. But most in fact stayed within the safe and respectable bounds of logic and epistemology. Of those who had been closely touched by Moore's example, Keynes alone became a social thinker of the first rank.[5]

Thus while Marshall and Wallas in one type of intellectual endeavor, and Moore and Russell in another, revitalized the central British tradition—empirical and nominalist—descending from Locke and Hume, no such philosophically grounded social science as Weber and Durkheim had inaugurated developed at the universities of England and Scotland. Keynes was equipped to play the role of founder, but he chose to devote his energies to public service and technical economics instead. It was rather a man whom Keynes had befriended and even financially aided—Ludwig Wittgenstein—who late in time and in tantalizing fragments gave his British students a glimpse of the possible connection between rigorous philosophical analysis and speculation on the nature of society.

Wittgenstein was not a refugee from political or "racial" persecution. Although of Jewish ancestry, he had never suffered discrimination on account of his origins. Moreover, his definitive move to England preceded by four years the advent of Hitler in Germany. Yet the function he performed among the British was the precise counterpart to—and even surpassed in influence—the work of the émigrés from Central Europe in the United States.

Britain's educational institutions were less receptive to the foreign-born than those of America. Far fewer in number, for the most part literary or classical in their curriculum, the British universities could absorb only a handful of the social scientists who emigrated from the Continent in the 1930's. It was not merely that teaching positions were scarce. It was also that the whole notion of formal graduate education was just beginning to take on in Britain and that a majority of the research students enrolled in

5. For Moore's influence on Keynes, see R. F. Harrod, *The Life of John Maynard Keynes* (London, 1951), pp. 75–81; see also on the wider significance of the two founders of British analytical philosophy, A. J. Ayer, *Russell and Moore: The Analytical Heritage* (Cambridge, Mass., 1971).

the universities were specializing in the natural sciences. Still more, the major discipline of sociology languished in obscurity. In these discouraging circumstances, it was natural that most Central European scholars preferred to cross the Atlantic.[6] And it was also not surprising that the most influential of the Continentals located in England should have been a man at work in the impeccably legitimate field of philosophy and one whose university connections dated back to before the First World War.

In his mid-twenties Ludwig Wittgenstein had studied at Trinity College, Cambridge, for three terms of the year 1912 and two terms of the year following. Here he had known both Moore and more particularly Russell. Lord Russell has recalled his consternation at the young visitor who came to him after one term of study and asked him point-blank:

> "Do you think I am an absolute idiot?" I said: "Why do you want to know?" He replied: "Because if I am I shall become an aeronaut, but if I am not I shall become a philosopher." I said to him: "My dear fellow, I don't know whether you are an absolute idiot or not, but if you will write me an essay during the vacation upon any philosophical topic that interests you, I will read it and tell you." He did so, and brought it to me at the beginning of the next term. As soon as I read the first sentence, I became persuaded that he was a man of genius, and assured him that he should on no account become an aeronaut.[7]

So Wittgenstein settled down in Cambridge to read systematically in philosophy. But this decision did not end Russell's bewilderment at his behavior:

> He used to come to see me every evening at midnight, and pace up and down my room like a wild beast . . . in agitated silence. Once I said to him: "Are you thinking about logic or about your sins?" "Both," he replied, and continued his

6. Helge Pross, *Die Deutsche Akademische Emigration nach den Vereinigten Staaten 1933–1941* (Berlin, 1955), pp. 34–37.

7. *The Autobiography of Bertrand Russell*, II: *The Middle Years: 1914–1944*, Bantam paperback ed. (New York, 1969), p. 133.

pacing. I did not like to suggest that it was time for bed, as it seemed probable both to him and me that on leaving me he would commit suicide.

Apparently Russell's conviction of Wittgenstein's genius—"passionate, profound, intense, and dominating"—enabled him to sustain so taxing a relationship. He even put up with technical criticism from the younger man that gave him "a sense of failure" and for a while convinced him that he "could not hope ever again to do fundamental work in philosophy." Yet years later—and when the end of the war had once again made intellectual exchange between Englishmen and Austrians possible—Russell was the prime mover in the long battle to get Wittgenstein's *Tractatus Logico-Philosophicus* published. The two met in The Hague and "spent a week arguing" the book "line by line."[8] And Russell wrote for it a laudatory introduction.

This introduction marked the beginning of a slow estrangement. Wittgenstein was furious at what he felt was Russell's distortion of his own intentions and even considered withdrawing his work entirely. Their friendship could not survive the strain. After a decade had passed, with the book in question now a modern classic and its author preparing to return to Cambridge, his former teacher's assessment of Wittgenstein's ideas had grown less enthusiastic. While they might "easily prove to constitute a whole new philosophy," Russell wrote, it was unclear whether they were true. "As a logician" who liked "simplicity," the older man added, he preferred to think that they were not. This was the nub of the disagreement, since Wittgenstein for his part had come to the conclusion that Russell's philosophy—and with it his own early work—consisted largely of tautologies. As Wittgenstein's fame spread, his former teacher's distrust of his new style of thought settled into detestation. And one by one the rising luminaries in British philosophy shifted their allegiance from Russell to Wittgenstein. The man who had begun as his pupil, the senior ruefully noted, had "ended as his supplanter."[9]

8. *Ibid.*, pp. 64, 90, 132, 134.
9. Michael Frayn, "Russell and Wittgenstein," *Commentary*, XLIII (May 1967), 73–74; Russell, *Autobiography*, II, p. 288.

With Moore, Wittgenstein's relations had been calmer. At the start the visitor from Austria had been less impressed by Moore than by Russell. Many years later he confessed that he had found the former's lectures repetitious, although he had in fact pleased Moore by looking "puzzled" during them. After his return to Cambridge, Wittgenstein's judgment was more even-handed: he concluded that while Russell might be "bright," Moore was "deep" and particularly adept at destroying "premature solutions" of philosophical problems. In their later years, when Wittgenstein had succeeded Moore as professor of philosophy at Cambridge, the two saw each other frequently. Their minds still worked in different fashions, and Wittgenstein still found Moore "childlike," but he evidently set a high value on their conversations. Indeed he was "extremely vexed" when Moore's wife, solicitous for her ailing husband's health, put a time limit upon them. The old philosopher, Wittgenstein maintained, "should discuss as long as he liked. If he became very excited or tired and had a stroke and died—well, that would be a decent way to die: with his boots on."[10]

This anecdote tells us a great deal about Wittgenstein's attitude toward life and death. It also suggests that he never adapted to the urbane style of the older English universities. One of his closest associates has gone so far as to say that he had a "great distaste . . . for English culture and mental habits in general."[11] While such may well have been the case, it did not limit his intellectual attraction. On the contrary, Wittgenstein's stubborn refusal to be assimilated to Cambridge ways constituted an integral part of his unique role as mediator between the Continental and the Anglo-American philosophical traditions.

II. *Ludwig Wittgenstein and Vienna*

Wittgenstein had been and remained authentically Viennese in his inbred familiarity with "high" culture and the life of the mind.

10. *Ibid.*, p. 133; Norman Malcolm, *Ludwig Wittgenstein: A Memoir* (London, 1958), pp. 66–68, 73.
11. *Ibid.*, p. 28.

The offspring of a wealthy and richly educated family, he had grown up in a milieu in which the fostering of artistic talent and the refinement of aesthetic appreciation had come more and more to rank as the main business of life. His home had been distinguished even in Vienna for the level of its conversation and the discrimination of its taste; Brahms had been a friend of his parents, and Schopenhauer's works a frequent subject of discussion. Jewish in origin like so much of Vienna's high bourgeoisie, the Wittgensteins had no sense of cultural separateness. They were typical, rather, of a society in which an understanding of the representational arts was taken for granted as the single clearest badge of status.[12] Ludwig Wittgenstein acquired by right of birth a cultural endowment that someone less privileged might have struggled a lifetime to obtain; his competence in music and in architecture commanded the respect of professionals. Yet he carried such accomplishments lightly and seldom spoke of them; his self-esteem as an intellectual was concentrated on the perceptions he had wrung from himself by his own unaided efforts.

Both Ludwig and his father Karl had been brought up as Christians. But they were Protestants rather than Catholics, and there was in the family a streak of puritanism that was far from characteristic of Austrian Catholicism. The atmosphere of the household—from which the children seldom ventured forth, since they were educated by tutors—was ultraserious and even somber. With no fewer than three older brothers having committed suicide, it was small wonder that Ludwig took a grave view of life and that he never felt at ease with the brittleness and irreverence of his Cambridge contemporaries. On such a man Oswald Spengler's *Decline of the West* made an immediate and strong impression.

Among his numerous brothers and sisters, Ludwig did not rank in the family estimate as particularly gifted. Rather curiously the Wittgensteins "thought of themselves as entirely Jewish in character"—defining their Judaism as "a tradition of aesthetic idealism." And within this self-definition music apparently held the highest

12. Carl E. Schorske, "The Transformation of the Garden: Ideal and Society in Austrian Literature," *The American Historical Review*, LXXII (July 1967), 1298–1300.

position. As a mere amateur in the field, Ludwig could not approach the virtuoso ability of his brother Paul, who despite the loss of one arm became a concert pianist and for whom Maurice Ravel composed his "Concerto for the Left Hand." In the future philosopher's mind music served rather as an indirect and even mystical form of communication. Following Schopenhauer, he considered it a way of transcending "the limits of representations" and of conveying the deeper matters which formal philosophical language could never express. In his ingrained concern with the nature and scope of the "sayable," Ludwig Wittgenstein was at one with a number of similarly perplexed young Viennese.

Although the son's eventual course diverged sharply from that of his father, the two Wittgensteins shared a personal modesty and dislike of show. An engineer, a highly successful founder of the Austrian iron industry, and the author of influential newspaper articles on economics, Karl Wittgenstein refused an imperial offer of ennoblement and limited the circulation of his collected essays.[13] His son, born in 1889, early showed an even greater talent for self-effacement. His impatience with outward forms— even of ordinary civility—was already apparent during his first stay in Cambridge. It evidently deepened during the First World War, when he quite literally carried the manuscript of his *Tractatus* in his knapsack and shouldered the burden of military life without complaint.

Wittgenstein's attitude toward his wartime service was free of the revulsion and protest voiced by so many of his generation. He accepted the hardships and dangers to which he was subjected as facts of life or as a simple matter of duty to the state. From all accounts he was a model soldier, cool under fire and decorated more than once for bravery. As an enlisted man he was a "good comrade." When he subsequently became an officer, he knew how to calm the men under his command and to get "the best out of them." Torn from the hothouse environment of Viennese high culture, Wittgenstein seems to have experienced the war as a kind

13. Allan Janik and Stephen Toulmin, *Wittgenstein's Vienna* (New York, 1973), pp. 117, 166, 169–177, 191; Paul Engelmann, *Letters from Ludwig Wittgenstein: With a Memoir*, trans. by L. Furtmüller, ed. by B. F. McGuinness (Oxford, 1967), pp. 119–121.

of liberation. Its "harsh circumstances . . . imposed a naturalness and a freedom from artificiality which were congenial" to his nature.[14] When Wittgenstein returned to civilian life in 1919, he had left his adolescence of wealth and privilege far behind him; he had even stripped himself of the large fortune he had inherited from his father. As he turned thirty, his sense of personal independence had become almost total. The publication of his *Tractatus* was the outward and visible sign of the transformation that had gone on within.

It is possible that from the start Wittgenstein's fellow Austrians —the young philosophers of what came to be called the Vienna Circle—misunderstood the deeper-lying drift of the *Tractatus*. Its famous concluding words were susceptible of a variety of interpretations:

> My propositions are elucidatory in this way: he who understands me finally recognizes them as senseless, when he has climbed out through them, on them, over them. (He must so to speak throw away the ladder, after he has climbed up on it.)
> He must surmount these propositions; then he sees the world rightly.
> Whereof one cannot speak, thereof one must be silent.[15]

At first and for a generation thereafter, nearly everyone assumed that Wittgenstein was propounding a radical positivism. This was why the Logical Positivists of Vienna were attracted to his work and why they held him in such great respect. Similarly in England, misled by Russell's introduction, the philosophers of logical analysis found in the *Tractatus* a thoroughgoing rejection of metaphysical or ethical inquiry; in their view, all that Wittgenstein had left standing was epistemology and linguistic exercises. From such an interpretation, the path was clear to the full-scale demolition of speculative philosophical concerns that characterized such influen-

14. *Ibid.*, pp. 73 and (editor's appendix) 140–142.
15. *Logisch-Philosophische Abhandlung* (Vienna, 1921), trans. with parallel German text as *Tractatus Logico-Philosophicus* (London, 1922), p. 189.

tial books as A. J. Ayer's *Language, Truth and Logic*, published in
1936, and Gilbert Ryle's *The Concept of Mind*, which followed
thirteen years later. Not until another two decades had passed did
an Englishman educated in the analytical tradition venture to
assert that Wittgenstein had never been a positivist, that it was
incorrect to make a sharp distinction between the early Wittgenstein of the *Tractatus* and the late Wittgenstein of the 1930's and
1940's, and that the puzzling obiter dicta of Wittgenstein the
"thinker" were similarly of a piece with his statements as a technical philosopher—in short, that the "80% of the *Tractatus*" which
"could, without obvious misrepresentation, be used as a source of
forthright, no-nonsense, positivist slogans" was not necessarily the
most important part of that work.[16]

The book's conclusion had enjoined a philosophical silence: it
was the nature of the silence that was in question. A careful
reading of the injunction to "surmount" Wittgenstein's own
propositions suggested that they were merely "elucidatory" and in
no sense definitive. Beyond them lay what could not be spoken.
Already before the *Tractatus* had appeared in print, Wittgenstein
had explained to one of its prospective publishers the deeper
purpose of his work:

> The book's point is an ethical one. I once meant to include in
> the preface a sentence which is not in fact there now but
> which I will write out for you here, because it will perhaps be
> a key to the work for you. What I meant to write, then, was
> this: My work consists of two parts: the one presented here
> plus all that I have *not* written. And it is precisely this second
> part that is the important one.[17]

Thus Wittgenstein's silence was one not of mockery but of respect. "Far from equating the important with the verifiable, and
dismissing the unverifiable as 'unimportant *because* unsayable,'
Wittgenstein took exactly the opposite stand. In the concluding
section of the *Tractatus*, and repeatedly thereafter, he kept insist-

16. Stephen Toulmin, "Ludwig Wittgenstein," *Encounter*, XXXII (Jan.
1969), 60.

17. Engelmann, *Letters from Wittgenstein* (editor's appendix), p. 143.

ing—though to deaf ears—that *the unsayable alone"* had *"genuine value."*[18]

For the time being, however, he saw no alternative to leaving the unutterable alone. Declining an invitation to return to Cambridge, he gave up philosophy and turned to pursuits that he apparently regarded as of greater human importance. For more than half a decade he taught elementary school in a succession of Austrian villages; subsequently he worked as a gardener and an architect. In his teaching he felt lonely and isolated: stranded among uncomprehending rural folk, he was thrown back utterly on his own resources. His letters from these years bespeak acute misery; even as a teacher he had a sense of failure. Yet for all his wretchedness he was learning something that would be of infinite value when he returned at last to philosophy. He had learned to know children, to listen to them, and to ask questions. Most of the time he got no clear answers—but the same would be true of his teaching in Cambridge. Working with children, he had begun to pose questions that would strike adults as senseless—questions that could be approached only in a language simpler than the language of convention and that suggested meanings even when they could not be answered at all. Like Sigmund Freud before him, Wittgenstein had learned from children how humanity spoke and thought when it had not yet put on the trappings of civilization. And in so doing he had shifted the axis of his philosophy from the categorical propositions of the *Tractatus* to the Socratic form of his later writings.[19]

At the end of 1924, Moritz Schlick, on behalf of the Vienna Circle that had been informally organized earlier in the year, wrote to Wittgenstein in admiring terms in the hope of arranging a meeting. The *Tractatus* was already well known within the Circle, where, since copies were lacking, it was "read aloud and discussed sentence by sentence." And of the young philosophers who had been captivated by it, Schlick was the one best qualified to approach its elusive author. Kind, modest, and diplomatic, Schlick knew how to reassure the skittish Wittgenstein and persuade him

18. Toulmin, "Wittgenstein," p. 61. These statements reappear almost verbatim in Janik and Toulmin's *Wittgenstein's Vienna*, pp. 219–220.
19. Engelmann, *Letters from Wittgenstein*, pp. 114–115.

to speak of his ideas. Even so the meeting took more than two years to arrange. Not until early 1927, when Wittgenstein had moved to Vienna to design a house for his sister, was Schlick at last able to see him—a meeting to which he went in the "reverential attitude" of a pilgrim and from which "he returned in an ecstatic state."[20]

It was one thing to talk in private with Schlick, another to speak with the rest of the circle and more particularly with its dominating personality, Rudolf Carnap. By the summer of 1927 Wittgenstein had indeed met Carnap, and subsequently there seem to have been a few sessions with the Circle as a whole. But such encounters had to be hedged with careful protocol. Schlick made sure that his friends did not indulge in the uninhibited philosophical give and take that marked their discussions among themselves. Wittgenstein, he explained, was "very sensitive and easily disturbed by a direct question. The best approach" was to let him "talk and then ask only very cautiously for the necessary elucidations." Conforming to this procedure as best he could, Carnap eventually came to the conclusion that Wittgenstein would tolerate "no critical examination by others," once he had gained an "insight . . . by an act of inspiration." And Wittgenstein himself had confessed to Schlick that "he could talk only with somebody" who "held his hand." Evidently the militantly scientific and positivist tone of the Circle was in the end too much for Wittgenstein. In early 1929, shortly before his departure for Cambridge, he declared that he would see Carnap no more and would limit his contact to Schlick and one other. Carnap "regretted" this decision: for all its difficulties, he had found his association with Wittgenstein "interesting, exciting and rewarding."

At the same time he was obliged to admit that his and Wittgenstein's minds were profoundly incompatible. Earlier, when the Vienna Circle had first read the *Tractatus* together, Carnap "had erroneously believed" that its author's "attitude toward metaphysics was similar" to his own. He "had not paid sufficient attention" to Wittgenstein's "statements . . . about the mysti-

20. *Ibid.* (editor's appendix), pp. 146–147; Rudolf Carnap, "Intellectual Autobiography," in *The Philosophy of Rudolf Carnap*, ed. by Paul Arthur Schilpp (La Salle, Ill., 1963), p. 24.

cal." Subsequently he had discovered that the latter's "point of view and . . . attitude toward people and problems, even theoretical problems, were much more similar to those of a creative artist than to those of a scientist; one might almost say, similar to those of a religious prophet or a seer."[21] Between Wittgenstein and his Viennese admirers there had opened up a philosophical chasm that Schlick's diplomacy could never bridge.

Yet for all their ambiguity and eventual collapse, Wittgenstein's encounters with the Vienna Circle had achieved one decisive result—they had led him back to philosophy. The conversations with Schlick and Carnap and the others had shaken him out of his state of intellectual suspension and self-doubt and forced him to confront once more the problems he had intended to lay to rest in his first book. The revelation that he was not *their* kind of philosopher obliged him to begin the slow process of defining just what kind of philosopher he was.

In 1936 Schlick was murdered by a deranged former student. The shock of his death not only snapped the tenuous link with Wittgenstein; it demoralized the remaining members of the Vienna Circle, who were already beginning to scatter. Five years earlier, Carnap had been appointed professor at the German University of Prague, and in the very year of Schlick's murder, he moved permanently to America. In 1938 the Nazi annexation of Austria finished off the Circle in the same definitive fashion in which it broke up the headquarters of Sigmund Freud. Vienna ceased to be a center either of philosophy or of psychoanalysis, and in neither did it regain its preeminence after the Second World War.

With the departure for the United States of Carnap and a number of the other adherents of the Circle, its intellectual affinities with Wittgenstein were weakened still further. During the war years, it was impossible for philosophers living in Britain and those who had settled in America to talk with each other. Still more, the cordial reception that the Viennese (and Viennese by adoption, such as Carnap himself) had received in America rein-

21. *Ibid.*, pp. 25–27.

forced their strictness of method. The analytic current in philosophy, as in the broadest terms it had come to be called, began to
diverge on the two sides of the Atlantic. In the United States it
remained aggressively empirical and "no-nonsense"; in Britain it
took on the more informal tone of the analysis of ordinary
language.[22] And while in America neither the émigrés nor the
native-born were particularly inclined to extend their investigations into the field of social thought, at the English universities
the possibility remained open.

This possibility entailed some clear reckoning with the realm of
value. For the members of the Vienna Circle, as for those who
followed their example in Britain and the United States, the base
point for such a discussion was Hume's classic distinction between
"is" and "ought"—in contemporary language, the assertion that
normative statements could not be derived from factual descriptions.[23] On so simple and fundamental a delimitation of the field
of inquiry there was no divergence of opinion. And it was also
natural that most of the philosophers who subscribed to Hume's
principle should have chosen to stay on the safe side of the line in
the realm of fact or science. Few followed Moore's attempt to
define the "good in itself," which, since in his usage the good and
the beautiful were nearly identical, amounted to taking up once
more the traditional concerns of ethics and aesthetics. The majority not only agreed with Wittgenstein in classifying such matters
as unsayable; it dismissed them with the scorn they wrongly
attributed to the author of the *Tractatus*.

Yet one at least of the Vienna Circle had sketched the nature of
the statements that lay beyond the boundary of the verifiable. In
the year following his move to Prague, Carnap undertook to describe what he called the "philosophy of norms" or the "philosophy of value." If this could not be couched in the language of
empirical statements, was there another language in which it could
properly be expressed? Was there a different method by which a

22. *Ibid.*, pp. 28–29; Herbert Feigl, "The Wiener Kreis in America," *The
Intellectual Migration: Europe and America, 1930–1960*, ed. by Donald Fleming and Bernard Bailyn (Cambridge, Mass., 1969), p. 639.
23. A. J. Ayer, editor's introduction to the anthology *Logical Positivism*
(Glencoe, Ill., 1959), p. 22.

person could voice his "general attitude . . . towards life"? Usually this had been done in the language that the Vienna Circle characterized as "metaphysical"; and metaphysics, Carnap argued, offered "an inadequate means for the expression of the basic attitude." It was art, rather, that was equipped to convey the philosophy of value. And among the arts, "perhaps music" offered "the purest means of expression" because it was "entirely free from any reference to objects." This Nietzsche alone had understood: "the metaphysician who perhaps had artistic talent to the highest degree . . . almost entirely avoided the . . . confusion" into which the run of philosophers had fallen. When Nietzsche left the realm of "historical-psychological analysis," when he tried to express what others had clothed in the language of metaphysics or ethics, he did not "choose the misleading theoretical form"; he chose "the form of art, of poetry."[24]

Nietzsche had been the most musical of philosophers. Wittgenstein was musically gifted to the point of being able to conduct a chamber orchestra or whistle a full sonata without mistake. The example of Nietzsche was virtually the only one available to him as he embarked on his agonizing quest for the unutterable.

III. Ludwig Wittgenstein and Cambridge

In early 1929 Wittgenstein arrived in Cambridge in the anomalous role of a research or graduate student. From the standpoint of the university officialdom, the author of one of the most influential philosophical works of the decade was simply beginning his apprenticeship as a scholar. Apparently the incongruity soon struck those in charge of his studies: it was found possible to give him credit for his prewar residence and to consider the *Tractatus* his doctoral thesis. In June of 1929 Wittgenstein was awarded his degree, and in the following year he became a fellow of Trinity College.

24. "Überwindung der Metaphysik durch Logische Analyse der Sprache," *Erkenntnis*, II (1932), trans. by Arthur Pap as "The Elimination of Metaphysics through Logical Analysis of Language" for *Logical Positivism*, pp. 77–80.

Nine years later he received a professorship, which he held for the better part of a decade thereafter. But it would be quite wrong to assume that this series of administrative steps tamed the restless Wittgenstein or converted him into any sort of "normal" academic. He continued to treat the conventions of university life with the impatience with which he regarded all outward forms; although he lived in Trinity, he refused to dine there, and he neither behaved nor dressed like a professor. "One could not imagine Wittgenstein in a suit, necktie, or hat."

> His face was lean and brown, his profile was aquiline and strikingly beautiful, his head was covered with a curly mass of brown hair.
>
> Whether lecturing or conversing privately, Wittgenstein always spoke emphatically and with a distinctive intonation. He spoke excellent English, with the accent of an educated Englishman, although occasional Germanisms would appear in his constructions. His voice was resonant, the pitch being somewhat higher than that of the normal male voice, but not unpleasant. His words came out, not fluently, but with great force. . . . His face was remarkably mobile and expressive when he talked. His eyes were deep and often fierce in their expression. His whole personality was commanding, even imperial.[25]

For such a man it was sheer torture to conform even in minimal fashion to what was expected of him. There remained something provisional and desperate about Wittgenstein's career as an academic. In the mid-1930's he visited the Soviet Union and thought of settling there. The outbreak of the Second World War gave him another chance to break away from university routine, and his service as a medical technician brought him back once more to the world of physical fact that he had always respected; his earliest subject of study had been engineering, and throughout his life he loved to tinker with machinery. After the war's end, he found two

25. Malcolm, *Wittgenstein*, pp. 23–25 (there are further details in the "Biographical Sketch" by Georg Henrik von Wright included in this volume, pp. 1–22).

more years of teaching all that he could bear; in 1947 he resigned his professorship.

He was still under sixty and looked younger than he actually was. As though suspecting that he had only a few years to live, he decided to devote his full energies to completing the work which he had undertaken in Cambridge. This ultrasensitive, "difficult" man finished his intellectual life as he had begun it—as a lonely wanderer. Never marrying, confined to male friendships that were often troubled and passionate, Wittgenstein lived, like Nietzsche or Weber, close to the edge of madness. Apparently the fear of slipping over that border never left him. Nor did a sense of his own moral uncleanliness. Yet his last words, as he lost consciousness forever, were these: "Tell them I've had a wonderful life!"[26]

Until the posthumous publication of his later writings, Wittgenstein's intellectual situation was anomalous in the extreme. "A philosopher who was known to be one of the greatest, if not the greatest alive, had changed his mind, but the only people who had any direct knowledge of the change were the privileged few who had heard him lecture or had had discussions with him."[27] The change was not so much in the content of his thought—he repudiated the *Tractatus* only in part—as in his view of what constituted "doing" philosophy in the first place. Philosophers, Wittgenstein had learned, ordinarily went about their business in a clumsy way: they behaved like "savages, primitive people, who hear the expressions of civilized men, put a false interpretation on them, and then draw the queerest conclusions from it." They allowed themselves to be seduced by their own reasoning processes into the illusion that the world was fully susceptible of logical explanation. And in succumbing to this particular form of self-deception, they found themselves trapped in a set of problems which appeared insoluble—problems which could "only be removed by turning" the "whole examination round."[28]

26. *Ibid.*, pp. 3, 16–18, 100.
27. David Pears, *Ludwig Wittgenstein* (New York, 1970), p. 40.
28. *Philosophische Untersuchungen*, trans. with parallel German text by G. E. M. Anscombe as *Philosophical Investigations*, 3d ed. (New York, 1958), ¶ 108, 194.

"A person caught in a philosophical confusion," Wittgenstein explained one day to a favorite student, "is like a man in a room who wants to get out but doesn't know how. He tries the window but it is too high. He tries the chimney but it is too narrow. And if he would only *turn around*, he would see that the door has been open all the time!" The imagined incident elaborated on one of Wittgenstein's dicta that became famous after his death: "What is your aim in philosophy?—To show the fly the way out of the fly-bottle." It also suggested his new view of the philosopher as a therapist, a healer of the ills of understanding. "Philosophy"—so ran another of Wittgenstein's most celebrated aphorisms—"is a battle against the bewitchment of our intelligence by means of language." This battle—to change the metaphor—entailed the destruction of most that seemed "great and important" which philosophers had built before, "as it were . . . leaving behind only bits of stone and rubble." But what was destroyed was in fact "nothing but houses of cards," which were knocked down in the process of "clearing up the ground of language" on which they stood.[29]

Language, then, was the terrain on which Wittgenstein chose to do battle. Yet it would be wrong to call his investigation linguistic in a narrow or merely technical sense. His assault on language was part of a wider inquiry into the way in which words functioned in the lives of human beings. More particularly, Wittgenstein was trying to clarify how his own ideas had changed since writing the *Tractatus*. At that time he had maintained that language proceeded from reality—that the structure of the real world determined the structure of speech. Now he had come to believe that the reverse was the case: language, as the vehicle for understanding reality, determined the way in which people saw it. Nor was it true, as Wittgenstein had once thought, that philosophical analysis could reveal an underlying uniformity in the logical structure of language. There was no such uniformity: all that the philosopher could do was to try to get at the deeper nature of language by examining its uses in their infinite diversity.[30]

29. Malcolm, *Wittgenstein*, p. 51; *Philosophical Investigations*, ¶ 109, 118, 309.
30. Toulmin, "Wittgenstein," p. 62; Pears, *Wittgenstein*, pp. 3–4.

"How many kinds of sentence are there?" Wittgenstein asked. There were "*countless* kinds," and with them "countless different kinds of use of what we call 'symbols,' 'words,' 'sentences'." And "this multiplicity" was not "fixed, given once for all; . . . new types of language, new language-games" were coming into existence all the time, as others dropped out of circulation.

> Language games are the forms of language with which a child begins to make use of words. The study of language games is the study of primitive forms of language or primitive languages. If we want to study the problems of truth and falsehood, of the agreement and disagreement of propositions with reality, of the nature of assertion, assumption, and question, we shall with great advantage look at primitive forms of language in which these forms of thinking appear without the confusing background of highly complicated processes of thought. When we look at such simple forms of language the mental mist which seems to enshroud our ordinary use of language disappears. We see activities, reactions, which are clear-cut and transparent. On the other hand we recognize in these simple processes forms of language not separated by a break from our more complicated ones. We see that we can build up the complicated forms from the primitive ones by gradually adding new forms.[31]

Such "language games" constituted the core of Wittgenstein's highly unorthodox method of teaching. He held his classes in his own rooms in Trinity and always in the late afternoon. What he called his lectures, but which in fact were closer to informal seminars, met twice a week for two hours. He supplemented them with "at homes" in which he discussed more speculative topics, but the line between these and his regular classes was not as sharp as Wittgenstein supposed. He also invited his students individually to tea. The result was a heavy teaching burden, which was all the greater because of the ruthless intellectual demands that Wittgenstein made on himself and on those who were trying to learn from him.

31. *Philosophical Investigations*, ¶ 23; *The Blue and Brown Books*, Torchbook paperback ed. (New York, 1965), p. 17 (*Blue Book*).

These would sit tightly packed on folding chairs. On one occasion at least their number reached as high as thirty, "wedged together without an inch to spare." Usually, however, the total would shake down to between ten and fifteen, once the "tourists," as Wittgenstein angrily called the more casual students, had had their curiosity satisfied and had given up trying to follow him. For it was a formidable task to understand exactly what was going on: one former student recalled that it took "at least three terms . . . before one could begin to get *any* grasp" of it. Wittgenstein spoke "without preparation and without notes"; when he had tried to proceed in a more conventional fashion, his words had appeared to him like "corpses." Thereafter he simply spent a few minutes before class "recollecting the course that the inquiry had taken at the previous meetings" and starting from there. One problem led naturally and spontaneously into another—although the transition was not always clear to his listeners. "There were frequent and prolonged periods of silence, with only an occasional mutter from Wittgenstein, and the stillest attention from the others. During these silences, Wittgenstein was extremely tense and active. His gaze was concentrated; his face was alive; his hands made arresting movements; his expression was stern."

While thus carrying on "a visible struggle with his thoughts," Wittgenstein associated the class in the battle by asking questions of individual students or engaging them in dialogue. Fear of their teacher kept them ever on the alert. Wittgenstein could be peremptory and crushing with what he took to be a stupid remark or objection—but by the same token he could refer to himself as a fool when he thought that his mind was not in good working order. Two hours of relentless probing left both teacher and students exhausted. After it was over, Wittgenstein himself would frequently ask a friend to go off with him to a film.

The students who became his friends, while they never ceased being frightened of him, were utterly devoted. They bore his severity and his gloom and enjoyed the rare moments in which he was positively merry. They appreciated his unsparing integrity, both intellectual and moral, and the fact that he was harder on himself than on those around him. "In talking about human greatness, he once remarked that he thought . . . the measure of

a man's greatness would be in terms of what his work *cost* him."
(One might compare this with Weber's assessment of his own
scholarly endeavor: "I want to see how much I can endure.") The
students who knew Wittgenstein well had no doubt of the fearful
price he had paid for what he himself regarded as mere glimmer-
ings of understanding in a dark world.[32]

It was to such student friends that Wittgenstein dictated (in
English) the preliminary studies which from the color of their
covers became known as the Blue and Brown Books. The first
dated from the academic year 1933–1934, the second from the year
following. Both circulated quite widely, in typed or in mimeo-
graphed form, in British philosophical circles, although neither
was regularly published until more than a half-decade after Wittgenstein's death. There were also in existence a number of notes
taken down by his students—which unlike the Blue and Brown
Books had not been checked over by Wittgenstein himself; selec-
tions from these jottings also began to appear in print in the
1960's. The most important from the standpoint of social thought
were lectures on aesthetics and religion dating from 1938 and
conversations about Freud held in the mid-1940's.

The Blue Book differed from the Brown Book in being a mere
set of notes never intended for publication; as such it had a simplicity that made it the most accessible of Wittgenstein's later
works. The Brown Book was a rough draft of what Wittgenstein
had projected as a major philosophical treatise. After trying more
than once to turn it into German—the language he always used
for his finished products—he gave up the attempt in 1936 and set
about writing the *Philosophical Investigations* that were to give
the full measure of his late thought. The first part was finished in
1945; the second remained incomplete at his death in 1951; both
were published posthumously in 1953.

In the preface he wrote to the first part of the *Investigations*,
Wittgenstein explained his purpose in returning to the notion of
publication after having given it up for so many years. His "van-
ity" had been "stung" by the fact that his ideas, "variously mis-

32. Most of the foregoing is derived from Malcolm, *Wittgenstein*, pp. 24–
29, 32, 55, 62, 72.

understood, more or less mangled or watered down," were already in circulation in fragmentary form; it was incumbent on him to set the record straight. Moreover, people were bound to be puzzled by the relation between the "old thoughts" in the *Tractatus* of nearly a quarter-century earlier and the "new ones" he had developed at Cambridge: although he had been "forced to recognize grave mistakes" in his early work, he did not want to discard it entirely; he wished rather to put his new ideas "in the right light . . . by contrast with and against the background of" his "old way of thinking." Yet the very structure of the two books betrayed the magnitude of the change that had occurred. The *Tractatus* had had the beauty of a finished and detached perfection; the *Investigations* was a report on work in progress. His second book, Wittgenstein explained, consisted of "*remarks*, short paragraphs," sometimes running in "a fairly long chain about the same subject," sometimes "jumping from one topic to another." It could be compared to an "album" of pictures, "sketches of landscapes which were made in the course of . . . long and involved journeyings" and which crisscrossed "in every direction."[33]

It was unfortunate that the majority of Wittgenstein's readers were to know the *Investigations* only in the parallel English text which was published, as had been done with the *Tractatus*, alongside the German. But even a casual glance across the page at the original could give some impression of its author's mastery as a stylist. His German was direct and supple; he eschewed involved constructions, literary phrases, and technical terms; he shifted easily from dialogue to aphorism and back again. Underlying the flow of his sentences and the surprising turns of his thought was a musical quality which reminded those who knew him well that his favorite composer was Schubert.[34]

Yet his writing gave him little but agony. After he had resigned his Cambridge professorship, he turned himself wholly to the second part of his *Investigations*. He went to live in Ireland, first in the remote countryside, subsequently in a hotel in Dublin. In 1949 he made his first and only trip to the United States. Here he

33. *Philosophical Investigations*, pp. ix–x.
34. Von Wright, "Biographical Sketch," p. 21.

discovered that he was gravely ill, an illness which was diagnosed
on his return as cancer. He had been in a "frenzy" at the thought
he might die in America: he was a European, he insisted, and he
wanted to die in Europe. A year and a half later he died, as he had
wished, in Cambridge close to his friends. Throughout the last
period of his life, his work had progressed only intermittently. He
was tormented by the thought that his mental powers were waning
and by the question of what he should do with his existence if his
talent was gone. He may even have feared that what he called
"loss of problems" was setting in—a philosophical malady which
he attributed to Russell and which made the world become "broad
and flat" and writing about it "immeasurably shallow and trivial."[35]

For the task he had set himself had proved even harder than he
had believed when he had originally struggled with his thoughts in
the early 1930's. At that time he had imagined that his language
games could proceed in a cumulative fashion—that it would be
possible to "build up the complicated forms from the primitive
ones by gradually adding new forms." As early as the Brown Book
he had begun to doubt the feasibility of such a work of construc-
tion. By the time he was in difficulties with the *Investigations*, he
had come to see that his games did not add up to anything—they
simply pointed to the "big question" of what language was in the
first place. The further Wittgenstein pushed his pursuit, the fewer
answers it afforded him. In the end he was obliged to conclude
that the various "phenomena" called language had "no one thing
in common," only the "relationships" whose crisscrossed paths he
had endeavored to follow.[36]

The new view of philosophy that Wittgenstein embodied in his
Investigations was "empirical, pedestrian, and even homely." Its
full effect demanded a "personal involvement"—as had been true
between Wittgenstein and his students; it worked itself "into
people's lives." Abandoning the high ground on which nearly all

35. Malcolm, *Wittgenstein*, pp. 93–100; Ludwig Wittgenstein, *Zettel*, ed.
by G. E. M. Anscombe and G. H. von Wright, trans. with parallel German
text by G. E. M. Anscombe (Berkeley and Los Angeles, 1967), ¶ 456.
36. Preface by Rush Rhees to *The Blue and Brown Books*, pp. ix–xi; *Philosophical Investigations*, ¶ 65.

previous philosophizing had been conducted, the author of the *Investigations* had given up "*striving after* an ideal." As early as the Blue Book, he had renounced the "craving for generality" that derived from a "preoccupation with the method of science." It could "never be" his "job," he had insisted, "to reduce anything to anything" or indeed "to explain anything." His job, rather, was to combat "the contemptuous attitude towards the particular case" which had characterized most previous philosophers.[37]

If one focused, then, on the particular case, one soon discovered that even the simplest terms one employed had no single meaning. In a "*large* class of cases . . . the meaning of a word" was "its use in the language"; the very word "meaning," as Wittgenstein had earlier explained, caused "philosophical troubles" by the way in which it did "odd jobs." Precise definition made matters worse: it was only the context (*Zusammenhang*), the circumstances in which a word or phrase came out, that counted. In such a fluid universe of discourse, there were no fixed rules. Yet at the same time there was no disorder. If a sentence, however vague, in practice made sense, then "there must be perfect order" in it. And similarly with the great problems that had vexed philosophers for centuries. The "most important . . . aspects of things" had been "hidden because of their simplicity and familiarity." Philosophy, Wittgenstein asserted, merely put "everything before us. . . . Since everything" lay "open to view," there was "nothing to explain." Eventually one might make "the real discovery"—the one that would enable men to stop "doing philosophy," the one that would make "philosophical problems . . . *completely* disappear," the one that would give philosophy "peace."[38]

The "extreme anthropocentricism" of such a view left Wittgenstein's readers dizzy. It was hard to grasp a world in which there were "no independent, objective points of support," and in which "meaning and necessity" were "preserved only in the linguistic practices" which embodied them. Yet at the same time, from the standpoint of social thought, Wittgenstein's method offered

37. Pears, *Wittgenstein*, pp. 109, 113–114; *Philosophical Investigations*, ¶ 98; *Blue Book*, p. 18.
38. *Philosophical Investigations*, ¶ 43, 98, 126, 129, 133; *Blue Book*, pp. 43–44.

marked advantages. It reopened old vistas that Russell and the
Vienna Circle had threatened to close off. It drew philosophy back
to the concrete case and to the actual process of living: "to
imagine a language," Wittgenstein surmised, meant "to imagine a
form of life." In its tolerance for imprecision of discourse it
encouraged the philosopher to discuss everyday human concerns in
a way that tried to follow the contours of the concerns in question.
While it did not denigrate science, as Carnap and his friends had
feared, it did suggest that there were enormous areas of men's
thought and conduct which remained relatively immune from
what was ordinarily understood as scientific analysis—and were
none the less important for that.[39] This was the artistic or mystical side of Wittgenstein's speculations which had disconcerted his
Viennese admirers.

Aesthetics, ethics, metaphysics—these matters of value, Wittgenstein agreed, lay in the realm of the unutterable. But it was
natural and inevitable that men should speak of them, and much
could be learned from the way in which people went about their
foredoomed task of trying to say the unsayable. Moreover, it would
not be clear where the boundary of sanctioned speech lay until an
attempt had been made to cross it and that attempt had failed.
Such efforts Wittgenstein regarded with benevolence. He treated
them as reconnaissance expeditions, perilous to be sure, but well
worth the effort expended on them. His *Investigations* aimed to
"retrieve" some portion at least of what his contemporaries had
banished from philosophical discourse—and at the price of posing
riddles that even he could not answer.[40]

Thus he refused to drop the word "soul" or "spirit" (*Geist*)
from his vocabulary. "Where our language suggests a body and
there is none: there, we should like to say, is a *spirit*." One of the
psychological tricks Wittgenstein detected in his own meditations
was observing his "soul out of the corner" of his eye. In his conversation he expressed sympathy for St. Augustine and Kierkegaard—and even Heidegger.[41] Indeed his *Investigations* began

39. Pears, *Wittgenstein*, pp. 179, 193; *Philosophical Investigations*, ¶ 19.
40. Pears, *Wittgenstein*, pp. 22–23, 104, 126–127.
41. *Philosophical Investigations*, ¶ 36, Part II, p. 188; Toulmin, "Wittgenstein," p. 60.

with a quotation from Augustine which indicated his knowledge of the Christian tradition and the peculiar fascination that religion held for him.

Wittgenstein's personal view of religion, like so much else in his outlook on life, was bleak and comfortless. It was Augustinian in its conviction of sin and in its image of God as a "fearful judge." These were the emotional residues that Wittgenstein's puritan childhood had left with him. On the intellectual level, his characteristic reaction to talk of religion was puzzlement. Unable to subscribe to any particular belief himself, he respected those who did believe and kept wondering what the grounds of their faith might be. He was quite sure that it could not be rational argument: religious belief not only was "not reasonable": it didn't even "pretend to be" so. Yet he defended himself against the notion that he was a complete skeptic, and he had two converted Catholics among his loyal followers. Religion he apparently regarded as one of those "forms of life" whose linguistic networks he was endeavoring to trace; it hovered in the back of his mind as a possibility that others might grasp but whose "essence"was forever eluding him.[42] Like James or Durkheim a generation earlier, Wittgenstein saw the need for calling attention to the *fact* of religion that his positivist-minded contemporaries left out of their reckoning.

When it came to ethics, Wittgenstein found a firmer footing. Religion had puzzled him in that it possessed a language of its own whose meaning he could not penetrate. (Yet he could "quite well imagine" a religion in which there were neither doctrines nor speech.) With ethics it was unavoidable that one should "go beyond" language entirely. Indeed, the human "urge to thrust against the limits of language" was what constituted ethics. This expression of "thrusting" or "running" against the boundaries of speech kept recurring in Wittgenstein's lectures and conversation in the period immediately following his move to England. It figured at the start of the only "popular" lecture he ever gave, an

42. Ludwig Wittgenstein, *Lectures and Conversations on Aesthetics, Psychology and Religious Belief*, ed. by Cyril Barrett from notes taken by Yorick Smythies, Rush Rhees, and James Taylor (Berkeley and Los Angeles, 1967), pp. 58, 70. See also Von Wright, "Biographical Sketch," p. 20, and Malcolm, *Wittgenstein*, p. 72.

informal talk on ethics delivered at the end of his first Cambridge year. Ethics, he explained, could be thought of in a wide sense as including "the most essential part" of what was generally called aesthetics; it was an inquiry that extended beyond the "good" into what was "important" or "valuable"—in short, it was an excursion into the realm of value. But these matters could never be defined, as even the intellectually fastidious Moore had supposed. They could be spoken of only in terms of metaphor or simile. Such similes, however, as opposed to the figures of speech in ordinary discourse, had no facts standing behind them. They were "supernatural": they gave evidence of man's "perfectly, absolutely hopeless"—yet deeply respectable—effort to burst the bonds of his "cage." It was impossible to write about ethics "a scientific book, the subject matter of which could be intrinsically sublime and above all other subject matters. . . . If a man could write a book on Ethics which really was a book on Ethics, this book would, with an explosion, destroy all the other books in the world."[43]

There was of course the alternative possibility of writing a "natural" or scientific work about how men behaved. But this would be simply a description or analysis of "facts," which could be subsumed under the heading of psychology. Sooner or later Wittgenstein was bound to make his reckoning with psychology— and with his great fellow Viennese, Sigmund Freud. The two already had something in common in combining what amounted to ethical relativism in the intellectual sphere with a stern view of morality in practice. Freud had said that morality was self-evident. Wittgenstein believed that "relativity must be avoided at all costs, since it would destroy the *imperative*" in ethics.[44] In their dealings with those close to them, both delivered harsh and absolutist judgments; both were convinced that the run of mankind was evil.

Like so many other leading twentieth-century intellectuals,

43. "A Lecture on Ethics," *The Philosophical Review*, LXXIV (Jan. 1965), 4–5, 7, 9–12. This is followed by a translation by Max Black of the key passages on ethics in the notes on talks with Wittgenstein taken down by one of the members of the Vienna Circle: Friedrich Waismann, *Wittgenstein und der Wiener Kreis*, ed. by B. F. McGuinness (Oxford, 1967), pp. 68–69, 115–118.

44. "Lecture on Ethics" (commentary by Rush Rhees), p. 23.

Wittgenstein could well have had recourse to psychoanalytic therapy. It might have mitigated his personal torment and enabled him to come to terms with the dark side of his nature. It was not that Wittgenstein misunderstood his own emotional life; in his capacity for self-awareness he was comparable once again to Nietzsche. But for him, as for Nietzsche, this awareness caused intense suffering. In his lecture on ethics, when groping for an example of what one meant by a term like "absolute good," he came up with "the experience of feeling *absolutely* safe," the sense of safety *whatever* happened. Wittgenstein freely granted that such an expression was "nonsense"; yet the vivid way in which he depicted the experience behind it suggested how rare and cherished a privileged moment of the sort must have been for him.[45] And he was far too stoical to seek professional counsel in his desolation.

Hence it was to be expected that his judgment on Freud should have been ambivalent. Basically he was skeptical of all psychology, characterizing it on the very last page he ever wrote as in a state of "conceptual confusion." (He had earlier noted the difficulty one encountered in dealing with the "unbridgeable gulf between consciousness and brain-process.") Although the similarity of his and Freud's methods was readily apparent, and although he himself in the preface to his *Investigations* described his approach in terms which resembled free association, he angrily dismissed the notion that the two techniques could be equated with each other. Psychoanalysis he called "a powerful mythology"; it was a "way of thinking" which needed "combatting." Yet he spoke of himself as "a disciple of Freud," "a follower of Freud," and ranked him among "the few authors he thought worth reading."[46]

Freud was worth reading because he possessed the rare quality of "having something to say": his "way of thinking" should be opposed because of the "subservience" it fostered. This contrast gave the key to Wittgenstein's divided mind. On the negative side, he found Freud clever but not wise and his claim to scientific validity unfounded. What Freud had given, rather, was *"specula-*

45. *Ibid.*, p. 8.
46. *Philosophical Investigations*, ¶ 412, Part II, p. 232; Malcolm, *Wittgenstein*, pp. 56–57; *Lectures and Conversations*, pp. 41, 50, 52.

tion—something prior even to the formation of an hypothesis."
More specifically Wittgenstein rejected the central psychoanalytic
precept that nothing in the human mind was guided by chance; he
himself was inclined to believe that there was no such thing as a
law governing mental phenomena. And similarly with the unconscious: the Freudians had obscured the whole issue by speaking of
"unconscious thought"; the clearer way to have expressed it would
have been to reserve the word "thought" for what went on in full
consciousness and to speak of the unconscious in terms of "newly
discovered psychological reactions." Wittgenstein's finely honed
mind took offense at the slippery use of language in psychoanalytic
theory—just as his prudishness recoiled from the sexual emphasis,
the "bawdy," in Freud's work. But what annoyed him most was
the role "persuasion" played in the acceptance of psychoanalysis.
To learn from Freud, one had to be critical—and this the psychoanalytic process ordinarily prevented.[47]

Wittgenstein's reading of Freud tended toward reductionism. It
also did not get much beyond *The Interpretation of Dreams.* It
was unfortunate that he had not studied psychoanalytic theory in
its fully developed and more permissive forms, that he was un-
acquainted, for example, with the work of still another Viennese
and his own contemporary, Heinz Hartmann, whose first statement of what subsequently became known as ego psychology had
been read to the Vienna Psychoanalytic Society shortly after
Wittgenstein himself began writing his *Investigations* and in the
year prior to the Nazi takeover in Austria. Wittgenstein's distrust
of psychoanalytic theory was of a piece with his doubts about the
Vienna Circle of philosophers: they smacked too much of positivism; they seemed to threaten the open universe of discourse
which his own late work was endeavoring to delineate.

Yet when all this has been said, it remains undeniable that
Wittgenstein acknowledged profound affinities between himself
and Freud, not so much as theorists—Wittgenstein, after all, had
discarded explicit theory—as in the human implications of what
they were trying to do. Both were negative and practical in their
aim. Both sought to strip away the illusions—or fantasies or
"pictures"—by which men ordinarily lived and to reveal the

47. *Ibid.*, pp. 23–24, 27, 41–42, 44, 51–52; *Blue Book*, pp. 57–58.

incongruence between avowed statement and the hidden meaning or intention behind it. Both were alert to the slips and tricks of language that could serve as clues in the search. Both argued that mere understanding was useless unless it was accompanied by a change within. In the broadest terms, Freud and Wittgenstein alike rejected the ideal images of man to which earlier thinkers had tried to make the intractable raw material of humanity conform. Freud had shown that a recognition of man's animal nature was essential to comprehending—and accepting—the burden of civilization. Wittgenstein taught that the gift of language which distinguished men from beasts and which offered them everything they really knew of the world about them could be appreciated at its full worth only if it too were accepted in all its ambiguity and imprecision.[48]

It would be incorrect to classify Wittgenstein as a social theorist in the usual sense of the term. His mind was far too nominalist for that. The very word "society" would have had little meaning for him; he would have experienced great difficulty in focusing on so amorphous a concept, since he himself preferred to deal with concrete, particular cases studied in their individual context. And his attitude toward society in practice was not without contradictions: although scorning conventions and hating all humbug, he had nothing but respect for "genuine" or legitimate authority and regarded as "immoral . . . revolutionary convictions of whatever kind."[49]

Yet subsequent social thought could not escape the responsibility of digesting what the young philosophers of Britain and America had learned from Wittgenstein. He himself was far from sure how much he had accomplished, and he chose as the motto for his *Investigations* the remark of the Austrian writer Johann Nestroy that it was "in the nature of every advance" to appear "much greater than it actually" was. The formula neatly embraced

48. For reflections in this vein, see Frayn, "Russell and Wittgenstein," pp. 74–75, and Stanley Cavell, "The Availability of Wittgenstein's Later Philosophy," *The Philosophical Review*, LXXI (1962), reprinted in *Wittgenstein: A Collection of Critical Essays*, ed. by George Pitcher (Garden City, N.Y., 1966), pp. 184–185.
49. Engelmann, *Letters from Wittgenstein*, p. 121.

Wittgenstein's unremitting oscillation between despair and confidence in judging his own achievement. If he frequently doubted the value of what he had written, he at least suspected that he had seen farther than any of his predecessors. If he was almost always dissatisfied with the way he finally put matters into words, he could rest assured that he had brought the meaning of those words into question with unprecedented thoroughness and penetration. If he sometimes thought himself foolish in his teaching, he ordinarily dismissed his fellow philosophers as still greater fools than he. Convinced that he had made an advance—how great, how small, he did not know—he was tortured by the thought that his admirers might propagate a travesty of his intentions.

Thus it would be further incorrect to try to find in Wittgenstein precepts to "apply" to the study of society. It was rather that he offered a new perspective for social thought that was both revolutionary and reconciliatory. His work inaugurated—or better, epitomized—a revolution by undercutting the entire vocabulary in which human beings commonly spoke of their own doings; it relativized not merely the words in ordinary use but, by implication, the more formal language of the sciences of man. And thereby it suggested a way to heal the schism in Western thought that Wittgenstein's own early writing had done so much to bring about.

In his youth, with his *Tractatus*, he had given twentieth-century neopositivism a rallying point. He had played a crucial role in establishing a new type of positivist thinking, more modest in aim than its nineteenth-century predecessor, a type of thinking which based its scientific credentials on logical rigor and a clear delimitation of "facts" rather than on the ascription of causal or lawful relationships to the universe of human affairs. Subsequently Wittgenstein gravitated toward an even more subtle type of positivism, close to the example of Hume and expressing itself in a "naturalistic" attitude to linguistic usage. In this late view, statements of fact retained a privileged position over value judgments. Yet since both were alike seen as mediated by the vast imprecision of language, the line between factual and value discourse became more fluid than most neopositivists supposed. The result of this "leveling" process was a refusal to discriminate "against any of the

modes of human thought. Each" was to be "accepted on its own
terms and justified by its own internal standards."[50] On the one
hand, Wittgenstein repudiated the "destructive" stance toward
the realm of value that so many of his early followers had derived
from his *Tractatus*. On the other hand, he would have disagreed
emphatically with the alternative neopositivist way of thinking,
primarily associated with structural linguistics and the anthropology of Claude Lévi-Strauss, which claimed to have discovered
beneath the phenomenon of language the immanent structure of
the human mind.[51] What Wittgenstein discarded and what he
ventured to assert were alike more tentative than was true of the
vast majority of his positivist-minded contemporaries.

Once these distinctions had been understood, it became immaterial whether or not one referred to Wittgenstein as a positivist.
From the standpoint of social thought, the most valuable aspect of
his legacy was the prospect it afforded of putting back into a single
intellectual universe the styles of thinking that had split apart in
the 1920's—analytical philosophy and logical positivism on the one
side, phenomenology and existentialism on the other. A man who
was a mystic as well as a logician had shown how it was possible to
read Heidegger and Moore with equal respect.[52] Still more, in his
attitude toward language, he had suggested that one could readmit
into the company of serious thinkers the practitioners of disciplines whose vocabularies were of necessity imprecise. Wittgenstein was not particularly concerned with history and seldom spoke
of it; yet in his distrust of exact definition and his emphasis on the
full context in which events occurred, he came close to the loose
and permissive usage of the practicing historian. His operational
notions about language epitomized his appreciation of those who
labored in fields of investigation where unassailable rigor of
method was out of the question.

For the most part Wittgenstein's contemporaries in the social

50. Pears, *Wittgenstein*, pp. 29, 184–185.
51. See my *The Obstructed Path* (New York, 1968), pp. 270–271, 286,
291.
52. Cf. Janik and Toulmin, *Wittgenstein's Vienna*, p. 194, in which one of
his letters is referred to as unifying "Wittgenstein the formal logician with
Wittgenstein the ethical mystic."

sciences knew little of his work and went their own way without reference to him. Once he had been "discovered," however, it became apparent that he had put in the most plain and general terms what so many of them had been groping for in their specialized languages.[53] Within a decade of his death, his example was already established as that of the German-speaking intellectual who had done more than any other to unite the world of his origins to the Anglo-American cultural milieu which welcomed him. Yet there was one linkage that even Wittgenstein could not forge or prefigure: the bulky inheritance of Hegel fell outside his scope. And correspondingly the neo-Hegelians of the German emigration to the United States had no use for Wittgenstein; they misunderstood his teaching and did their best to maintain the old distinction between the philosophical tradition of Central Europe and that of Britain and America.[54]

It is finally noteworthy that Wittgenstein commented scarcely at all on public affairs or on the events of his day. In this apolitical stance, as in so much else about his life that he accepted without question, he remained an authentic representative of the pre-1914 Austrian intelligentsia. Unlike their counterparts in the Reich, the Austrians had seen no incompatibility between technical and cultural pursuits, nor had they found anything incongruous in combining total religious skepticism with an acceptance of Catholicism as the "normal" religious posture. And their corresponding loyalty to the state that guaranteed their German linguistic heritage had deterred them from revolutionary yearnings.[55]

After the breakup of the Hapsburg Empire, such attitudes had begun to change and to polarize. But Wittgenstein had stayed fixed in his earlier views. Although he obviously detested fascism and became a British subject when the annexation of Austria in

53. For example, Hanna Fenichel Pitkin, *Wittgenstein and Justice: On the Significance of Ludwig Wittgenstein for Social and Political Thought* (Berkeley and Los Angeles, 1972), p. 328, envisages "a Wittgensteinian political theory . . . addressed from one citizen to others" rather than delivered in the customary style from some intellectual eminence.

54. See Chapter 4.

55. See the unpublished Ph.D. thesis by David S. Luft, "Robert Musil: An Intellectual Biography, 1880–1924" (Cambridge, Mass., 1972), Chapter 2. Luft notes striking parallels between the family and intellectual backgrounds of Wittgenstein and of Musil.

1938 would have made him a citizen of Nazi Germany, he limited himself to speaking of the "dark" times in which he lived and to volunteering for civilian service in the Second World War. What was informal and commonplace in his approach seemed to preclude the kind of cataclysmic pronouncements that occurred so readily to people of his generation. It may also have been true that he hesitated to speak of matters of which he had no direct knowledge. The most probing commentary on fascism was to come not from minds of philosophical distinction such as Wittgenstein's but from men of a robust and combative intelligence who knew at first hand whereof they wrote.

CHAPTER

3

The Critique of Fascism

NOT A SINGLE PROPHET, during more than a century of prophecies, . . . ever imagined anything like fascism. There was, in the lap of the future, communism and syndicalism and what not; there was anarchism, . . . war, peace, deluge, pan-Germanism, pan-Slavism . . . ; there was no fascism. It came as a surprise to all. . . ."[1] Thus Giuseppe Antonio Borgese, musing on the convulsions that had driven him from his homeland, voiced the bewilderment of intellectuals before a phenomenon which none had predicted and which threatened to annihilate the bright anticipations the nineteenth century had bequeathed to its successor.

Europe's intellectuals were at a loss because they could get no handle on the movements that Mussolini and Hitler led. Writers and professors were accustomed to deal in words, and with fascism words gave little guide to what was occurring. Language functioned to deceive or to arouse or to lull rather than to explain; the gap between rhetoric and actuality went far beyond the normal bounds of political usage. More particularly, it was unclear whether fascism was revolutionary or reactionary, whether it belonged on the left or on the right. Most of those who studied it could see where it derived from the course of contemporary history: they could trace its origins to the delayed and unfinished character of Italian and German national unity, to the defeats and

1. G. A. Borgese, "The Intellectual Origins of Fascism," *Social Research*, I (Nov. 1934), 475–476.

disappointments the Italian and German peoples had suffered in the First World War, to the economic dislocations of the immediate postwar years and to the mass unemployment of the early 1930's. Those who probed deeper could note a lack of homogeneity in the societies of Italy and Germany as opposed to those of France and Britain, and a less widespread acceptance of middle-class or democratic values. Yet such fragments of an explanation were patently insufficient: the dynamics of fascism itself eluded any simple formula.

Of one thing, however, nearly everyone—both those who remained in Europe and those who emigrated to America—was sure: what had come to power in Italy in 1922 and in Germany eleven years later deserved to be called by the same name. No doubt it was significant that Mussolini had triumphed a decade earlier than Hitler; no doubt Hitler ran a tighter show and was infinitely more concerned about "race" than the Italian leader who had originally served as his model. But there were matters of timing and emphasis: to contemporaries it went without saying that German National Socialism should be considered a variant— an extreme variant—on the type of rule which the Italian Duce had invented and to which he gave the name eventually applied to his imitators throughout Europe. During the period when fascism was in power, those who had experienced it were scarcely in a position to think of it as some vague abstraction. Its rigors were far too real for that. It would have seemed absurd to indulge in the kind of nominalism—or obscurantism—that a decade or two later was to dismiss the comparative study of fascist regimes as a matter too complex for generalization. It was true that in the meantime, particularly during the Second World War, the term "fascist" had all too often been exploited for purposes of indiscriminate abuse. But this had gone on in the forum of partisan debate rather than at the level of scholarly analysis. The more conscientious students of fascism strove for intellectual rigor: although they had suffered under fascist tyranny and made no secret of their antipathy toward it, they did their best to amass their documentation and to weigh their evidence in accordance with accepted professional standards.

Thus movements and regimes which had mastered the arts of obfuscation and whose ideologies were a maze of contradictions presented a special and very personal challenge to the thought of the emigration. Far from engulfing those who studied it in its own semantic morass, fascism stimulated its critics to heroic efforts at clarification. It served as the precipitant directing social speculation toward immediate issues of a burning actuality. It raised in acute form the question of what should be considered the key features of modern industrial society and the extent to which Marxist or quasi-Marxist theory was appropriate for analyzing them. In the most general terms, the fascist systems posed the problem of whether it was possible to arrive at judgments that could claim any long-term validity, when the prior investigation, by force of circumstance and temperament, had been anything but "value-free."

I. *Initial Perspectives: Borgese, Mannheim, Fromm*

With three of the most influential critics of fascism, their accounts of its nature and prehistory did not rank as their chief literary production or the focus of their intellectual lives. Borgese, Mannheim, and Erich Fromm had in common the fact that study of the fascist phenomenon came at the end or at the beginning of careers devoted to other concerns. What they had to say about it was necessarily tentative. They offered suggestions, beginnings; they did not attempt a full-scale analysis.

Giuseppe Antonio Borgese was not quite fifty in 1931 when, on an American lecture tour, he refused to take the oath demanded of Italian university professors and chose to remain in the United States. Born in Sicily in 1882, he had earned the reputation of an *enfant terrible* of Italian letters, as critic, poet, novelist, and teacher of aesthetics. He had also been a publicist, independent and outspoken, who had broken with the philosophical doctrines of his master Croce and had pursued an isolated and eccentric anti-Fascist course.[2] In America he taught first at Smith College, later

2. For biographical details, see Sarah D'Alberti, *Giuseppe Antonio Borgese* (Palermo, 1971), pp. 25–38, 53.

at the University of Chicago, where he met and married a daughter of Thomas Mann. His father-in-law quickly recovered from his consternation at the thirty-six-year age difference in the bridal pair; Borgese, he wrote his brother Heinrich, was "a brilliant, charming, and excellently preserved man . . . and the bitterest hater of his Duce."[3]

As was to be expected from a writer whose intellectual preparation had been preponderantly literary, Borgese's critique of fascism was vivid and impressionistic. It also made extremely good reading: Borgese had acquired a command of written English that was astounding in a man who had begun to use it so late in life; his work bubbled over with surprise effects, telling anecdotes, and arresting figures of speech. And the same theatrical inclination led him to stress those features of fascism that lent themselves to a consciously artistic presentation—the vicissitudes of its march to power and the cultural-historical context from which it derived. Borgese's experience of Mussolini's rule had convinced him that its acceptance by the Italian people was primarily due to weakness of character; "the specific elements of fascism" were "of a mental and sentimental nature"; it had "happened first in the mind" and only subsequently "found its way into the facts of mass history."[4]

In the year following the advent of Hitler, Borgese published an essay on fascism's intellectual origins. While it dealt primarily with his own country, it made frequent reference to what was going on in Germany and traced to the same cultural sources the movements that Hitler and Mussolini had founded. These sources Borgese discovered in the "ideal and emotional backgrounds" of people with a "middling" education. Fascism had "nothing to say" to "the proverbial peasant." Nor could it appeal to "real minds," which wanted a "critically clean food." But to those suffering from "intellectual starvation," it gave a "daily spiritual meal." Fascism was "first of all a degradation of romanticism, both cultural and political, . . . not a revolution . . . but an involution." As such, it taught that "change" was "substance" and "passion . . . virtue." In its belief that force made right and in its "substitution of

3. November 26, 1939, *Letters of Thomas Mann 1889–1955*, selected and trans. by Richard and Clara Winston (New York, 1971), p. 320.
4. "Intellectual Origins," p. 463.

the idea of power for the idea of justice," it had become "the creed of the lower middle classes."[5]

Why, then, had fascism triumphed first in Italy? Borgese gave no simple answer, but he was inclined to believe that it was because his countrymen had had a spectacularly mixed history of glory and degradation:

> accustomed through two thousand years of world empire and universal church . . . to loftiness of political imagination, and at the same time to the most dejected renouncement of personality in public life, . . . they were prepared to accept anything strange and new, particularly if the novelty promised somehow to revive the hereditary complex of Roman superiority and to check the stubborn . . . complex of modern inferiority.

Borgese's psychological pronouncements did not rise above the clichés available to any educated layman in the 1930's. But they indicated his appreciation of the emotional disorientation that characterized both leaders and led in the fascist movements. Mussolini, he was later to suggest, should be studied in "the perspective of the good novelist." Freud, Borgese added, "would not have very much to say" about the Italian Duce. "He would probably hand over the case to his colleague Jung" (an unlikely event, one may note, to have occurred a quarter-century after the break between the two), a seer whom Borgese thought peculiarly qualified to handle "the all-embracing ego problem."[6]

The book entitled *Goliath* that Borgese published three years after his essay about intellectual origins enlarged on a number of the latter's themes, concentrating this time almost exclusively on the Italian experience. He took pains to refute the Marxian interpretation of fascism, which in the meantime had been gaining currency: "social and economic factors," he contended, explained the phenomenon "as little as the mushrooms crowding at the foot of the tree or the mistletoe clambering on its branches" explained "the tree itself." Borgese had declared fascism to be "an outburst

5. *Ibid.*, pp. 463, 467, 474.
6. *Ibid.*, p. 477; *Goliath: The March of Fascism* (New York, 1937), pp. 171, 195.

of emotionalism and pseudo-intellectualism," and he stuck by the definition: "the sin had been in the mind; and from the mind should have come redemption." Hence he deemed it crucial how his fellow intellectuals had reacted to Mussolini's rule. Most of them, he observed with bitterness, had behaved like cowards. Even Croce, whom the outside world viewed as the symbol of intellectual resistance, had failed to give the guidance that his juniors had the right to expect of him—first, by never repudiating the ethical Machiavellianism of his writings of the prefascist era; second, by appeasing the consciences of the young with the assurance that "working for culture" was an adequate response to tyranny.

"All strongholds of Italian intelligence," Borgese concluded, "were razed to the ground: because they had not been strong at all."[7] We now know that this verdict was unduly pessimistic. But we may also understand the personal reasons why Borgese wrote as he did. Alone in a strange land, unattached to any émigré political movement, and without the training for close ideological or social analysis, Borgese fell back on the intellectual equipment he had, his literary gifts and his thorough knowledge of European cultural history. His *Goliath* was an engrossing human chronicle; the product of a lofty idealism in both the philosophical and the ordinary moral meaning of the term, it scored an immediate popular success. If it did not go very far beyond a spiritual interpretation of the fascist appeal, it at least located those whom that appeal had touched and for whom future investigators were to show a special concern.

In the last two decades of his life, Karl Mannheim never recaptured the intellectual heights he had attained at the end of the 1920's with his *Ideology and Utopia*. His emigration to England in 1933 led him to neglect the theoretical concerns that had made him after Weber's death the most inventive sociologist in Germany. Virtually abandoning his longstanding interest in the sociology of knowledge, he turned to applied and even propagandist pursuits. He persuaded a London publishing house to support his editing of an "International Library of Sociology and Social Reconstruction"—a collection of works, many of them Continental

7. *Ibid.*, 217–218, 289, 299–302, 305.

or American, which ranged from demography, education, and law to anthropology and religion—and he lectured and wrote voluminously in behalf of the "democratic planning" which he was convinced offered the only hope for rescuing Western society from the grip of dictatorship and war.

If the influence of his adopted country was apparent in Mannheim's later writings—if the pragmatic, reform-minded bent of English social thought guided him toward a more direct and accessible presentation of his ideas—there could also be discerned in his new sense of mission a return to his origins. As a young man in Budapest before the First World War, Mannheim had belonged to a coterie of left-oriented writers, a large number of them Jewish like himself, who had followed the lead of Lukács in regarding intellectuals as the future saviors of society. This attitude was thoroughly comprehensible in a situation such as the Hungarian where the ruling aristocracy and gentry remained adamant against every type of change and the educated bourgeoisie was small and lacking in influence;[8] it was to lead Lukács himself into his lifelong association with Communism. In Mannheim's case, the relationship to Marxism and the political left was always more nuanced. And after his move to Germany his view of his own situation as a "free-floating" mind was reflected in a concept of intellectuals as mediators among classes and interests rather than as social innovators in their own right; such had been one of the central contentions of his *Ideology and Utopia*. With Mannheim's second transplantation, however, his old messianic feelings returned: jumping over the aloof, academic stance of his central years in Germany, he arrived at a curious and highly personal combination of his early Hungarian intellectual elitism and an Anglo-Saxon insistence that for a given social or political problem an appropriate remedy must exist.

The book entitled *Man and Society in an Age of Reconstruction* marked the transition from Mannheim's German to his British

8. For Mannheim's Hungarian background, see Zoltán Horváth, *Die Jahrhundertwende in Ungarn: Geschichte der zweiten Reformgeneration* (1896–1914), trans. from the Hungarian by Géza Engl (Neuwied and Berlin, 1966), and for a general biographical sketch, Lewis A. Coser, *Masters of Sociological Thought* (New York, 1971), pp. 441–449, 457–463.

phase. Originally published in German in the Netherlands two years after its author's emigration, it appeared in English in 1940 in revised and enlarged form. At the very start of the work Mannheim explained how the circumstances of its composition had affected its content. As one of "those to whom destiny" had "given the opportunity of living in many different countries and of identifying themselves with various points of view," he had thought it his task to blend these views "in a new synthesis"—and more particularly to reconcile his firsthand, German-based sense of "sitting on a volcano" with the optimism derived from the British experience of "living in a country where liberal democracy" functioned "almost undisturbed." If his stay in England had enabled him "to free himself from his deep-rooted scepticism as to the vitality of democracy" in his own age, he had not changed his former conviction that profound structural changes had eroded the social foundations which democratic apologists ordinarily took for granted.[9]

In trying to define these changes, Mannheim felt that he was "only groping his way"; his work remained incomplete and without any "illusion of finality or absolute proof." Yet in the most general terms he found it undeniable that the "last decades" had witnessed a retreat from "moral and rational progress." In common with the Frankfurt Hegelians Adorno and Horkheimer, Mannheim associated the advent of authoritarian rule with an eclipse of rationality. And the danger of such a lapse, he thought, lay in the very nature of large-scale industrial society. As Weber had already observed, that society had created "a whole series of actions" which were "rationally calculable to the highest degree" and which depended on a corresponding "series of repressions and renunciations of impulsive satisfactions." It had so refined "the social mechanism that the slightest irrational disturbance" could "have the most far-reaching effects"; concomitantly it had produced "an accumulation of unsublimated psychic energies" which threatened "to smash the whole subtle machinery of social life."[10]

9. *Man and Society in an Age of Reconstruction*, trans. from the German by Edward Shils (London, 1940), pp. 3–5, 9.
10. *Ibid.*, pp. 32, 51, 61.

In the fatal antinomy of technical rationality and mass emotion—in the dialectical play between sophisticated equipment and latent barbarism—Mannheim discerned the psychosocial dimension of fascist movements.

"Up till now," he surmised, people had been able to believe that "relatively free competition between different forms of education and propaganda would, by natural selection, allow the rational, educated type of man, best fitted for modern conditions, to rise to the top." The experience of the 1920's and 1930's had proved this confidence unfounded; the "normal mechanism" of choice had failed to operate. There had come about instead a "negative selection of the élites": the "earlier bearers of culture" had begun "to be ashamed of their . . . values" and "to regard them as the expression of weakness and . . . a form of cowardice"; meanwhile "the representatives of local culture" were discrediting the intellectuals' cosmopolitan ideal with appeals to xenophobia and primitive virtue.[11]

Mannheim had never ceased to believe in the association of high culture with aristocratic values. In Britain he found it still possible for the upper orders to assimilate "a gradual influx from the lower classes" while maintaining their own traditional standards. On the Continent, however, he saw the older intellectual groups losing "their assimilative power." They were being submerged by numbers and forfeiting political and cultural leadership to the lower middle class—"the minor employees, petty officials, artisans, small business men, small peasants, and impoverished *rentiers*." And this composite stratum was of necessity reactionary: threatened from every quarter, it was attempting "to rescue itself by using all the political techniques at its command in order . . . to restrict the extension of rationalized industry, and to prevent the development of the modern rational type of man with . . . his humane ideals."[12]

Thus by a very different route from Borgese's, Mannheim arrived at the same social class as his focus of primary concern. Whereas the Italian littérateur had traced from its nineteenth-

11. *Ibid.*, pp. 74, 95–96.
12. *Ibid.*, pp. 101–102, 105.

century origins the neo-Romanticism of the half-educated, the Hungarian-Jewish-German-Englishman-by-adoption followed a Freudianized version of Max Weber in delineating the "negative selection of the élites." But in fastening like Borgese on the lower middle class, Mannheim did not limit himself to trying to understand the fears and resentments that made it fascism's major reservoir of recruits. He peered behind the frightened little people to see who else might be lurking in the shadows. In the turmoil of mass psychic breakdown, he suggested, there must be some who stayed cool and kept their power of rational calculation. Such men of substance as army leaders, large businessmen, and high officials might still hope to turn the general insecurity to their own advantage. And they might also locate and support those better endowed than they with the gift of popular leadership:

> It is not to be expected that the old bureaucracy . . . or the former commercial and industrial leaders trained in the ways of rational calculation will find the secret of symbol-manipulation. They need an alliance with a new kind of leader, and this leader, and the petty leaders, must come chiefly from those holes and corners of society where even in normal times irrational attitudes prevailed and where the catastrophe of unorganized insecurity was most severe and prolonged. Thus the leader must himself have experienced that emotional rhythm which is common to those who have been most exposed to the shocks of a partial dissolution of society.[13]

The fascist leaders had learned at first hand to play upon the mass anxieties of their countrymen. At the same time they were obliged to cultivate their own calculating faculties and to gain the sympathies of those who possessed such faculties to the highest degree. Mannheim merely sketched the alliance of disparate partners that lay behind the garish façade of fascist rule; he held his analysis to the generalized, schematic level of a psychosocial ideal type. The configuration he had marked out was to be filled in by a different variety of scholar, one with an eye for detail and a convic-

13. *Ibid.*, pp. 135–136, 138.

tion that a thorough empirical investigation could alone give the full measure of the fascist phenomenon.

Eleven years younger than Borgese, Mannheim was in terms of historical experience a member of the same generation. Both had come to intellectual maturity before the First World War; both had their base point in the prewar sense of economic security and social deference that the cultivated had enjoyed. The smaller age gap which separated Mannheim from Erich Fromm marked on the contrary a real psychological watershed. Born in 1900, Fromm belonged to the generation that went through the war as adolescents and whose decisive intellectual encounters were to occur in the tormented early years of the 1920's.

A psychoanalyst by training, Fromm had evolved away from Freud. He also broke with the Frankfurt Hegelians with whom he had been associated both before and after his emigration to the United States in 1934. By the time he published his first book in English, *Escape from Freedom,* seven years later, he had worked out a personal blend of a revisionist Freudianism and a similarly diluted Marxism that won him a wide audience in his new country.[14] *Escape from Freedom,* like Borgese's *Goliath,* was easy to read and attuned to the unspecialized; it had in common with Mannheim's work a characteristically German substructure of social and psychological theory.

Dissatisfied with purely psychological explanations and equally unwilling to accept any rudimentary Marxian schema, Fromm sought to combine elements of the two in a long-range historical assessment of fascism's appeal. Disregarding entirely the Italian experience, he found in his own native land the acute and extreme manifestation of a pervasive modern unease. And this in two separate epochs: the most original feature of Fromm's book was the simplistic and anachronistic suggestion that Reformation Germany prefigured the social history of the Weimar and Nazi periods. In each case, the line of reasoning ran, sudden economic change dislocated the traditional structure of society; in each case "the individual's feeling of powerlessness and aloneness . . . in-

14. For Fromm's intellectual autobiography, see *Beyond the Chains of Illusion: My Encounter with Marx and Freud* (New York, 1962).

creased, his 'freedom' from all traditional bonds" became "more pronounced, his possibilities for individual . . . achievement . . . narrowed down," and he felt "threatened by gigantic forces." The result, in the sixteenth century as in the twentieth, was a "compulsive quest for certainty," a "desperate escape from anxiety" into the arms of a religious or ideological leader, a Luther or a Hitler.[15]

Such a flight from a freedom seen as spurious, Fromm argued, characterized the lower middle class in particular. "The isolation of the individual and the suppression of individual expansiveness . . . were true to a higher degree" of this class than of those above and below it. Nazism could appeal to its "destructive strivings" and use them "in the battle against its enemies." For the average member of the lower middle class did not comprehend his own situation: he thought that he was suffering from the defeat and humiliation of his nation rather than from economic obsolescence; he failed to appreciate the extent to which Hitler's rule worked against his own social survival.[16] In short, he offered a classic example of what Marx had labeled false consciousness.

Thus in the end, like Mannheim before him, Fromm arrived at a sociopsychological explanation that hinted at the cleavage between ideology and economic reality in the fascist movements. In delineating the emotional universe of the lower middle class, he was more precise than either of his predecessors. Convinced, as they were, that the little people's vulnerability gave the key to fascism's success, he knew that this was only the first part of the story. But to write the sequel would require a detailed knowledge of events and an economic expertise that Fromm did not possess. Diffuse, hortatory in tone, and replete with banal psychoanalytic explanations, *Escape from Freedom* looked more impressive when it first appeared than it did a few years later. Second thoughts were to suggest that it had stretched its historical parallel too far and put together too tidy an explanatory synthesis.

Those who had acquired the special qualifications for analyzing fascism that Borgese and Mannheim and Fromm in their different

15. *Escape from Freedom* (New York, 1941), pp. 77, 91, 123, 207–208.
16. *Ibid.*, pp. 184–185, 216, 221.

ways all lacked were not necessarily their intellectual superiors. But they were men whose severe intelligence admirably fitted them for the task of making sense out of an incoherent mass of contradictory data. Quite independently of each other, Gaetano Salvemini and Franz Neumann, from their contrasting Italian and German experiences, wrote accounts whose conclusions were mutually reinforcing and whose factual density and critical bite very quickly gave them an authoritative standing. Subsequently, in the 1950's, they were frequently dismissed as "leftist" and subjected to major correction. When a full generation had passed, they were retrospectively restored to honor as the classic examinations of fascism in power.

ii. *Gaetano Salvemini between Scholarship and Polemic*

Gaetano Salvemini has been described as the last of the now "extinct species" of Italy's intellectual "masters." He has similarly been characterized as the ideological spokesman of his country's radical petite bourgeoisie, with a role comparable to Croce's for its grand bourgeois liberals, and Gramsci's for its Marxists.[17] Simply as an intellectual, Salvemini bulks less large than either of these in the culture of his own country or in the history of social thought. His mind was of a coarser grain than theirs, and his expression less disciplined. Yet there fell to him the task that neither Croce nor Gramsci was in a position to accomplish—the job of exposing to the outside world the realities of the despotism under which the Italians lived for two full decades. Croce was both too prudent and too fastidious to grapple with the sordid day-to-day realities of Mussolini's rule; cut off from reliable sources of news, Gramsci was reduced to the cryptic, coded aphorisms of his writings from jail. Neither the eminent untouchable nor the wretched prisoner could speak his full mind. Only an exile could proclaim the whole truth,

17. Gaspare De Caro, *Gaetano Salvemini* (Turin, 1970), p. 425; Massimo L. Salvadori, *Gaetano Salvemini* (Turin, 1963), p. 8. The former, the fullest biographical study, is bitterly hostile to its subject; the latter is briefer but more judicious. See also the laudatory collaborative volume by Ernesto Sestan et al., *Gaetano Salvemini* (Bari, 1959), and Salvemini's own *Memorie di un fuoruscito* (Milan, 1960).

and among the Italian émigrés Salvemini soon emerged, as though predestined for the assignment, in the congenial guise of the Duce's critic-in-chief.

He was just short of fifty-two when in 1925 he left Italy for an absence that was to last more than twenty years, and he had behind him a quarter-century of active involvement in ideological strife. Along the way he had delivered himself of countless misjudgments and had repeatedly been obliged to revise or to disavow positions he had earlier espoused with passion. It has not been hard for critics two generations younger to ferret out the inconsistencies in his voluminous writings and to question the moralizing tone that came naturally to him. Loathing what was merely abstract and forever in search of the "concrete," Salvemini often ended up in his own peculiar form of ethical or political abstraction.[18] His corresponding distaste for industrial society led him to underestimate the dynamic force of Italian capitalism and to champion the egalitarian misery of small peasant proprietorship. In this as in so much else of his stubbornly held set of convictions, he looked like a holdover from the nineteenth century never fully at home in the intellectual world of the twentieth. Yet there was one aspect of Salvemini's character that his detractors could not belittle or deny—his transparent integrity. He spoke the truth as he saw it, and early experience with hardship and tragedy had left him almost without fear and detached from worldly considerations.

These were to be precious assets when it came time for Salvemini to pass judgment on the Fascist regime. Likewise his mistakes of the past could be mobilized and brought to bear in his rigorous self-appointed task. His very failings—his political amateurishness and his moral impetuousness—became sources of strength when his countrymen lost their bearings and when he undertook to piece together from inadequate information the fundamentals of an unprecedented ideological situation. His three decades in Italy's political arena, coupled with his labors as a professional historian, had given him an immense range of knowledge of men and events, a knowledge which made him confident that

18. Salvadori, *Salvemini*, p. 114.

he could finally understand and explain the facts about Fascism, where others were at a loss.

In the biographical elements contributing to a personality that remained disarmingly simple, the earliest and deepest impressions were those stemming from a precarious lower-middle-class origin in the Italian south. Salvemini was born in 1873 in the small Apulian city of Molfetta—one of those white Adriatic seaports that look so charming until one discovers the squalor of the back streets. His family had struggled up from the peasantry into the petite bourgeoisie, only to be reproletarized by the economic depression of the 1880's. As a boy he had known hunger and anxiety, and along with them a meager intellectual diet. An uncle who was a priest had steered him toward an ecclesiastical career—the classic fate of the bright sons of poor southern families from which he was saved by the timely award of a scholarship to study in Florence.

These origins naturally invite comparison with those of Croce and Gramsci—both of whom similarly came from Italy's under-privileged regions. But with Croce the comparison ends there: the latent hostility that marked a half-century of intermittent relations between Salvemini and the Neapolitan philosopher sprang not only from profound differences in intellectual temper; it reflected the social cleavage between a man born into the southern elite and far removed from the poverty of the southern masses and one who early set himself up as the champion of the oppressed peasantry. In this latter course, Salvemini's career anticipated that of Gramsci —whose Sardinian petit bourgeois childhood closely paralleled his own. Indeed Salvemini, who was a half-generation older, saw twenty years before Gramsci the need for Italian Socialism to concern itself at last with the peasants of the south and of the islands. Yet whereas Gramsci settled in Turin—the most advanced of Italy's industrial centers—and preached from there the virtues of an alliance between urban and rural proletarians, Salvemini remained stuck in his loyalty to what was economically retrograde in Italian society. His southerner's resentment at northern domi-nance and at the scorn that northerners heaped upon his people was reinforced by the conviction that the south should and could be spared the horrors of industrialization. It was only the patient persuasion of his mentor, the pioneering student of southern society Giustino Fortunato, that little by little cured him of his illusion that the *cafoni* unaided could "save Italy." And there was something primitive and earthy also in Salvemini's abiding distaste for the complexities of formal philosophy: it made him feel, he complained, like "a *pugliese* peasant who begins to suspect in the streets of Naples that someone is trying to deceive him."[19]

At first sight it might appear odd that such a man should have become at home in Florence and have made it his intellectual headquarters. Yet in fact Florence perfectly answered his requirements: it was there that he received his training as a historian, it was there that he passed his best teaching years, and it was to there that he returned when his exile was over. In Florence from the start people were kind to him; the reigning positivist tone he found congenial to his spirit, and despite his peasant ways, he early won acceptance in some of its more exalted social spheres. Moreover, in Florence he could square the circle of his conflicting needs. He could escape the cultural confinement of the south without selling out to the north. He could live in a highly civilized and advanced community that still remained uncontaminated by the industrial bustle of the larger cities farther north. In the Tuscan capital he found a sobriety and moral seriousness which offered a welcome contrast both to the political trafficking in Rome and to the business values of the triangle Genoa-Turin-Milan.

Hence when he became a Socialist—something which was almost inevitable for a young man in the 1890's with Salvemini's ardor and concern for the poor—he soon saw reason to quarrel with the national leaders of the party. It was not only that these leaders viewed Italy's problems in a northern and urban-industrial perspective which was alien to Salvemini's temper. It was also that he could not abide any sort of political orthodoxy. His encounter with Marx was brief and superficial: in his reading of the Marxian texts he never got beyond the *Manifesto* and the works on con-

19. De Caro, *Salvemini*, pp. 200–201; Enzo Tagliacozzo, "Nota biografica," in Sestan et al., *Salvemini*, p. 216. See also Salvemini's own retrospective comments in his preface to Bruno Caizzi, *Antologia della questione meridionale* (Milan, 1955), p. 10.

temporary French history. As opposed to Croce, who came to his
own measured assessment of historical materialism after years of
careful study, Salvemini rather hurriedly picked up from Marx the
notion of class struggle and left it at that. In the course of his
ideological battles it gradually became apparent that he was far
more a positivistically minded radical than a Marxist. Indeed it can
be argued that the imprint of Christianity upon his thought
remained more profound than anything he had learned from the
classics of socialism. In his childhood he had been struck by the
ethical force and poetic beauty of the Gospels—this was the
earliest source of his moralizing—and in his old age he was to
write with warm sympathy of the mystical tradition in Italian
Catholicism, the spiritual universe of charity and undogmatic faith
that kept itself blessedly unaware of the official pronouncements
issuing from the Vatican.[20]

Salvemini's historical writings illustrate his evolution from a
simple, quasi-Marxist schema of class conflict to a more nuanced
view in which the radical values of the eighteenth-century Enlightenment predominated. The book with which he established
his reputation, *Magnati e popolani a Firenze dal 1280 al 1295*, had
"undeniably a certain mechanical quality," despite the impressive
archival scholarship that had gone into it.[21] In its delineation of
the issues pitting the great against the "little people" in Florence
six hundred years earlier, it betrayed its author's anxiety about the
social struggles that were currently shaking his country. The date
of publication was 1899: at the turn of the century Italy was
tormented by civil strife and official repression. In such a situation,
Salvemini's Socialist comrades were quick to hail his book as
inaugurating a new type of class-oriented history. These hopes
Salvemini disappointed. The works with which he followed
Magnati e popolani, while written for a wider audience, could no
longer be described as Marxist in inspiration. In moving from the

20. *The Origins of Fascism in Italy* (New York, 1973), pp. 155–156. This
work, written in 1942 and based on one of the lecture courses that Salvemini
gave at Harvard University, was published three decades later under the
editorship of Roberto Vivarelli, who had already edited an Italian version entitled "Lezioni di Harvard: L'Italia dal 1919 al 1929," *Scritti sul fascismo*
(*Opere di Gaetano Salvemini*, VI), I (Milan, 1961).
21. Ernesto Sestan, "Lo storico," in Sestan et al., *Salvemini*, p. 13.

Middle Ages to the modern era, Salvemini reversed the usual pattern by becoming more rather than less cautious. His books on Mazzini and the French Revolution, both published in 1905, won their lasting popularity as models of lucid synthesis and reasoned exposition.

Yet they had in common with his earlier and his subsequent writings a point of departure in the controversies of his own day. In his study of Mazzini, Salvemini was clearly trying to distinguish for the benefit of his countrymen what was helpful and what was dangerous in the legacy of the Risorgimento hero: while applauding the man of action, he warned his readers against the dogmatic and the "theological" in Mazzini's thought. Similarly it was characteristic of Salvemini's didactic bent that he should have ended his account of the French Revolution in 1792—*before* the era of terror and foreign conquest. He quite evidently wanted to demonstrate that the permanent significance of the Revolution lay in its reforming phase and its destruction of privilege: what had followed was sound and fury. He also meant to admonish the governing classes of contemporary Italy that they must adapt to democracy and socialism while they still had time.[22] In arguing that there was nothing fated, inevitable, or necessary about the violent phase of the Revolution in France, Salvemini was already anticipating what he was to maintain two decades later about the advent of Fascism in Italy—just as in his study of Mazzini he foreshadowed the role of moral leader in exile that he himself was to assume after 1925.

Here lay a further reason for his strained relations with Croce. While the two might agree that the historian's most authentic and convincing products took their initial impetus from some deeply felt contemporary concern, they went about the historiographic task in very different fashion. Croce tried to free himself from polemical passion by lifting his account to a high level of philosophical generalization; in his work the narration of "facts" and the judgment passed upon them were fused in a continuous line of quietly persuasive prose. Such was the practical manifestation of

22. *Ibid.*, pp. 19, 24–25; Franco Venturi, preface to republication of *La Rivoluzione francese* (1788–1792) in Salvemini's collected *Opere*, II, Vol. I (Milan, 1962), pp. xi, xiv–xv.

his idealist canon in the historian's daily labors. With Salvemini, these successive phases of history writing remained distinct. In his reconstruction of factual sequences, he conscientiously tried to detach himself so far as was humanly possible from the work at hand—hence the crisp, no-nonsense clarity of the expository portion of his writings. But when this duty had been performed, he felt at liberty to indulge in partisan rhetoric. In Salvemini's mind, the historian was entirely justified in expounding his own moral or ideological position, providing he had first established his account with scrupulous accuracy. In thus juxtaposing polemic and historical scholarship, Salvemini remained true throughout his life to the tradition of the Enlightenment and of nineteenth-century positivism. Quite naturally Croce dismissed such a procedure out of hand as methodologically crude and philosophically untenable.[23]

Yet when personal tragedy struck Salvemini in 1908, Croce was among those most deeply affected. In the earthquake at Messina—where seven years earlier he had received his first university chair—Salvemini's wife and five children all perished. As an adolescent Croce had similarly lost his parents in an earthquake: he was in a nearly unique position to understand what Salvemini had suffered. More broadly, to Italians of all sorts the misfortune that had befallen Salvemini ranked as the supreme, the unspeakable disaster. For a society that cherished and honored the family above everything, the fact of having lost wife and children in one blow passed mortal comprehension. In his grief-stricken state his friends feared for Salvemini's sanity: after the Messina earthquake his career was to be marked—and possibly furthered—by the pity and sympathy with which he was surrounded.[24]

Still more significantly, the entire central portion of his life—the quarter-century until his move to America in the early 1930's—was delivered over to a frenzy of activity. Once the first shock was over, and virtually abandoning historical scholarship, Salvemini sought forgetfulness by plunging into the murky eddies of Italian politics.

23. See, for example, Salvemini's lectures delivered at the University of Chicago in 1938 and published under the title *Historian and Scientist* (Cambridge, Mass., 1939), pp. 75, 82–84, 160, and Croce's ironical, condescending review of the Italian edition: *Quaderni della "Critica,"* No. 13 (March 1949), pp. 93–95.
24. De Caro, *Salvemini*, p. 150.

The variety and feverishness of his pursuits are explicable only in terms of the despair that lay behind them. He denounced Italy's liberal parliamentary master, Giovanni Giolitti, as the "minister of the underworld"; he detailed the combination of corruption and threats of violence with which Giolitti's henchmen managed elections in the south; and as though to prove the point, he ran unsuccessfully for the Chamber of Deputies from his native Molfetta. His basic aim—and his great contribution to the understanding and awakening of the south—was to politicize the southern masses. Most of the peasantry were still disenfranchised: at the best their landlords' relations with them remained paternalistic. Universal suffrage alone, Salvemini argued, could mobilize the peasants to stand up for themselves and struggle in their own behalf. And it was for this that he did battle in the years of Giolitti's rule. It was not his fault if the ringleader of Italian politics reduced him to a state of "stupefaction" by granting from on high in 1912 the substance of the universal manhood suffrage that Salvemini had urged the southern peasantry to wrest from Italy's governing classes by their own exertions.[25]

In the previous year, with the foundation of the review *Unità*, he had assumed the role to which he adhered for the remainder of his life—the role of preceptor to his countrymen. Gathering about him a group of contributors drawn from a broad spectrum of political persuasions, Salvemini sought to make the new review a forum for technical, nonrhetorical analysis of Italy's political and social problems. Not surprisingly Croce found Salvemini's writings as editor "half naive and half unjust, and tinged with utopianism."[26] Others have characterized *Unità* as excessively eclectic. But unquestionably it raised the level of the discussion of public affairs in Italy, and in the range of subjects it dealt with admirably prepared Salvemini for his future task as dissector of the Fascist system. More immediately it occasioned a change in its editor's life that had been long in the making—his withdrawal from the Socialist party.

On the outbreak of the First World War, Salvemini broke

25. *Ibid.*, p. 177; Salvadori, *Salvemini*, p. 51.
26. *Storia d'Italia dal 1871 al 1915* (Bari, 1928), trans. by Cecilia M. Ady as *A History of Italy 1871–1915* (Oxford, 1929), p. 251.

completely with his former comrades by advocating Italian intervention on the side of Britain and France. He joined in the
agitation that at length led Italy into the conflict through the
street demonstrations of 1915 known to nationalist history as
"radiant May." Still more, he served as a volunteer at the front
until his health buckled under the strain. No action—or series of
actions—of Salvemini's has occasioned more subsequent controversy. Even his most admiring biographer has admitted that the
"resolute and aggressive . . . minority" in which he enrolled
"succeeded in dragging into the war" a people whose "great
majority" were opposed to intervention.[27] And Salvemini himself
was subsequently to grant that the Italian masses "asked only to be
left at peace in their daily life" and to describe radiant May as a
"coup d'état" and dress rehearsal for the extraparliamentary pressure which seven years later brought Mussolini to power.[28] While
he never precisely apologized for what he had done, he made it
clear that later events had shed doubt on the stand which in 1914
and 1915 had seemed to him—as to so many educated and public-
spirited Italians—a simple matter of loyalty to the memory of the
Risorgimento and to the embattled forces of Western democracy.

Alongside and reinforcing the growth of Fascism, what had
discredited democratically minded interventionists such as Salvemini had been their failure to persuade their countrymen of the
virtues of a "Mazzinian" or Wilsonian peace. As interventionists
they had always been a minority within a minority: by 1919, their
voices were drowned out by those who in the name of "sacred
egoism" clamored for Italy's full share of the victors' spoils. In that
same year, Salvemini was elected to the Chamber on a nonparty
"veterans'" ticket; but he soon learned that his running mates
were losing whatever enthusiasm they may once have had for a
peace of international reconciliation and were moving toward a
protofascist course. In 1921, he did not stand for reelection; in
1922 the March on Rome found him tired and disillusioned, with
a sense that age was overtaking him and that his own political

27. Tagliacozzo, "Nota biografica," p. 235.
28. "La diplomazia italiana nella grande guerra" (originally published in
1925), *Dalla guerra mondiale alla dittatura* (1916–1925), in Salvemini's collected *Opere*, III, Vol. II (Milan, 1964), p. 726; *Origins of Fascism*, p. 108.

mishaps and the collapse of Italy's popularly based political movements had borne out the contention of his countryman Gaetano
Mosca that active and determined elites alone knew how to
govern.

When Mussolini came to power, then, it might have seemed
that Salvemini's public career was finished. In fact within two
years he was to launch the third and greatest of his battles—
dwarfing his fights for universal suffrage and for a just peace—the
"implacable" battle he waged from exile against the Fascist
regime.[29]

In common with nearly everyone else of influence in Italy,
Salvemini had misjudged Mussolini. In the prewar years he had
viewed the future Duce as the gadfly the Socialists needed to stir
them out of complacency. There had even been a curious episode
linking Mussolini not only to Salvemini but to the former comrade
he would imprison, Antonio Gramsci. Just before the outbreak of
the war the *torinese* left Socialists with whom Gramsci was associated had proposed that Salvemini run for the Chamber in a by-
election from their city; his candidacy, they explained, would
express the solidarity of the northern industrial workers with the
peasants of the south. Salvemini, although "shaken and. . .
moved" by the proposition, had felt obliged to refuse. And in his
place he had suggested Mussolini.[30]

Subsequently the two former Socialists had been aligned together in the interventionist cause. As the gap had widened
between the Italian nationalists and the advocates of a Mazzinian
peace, Salvemini and Mussolini had gone their separate ways. By
1919 they were clearly enemies. But still Salvemini hesitated to
throw the full weight of his polemic against the approaching dictatorship. His uncharacteristic passivity during Mussolini's assumption of power was a sign of more than weariness: it showed
that he shared the illusion of most of the Italian elite that they
and the Duce lived in the same moral universe. Mussolini was a
familiar figure on the Italian political scene; Salvemini, like Bor-

29. Salvadori, *Salvemini*, pp. 28, 33.
30. For Gramsci's own account of this episode, see his posthumously published *La questione meridionale* (Rome, 1952), pp. 14–16.

gese and so many other critics of Fascism, had known him personally in his double capacity as politician and journalist. On the left
as on the right, there was a widespread conviction that the Socialist leader turned nationalist would remain substantially within
the tradition of Italian public life. This was a mistake that many
fewer German antifascists would make about Hitler, who was
easier to spot from the start.

It took the "great shock" of the murder of the Socialist deputy
Giacomo Matteotti in mid-1924 to convince Salvemini that his
own "inertia" amounted to complicity with an "infamous regime"
and that he "must say a resolute and public no to that regime."[31]
From this point on he hesitated no more: he became the guiding
spirit among the anti-Fascists of Florence, where he had lived
since 1909 and been professor of history since 1916; he edited the
first of Italy's clandestine journals; he was arrested, tried, released,
and then, with his life in danger, crossed the Alps into exile.
Shortly thereafter he resigned his university chair—on the grounds
that freedom of teaching no longer existed in his native land—and
began a wandering life that was to last the better part of a decade.

Shuttling back and forth between France and England, Salvemini labored ceaselessly to collect evidence on what was occurring
in his home country. To give himself any respite, he felt, would be
to let down his friends who had remained in Italy and who were in
far more peril than he. Yet among the emigration that made its
headquarters in Paris, Salvemini stood almost totally isolated. He
did not share the belief of most of his fellow exiles that the Fascist
regime would soon succumb to an internal crisis and that their
energies should be directed toward maintaining contact with the
opposition inside Italy and preparing for an eventual insurrection.
Salvemini foresaw that the job of fighting Mussolini from abroad
was a very long pull indeed, and he was skeptical of plans for
clandestine action. To his mind, the only way to topple Fascism
was to discredit it in the eyes of the great Western democracies. In
France and Britain and the United States, most solid citizens were
taking a benevolent view of Mussolini's rule; they were inclined to
disregard or to remain in ignorance of the Fascist terror. It was

31. *Memorie di un fuoruscito,* pp. 10, 106.

Salvemini's purpose to force them to look at the facts by presenting them with irrefutable proof.

Two myths which were in general circulation summed up the
conventional wisdom about Italy: that Mussolini had saved his
countrymen from "Bolshevism," near-chaos, and economic distress; and that the strong rule he had given them was precisely
what the Italians deserved. This was the line that the Fascist
propagandists were peddling and that foreigners were content to
swallow. In combating it Salvemini drew on his training and experience as a historian; by applying his ruthless critical technique
to the newspapers and official publications that reached him from
Italy he tried to expose the truth below the inflated rhetoric of the
regime. His preferred method was to let the documents speak for
themselves: with biting irony and marvelous comic effect he lined
up the Fascist pronouncements in all their intellectual vacuousness
and inconsistency.

The first of his books on Mussolini's rule, *The Fascist Dictatorship in Italy*, dealt primarily with the circumstances under which
the regime had come to power. It explained that the postwar
economic crisis was already past before the March on Rome and
that "the so-called Italian 'Bolshevism' of 1919–20 was nothing
worse than an outbreak of uncoordinated unrest among large
sections of the Italian people, to which the worse elements of the
ruling classes replied by an exhibition of cowardice out of all
proportion to the actual danger."[32] There had never been any real
peril of revolution from the left—the forces of Italian Socialism
were far too divided for that. Nor had the Italians accepted the dictatorship as spinelessly as most foreigners believed. The grisly facts
of police repression pointed, on the contrary, to the existence of a
stubborn internal resistance unknown to the world outside.

It was in its detailing of the crimes of Mussolini's followers that
The Fascist Dictatorship really hit home. This was its polemical
strength, and in this lay its analytical deficiency. From it the
Western public learned for the first time the full story of Matteotti's assassination and the acts of official violence that had
followed it. As he had earlier done with Giolitti, Salvemini
fastened on the scandalous and gangster features of his country's

32. *The Fascist Dictatorship in Italy*, enlarged ed. (London, 1928), p. 54.

new rulers—hence the sensational and episodic nature of his account.[33] Salvemini's first study of Fascism in power was a magnificent polemic; but it failed to reach the inner articulations or to analyze the structure of that power. It would require one further political disappointment and an assurance of continuity in his intellectual labors before Salvemini was in a position to offer to the English-speaking public his definitive critique of Fascism.

When the most dynamic of Italy's oppositionists, Carlo Rosselli, escaped to France in 1929, Salvemini temporarily abandoned his attitude of detachment toward militant anti-Fascist action. Won over by the charm and persuasiveness of a man who had been his student in Florence, he consented to help in the launching of a new political movement, Giustizia e Libertà. Rosselli's notion of fusing the liberal and the socialist traditions fell in with Salvemini's own ideas. For a few years the older and the younger man worked in harmony. But as Giustizia e Libertà, under the influence of its clandestine *torinese* adherents, began to move toward an understanding with the Communists—whom Salvemini always detested—his faith in Rosselli's movement waned. His personal "affection" and "admiration," he subsequently wrote his friend, remained unchanged. As he had witnessed, however, their joint venture "lose its bearings," he had "shut himself up" in his own concerns. He felt "old, . . . mistrustful," and at "the end of all hope."[34]

From this—the third of the shattering blows that had punctuated Salvemini's career—he was rescued in 1934 by the offer of a lectureship in Italian civilization at Harvard. For the decade and a half of his American sojourn, Salvemini lived in Cambridge in austere, sparsely furnished university quarters. His pay was low, but his teaching burdens were correspondingly light. His lectureship gave him what he needed—the minimum financial security he had lacked before and ideal working conditions. His real home was

33. As though to restore the spirits of the flagging opposition inside Italy, a few of its members, among them Benedetto Croce, received copies of the book, suitably disguised beneath a pornographic dust jacket: *Memorie di un fuoruscito*, p. 105.

34. Letter of September 29, 1935, quoted in De Caro, *Salvemini*, p. 388.

Widener Library, the "enchanted island," as he called it, the refuge from political disillusionment where he achieved at last a kind of despairing serenity.

Although Salvemini's own Ph.D. students were few, his indirect influence extended much more widely. The promising growth of American interest in modern Italian history following the Second World War sprang primarily from his example.[35] And it is as an exemplary figure that Salvemini is remembered in the United States. To the young people in his classrooms he was a curiously exotic and almost legendary character. His courses at Harvard avoided the contemporary topics that might have tempted him into controversy—he confined himself to the medieval communes and the Risorgimento—but he lectured with the same verve that marked his political writings. For a man who had learned to speak English when he was over fifty, Salvemini had an extraordinary command of the language. The humor and pungency of his Italian style passed over readily into his new tongue; one of his Italian editors has noted with how little difficulty Salvemini's ideas go from Italian to English and then back to Italian again. This ease of translation suggests a broader compatibility between Salvemini and the Anglo-American world—a *Wahlverwandtschaft* of shared simplicity, matter-of-factness, and distrust of abstractions.[36]

Such were the material and intellectual circumstances contributing to the writing of Salvemini's most important work on Mussolini's system, *Under the Axe of Fascism*. He had followed his account of the advent of the regime with a study of its foreign policy, *Mussolini diplomate*, published in France in 1932. Like its predecessor, it was a witty and devastating polemic. Yet its author must have sensed that in neither work had he risen to the full height of his analytical capacities. As his research deepened, he discovered that a social interpretation alone could bring into conceptual unity the massive bulk of previously scattered evidence he had gathered. The parallel work in this field by such scholars as Louis Rosenstock-Franck in France and Herman Finer in England

35. See my "Gli studi di storia moderna italiana in America," *Rassegna storica del Risorgimento*, XLV (April–June 1958), 274.

36. Roberto Vivarelli, preface to *Scritti sul fascismo*, I, viii.

reinforced his confidence and sharpened his conclusions.[37] His book appeared at the turning point of Mussolini's rule—in 1936, the year of victory in Ethiopia, the alignment with Nazi Germany, and the intervention of the two fascist powers in the Spanish Civil War. Although in fact the beginning of the long slide into defeat, it looked to contemporaries like a year of triumph.

The immediate stimulus for Salvemini's book was the bombastic proclamation in 1934 of the establishment of the "corporations" that were at last to give substance to what Mussolini had long called his "corporate state." Ostensibly these corporate bodies were to end—indeed, had ended—the strife of capital and labor. In actuality, as Salvemini demonstrated with an irrefutable array of facts, the corporations were patently one-sided. The representatives of capital who sat in them were the businessmen themselves; the representatives of labor were delegated by the Fascist bodies that enjoyed a monopoly in the trade union field. This position they had received nine years earlier under the terms of the Palazzo Vidoni agreement of 1925, a scarcely known transaction between the major Italian industrialists and Mussolini's government, which had completed the consolidation of the dictatorship in the social and economic sphere.[38]

Thus, Salvemini maintained, although the corporative institutions themselves were no more than an elaborate deception, they were worth studying for the key they gave to the way in which the Fascist system worked in practice. When one had penetrated behind the barrage of propaganda which enveloped them, one discovered that the beneficent innovations to which the regime laid claim amounted to extremely little. Far from being substantially modified or "transcended," Italian capitalism remained intact. Indeed, within the capitalist framework the position of the larger industrialists had been strengthened—and at the expense of small businessmen, the professional classes, and agrarian and industrial labor. In the corporative institutions the ordinary worker counted not at all; in the Fascist labor organizations the rank and

---

37. Louis Rosenstock-Franck, *L'économie corporative fasciste en doctrine et en fait* (Paris, 1934); Herman Finer, *Mussolini's Italy* (London, 1935).
38. *Under the Axe of Fascism* (New York, 1936), pp. 15–16.

file had "no greater authority than do the animals in a society for the prevention of cruelty to animals." And continuing with the zoological metaphor, Salvemini quoted Prince Metternich to the effect that in the desired cooperation between rider and horse it was well to "be the man and not the mount. In Fascist class cooperation the employer is the man and the worker is the mount."[39]

What, then, of the state intervention into the affairs of Italian capital that had marked the early years of the depression? This, Salvemini explained, had nothing collectivist or socialist about it. It was in fact no more than a series of rescue operations directed toward saving big business from bankruptcy. "When an important branch of the banking system, or a large-scale industry which could be confused with the 'higher interests of the nation,'" had "threatened to collapse," the government had "stepped into the breach and prevented the breakdown by emergency measures."

> In Fascist Italy the state pays for the blunders of private enterprise. As long as business was good, profit remained to private initiative. When the depression came, the government added the loss to the taxpayer's burden. Profit is private and individual. Loss is public and social.[40]

"Must we conclude from these facts," Salvemini asked, "that Fascism is a capitalist dictatorship?" His answer was more qualified than the reader might have been led to expect from the analysis that had preceded it. Mussolini's Italy, Salvemini explained, was a conglomerate oligarchy whose main components were "army chiefs, high civil servants, big business men, and Party leaders." The interlocking—and mutually reinforcing—interests of these four groups gave the regime its internal coherence and stability. "In this oligarchy the big capitalists" were "far from exercising an uncontested sway. . . . If the capitalists stopped playing the policies of the Party, the Party could easily steer to the left. Thus, although the employers" were "protected," they were "intimidated at the same time."[41]

39. *Ibid.*, pp. 66, 196.
40. *Ibid.*, pp. 379–380.
41. *Ibid.*, pp. 383–385.

Ultimately the Fascist party leaders called the tune. Yet their power—and that of the Duce himself—was limited by the needs and pressures of the other elements in the oligarchy with which they were obliged to work:

> Among these groups, therefore it behooves Mussolini to move warily and watchfully, now sacrificing the big business man to the high civil servant, now the civil servant to the big business man, conciliating them whenever he can with convenient compromises, never sacrificing the military chiefs, taking no unnecessary risks, and always yielding to the strongest pressure or to necessity.[42]

These were imperatives that the Duce forgot when he plunged his country into the Second World War. His desperate gamble failed: the men of substance in Italian society whom he had favored and who in return had given him their support slipped away from him one by one until at last in the summer of 1943 he was overthrown by his own party chieftains. Salvemini had not predicted in detail how the fall of Fascism would come about. But his dissection of its inner workings accorded precisely with the cumulative loss of confidence that ended in the collapse of the regime.

Mussolini's fall, like Giolitti's grant of universal suffrage a generation earlier, caught Salvemini unprepared. He seemed unable to grasp the new realities that emerged from the slow liberation of his country and the exploits of the armed Resistance in the north. He bitterly denounced the unavoidable tactical compromises of anti-Fascist leaders who had once been his friends. When the war ended, Salvemini was more isolated than ever before, boxed in by the stern demands of his own moral rigor.[43] Hence it was understandable that he should have hesitated about returning to Italy, where his old university chair in Florence had been restored to him. A reconnaissance trip in 1947 convinced him to go

42. *Ibid.*, p. 386.
43. For a balanced assessment of Salvemini's writings during the war years, see Gian Giacomo Migone, *Problemi di storia nei rapporti tra Italia e Stati Uniti* (Turin, 1971), pp. 155–156.

back: he was overcome with joy at seeing his native land again—
with pride in his countrymen's hard work of material reconstruction and admiration at the beauty of the Italian women. Two
years later, at the age of seventy-six, he took up his university
teaching once more.

Now, as in the past, he found an unworthy political regime to
belabor. For the third time in his life, Salvemini rose to do battle
against his country's rulers. Prime Minister De Gasperi's Christian
Democrats, with their covert clericalism and fostering of conservative interests, were no more to his liking than Giolitti had been.
Toward the latter, however, he had relented: he was now willing
to grant that in view of what had succeeded him, the great parliamentary corrupter was not wholly without merit.[44] Nor did he
find Christian Democracy's sins to be even remotely on a scale
with those of Fascism. Salvemini's last polemics had about them
an air of déjà vu. It was difficult for him to maintain his ethical
strenuousness when his fellow citizens of all ages and opinions
were treating him as a lovable old schoolmaster whose perplexing
vehemence had long ago been forgiven or forgotten.

With his health failing, Salvemini finally took refuge in the
Sorrento villa of an aristocratic friend of long standing, who had
already sheltered him prior to his emigration. Here he died in
September 1957, two days before his eighty-fourth birthday. His
death was serene and a source of inspiration to those who flocked
to visit him. Some found it Socratic, noting as they did so that in
physical appearance also Salvemini resembled Socrates. With his
snub nose, his enormous bald forehead, his little eyes that radiated
a mocking intelligence, he might have passed for some mythical
satyr. His broad, stooped shoulders, his squat torso, his heavy step,
his indelible *pugliese* accent, recalled his peasant ancestors. Or
perhaps one could see in him "the figure of the eternal emigrant
from the Italian South," whose capacity for exhausting labor
seemed without limit.[45]

44. For the vicissitudes of Salvemini's views on Giolitti, see A. William
Salomone, "Ritorno all' Italia giolittiana: Salvemini e Giolitti tra la politica e
la storia," *Rassegna storica del Risorgimento*, XLVI (April–Sept. 1959), 174–
223.
45. Ernesto Rossi, "Il non conformista," *Il Mondo*, September 17, 1957;
Sestan, "Lo storico," p. 5.

As early as 1899 Salvemini had revealed the complicity of northern capitalists with southern landholders in preserving the status
quo among the people from whom he had sprung.[46] He had
pointed out how it was to the advantage of both that the peasantry of the south should remain in political and economic sub-
jection: with nearly half of Italy reduced to institutionalized
inferiority, the northern leaders could keep their hegemony on the
national plane, the southern their local preeminence. This down-to-
earth approach, this realistic attention to those who profited and
those who suffered from policies ostensibly directed toward the
general interest, were to serve Salvemini well when he came to
unravel the complexities of Fascism. His peasant suspicion that
somebody was trying to put something over on him was exactly
what was required in exposing the truth about a regime which
specialized in mystification; it enabled him to drag out from
behind their façade of nationalist pieties the interlocking pressure
groups at the center of the Fascist phenomenon.

In such a task Salvemini's intellectual deficiencies—his eclecti-
cism and distrust of theory—no longer figured as handicaps; on the
contrary, they left him free to draw on his own long experience in
judging an enormously miscellaneous body of data. Even his
inveterate moralizing at last became appropriate when it was quite
literally a gang of bandits with whom he was dealing. Salvemini's
writings on Fascism, for all their fragmentary and polemical character, raised the basic questions. All subsequent students were
obliged to begin where he left off—with a class analysis of those
who benefited and those who lost out during the two decades of
Mussolini's rule.

III. *Franz Neumann between Marxism and Liberal Democracy*

By the end of the 1960's most American students of sociology,
history, or political theory were only dimly aware of who Franz
Neumann was. A half-generation earlier, in the late 1940's and
early 1950's, he had ranked as a major force in social science, a
man who from the start had given leadership to the intellectual

46. Rosario Villari, "Il meridionalista," in Sestan et al., *Salvemini*, pp. 108–
109.

emigration from Germany and had subsequently become one of the most respected professors in one of America's most prestigious universities. This contrast epitomizes what we may call in appropriately Germanic fashion "the Neumann problem." If Franz Neumann was enormously influential in his own time and began to suffer neglect very shortly after his death, the explanation lies only partly in the fact that the corpus of his published writing was small and that his powers of persuasion were exerted primarily through the spoken word; the change was also due to the ambiguity of the intellectual inheritance he left behind him. Beneath the force and clarity of his polemical style, his intimates had increasingly detected a profound hesitation and uncertainty. As long as Neumann himself was in charge of his theoretical output, he managed—at least in public—to impose order on his contradictions through the application of an inordinately powerful mind and a strict sobriety of method. After his death, all the ambiguities came to the surface, and it was difficult for his younger readers to find the thread of ideological and emotional consistency that held them together.

Thus the career of Franz Neumann suggests both what was tragic and transitory in the emigration experience and the fashion in which that experience passed into the wider currents of American intellectual life. Throughout the period when his work was neglected, his indirect influence persisted—and persisted largely through the work of men who considered themselves his students, whether or not they were ever formally enrolled under his direction. For this reason it is urgent for one of those in his intellectual debt to set down the record before memories grow blurred. Even in our century of unmanageable documentation, there are some events of the mind that remain almost entirely unrecorded. The influence of Franz Neumann was one of these: it should not be lost to the history of ideas.

The events of Neumann's life can be briefly told. Their relevance to his development as ideologist and theoretician is readily apparent. Born in Kattowitz (now Katowice) in 1900 of Jewish parentage, Neumann grew up in a border area which was contested between German and Pole and was to change from the hands of one to the other on three occasions in his own lifetime. For Neumann's family, as for most of Germany's eastern Jews, the preference for the Reich was clear; they were also more markedly Jewish than their highly assimilated coreligionists in the western part of the country or in Berlin. Neumann was never religiously observant; at the same time he never denied his Judaic origin. The fact that he entertained no doubts about and saw no contradiction in being both a German and a Jew may help to explain the self-confidence with which he adapted to American life and acquired American citizenship. However his external circumstances might change, he always knew precisely who he was.

As an adolescent, Neumann did military service at the end of the First World War, receiving his first ideological education in the Soldiers' Councils which sprang up in the wake of the armistice of 1918. After that he studied labor law in Frankfurt, and in 1927 settled in Berlin as a labor lawyer. Life in the capital evidently suited his tastes: for the rest of his life he spoke both German and English with the harsh tones of a Berliner, to which his increasing deafness gave an even more metallic character.

Had German democracy been preserved, there seems no doubt that Neumann would have attained a position of major political influence. In the last years of the Weimar Republic, he was simultaneously teaching at the Hochschule für Politik and serving as legal adviser to the executive of the Social Democratic party. In the latter capacity, he acted as an ideological gadfly, contemptuous of the routine-mindedness of the official leadership. It was only natural, then, that when the Nazis came to power, Neumann should have been one of the first they deprived of German citizenship and drove into exile.

On the road of emigration, his initial stop was London. Here, with his characteristic practical-mindedness, realizing that a knowledge of German law was of no use to him abroad, he converted himself into a scholar by taking a degree in political science with Harold Laski. Soon, however, in equally practical fashion, he saw that permanent residence in England would not do. He had, as he recalled two decades later, originally gone there "in order to be close to Germany and not to lose contact with her." Yet "it was precisely in England" that he "became fully aware that one had to bury the expectation of an overthrow of the [Nazi] régime from within. . . . The . . . régime, far from becoming weaker, would grow stronger, and this with the support of the major European powers. Thus a clean break—psychological, social, and economic— had to be made, and a new life started." But England, with its tight, homogeneous society, "was not the country in which to do it. . . . One could . . . never quite become an Englishman. . . . The United States appeared as the sole country where, perhaps, an attempt would be successful to carry out the threefold transition: as a human being, an intellectual, and a political scholar."[47]

Neumann arrived in the United States in 1936—at the high point of the New Deal—and he was frank to recognize that after the timidity of English politics, what he called "the Roosevelt experiment" made the same favorable impression on him that it did on Thomas Mann and so many of his émigré countrymen. But his interest or participation in American political life remained marginal to his chief concern. This was to assault Nazism with his lawyer's talents and the new intellectual skills he had acquired in London. Settling down with Adorno and Horkheimer's left-oriented Institut für Sozialforschung which had migrated from Frankfurt to Columbia University, he began work on *Behemoth*, a massive study of Hitler's system, for which he was to be chiefly remembered. After America's entry into the war, he moved to Washington, serving as principal expert on Germany for the Office of Strategic Services and subsequently for the Department of State; in the last years of the conflict his was widely recognized as the most authoritative analysis of the Nazi regime. And in a military sense the war followed the course he had predicted: Nazism was destroyed utterly, by the massed might of the Soviet and Anglo-American forces.

After 1945, however, Neumann's hopes for the postfascist world were disappointed all along the line: the cold war destroyed whatever lingering chance remained for the international order and the German society based on socialist principles which he had sketched in his wartime memoranda. For the West Germany that was emerging under Adenauer's guidance, Neumann never both-

47. "The Social Sciences," in Franz Neumann et al., *The Cultural Migration: The European Scholar in America* (Philadelphia, 1953), pp. 17–18.

ered to conceal his contempt. Toward Berlin, his former home, he was more indulgent: on repeated trips to the divided city he gave generously of his advice and encouragement to the Social Democratic leadership, the trade unions, and the newly established Free University. To the end of his life, Neumann never ceased to feel the emotional pull of Germany and of traditional European culture.

In the United States there was only one career that both appealed to him and was open to him—university teaching. He disliked his office chores as a State Department expert, and after shuttling for a while back and forth between Washington and New York, he decided for the latter without hesitation as soon as a full-time professorship of political science at Columbia became available to him. By the late 1940's Neumann seemed to be fully absorbed in American life: for more than a decade he had made the United States his home; he was married and had two young children; he lived in a prosperous suburb, to outward appearance thoroughly *embourgeoisé*.

Yet the new fit was never complete. Whatever Neumann's academic success—and it was very great—however warmly he might speak of the openness of American social and university life, he remained curiously detached from his surroundings. And by the same token he became increasingly melancholy. When roused to action, his old vigor and combativeness would return; when alone or with his intimates, he would lapse into silent meditation. He was evidently groping for a new life and a new style of thought— and he was beginning to think he could find them when on vacation in Switzerland in the summer of 1954 he was killed in an automobile accident.

A career such as Neumann's cut off in midcourse necessarily poses the question of what he would have said and done if he had lived another twenty or thirty years. And in Neumann's case the problem is complicated by the fact that his natural temperament was thwarted by events at two decisive points. The first was when the advent of Nazism forced him to transform himself from a political activist into a scholar; the second was when the cold war frustrated the vision which had inspired both his politics and his scholarship. It is only if we bear these two enormous disappointments in mind that we can properly assess the writings he left behind him.

Like his Italian counterpart Salvemini—whom he resembled in the verve with which he attacked the fascist system that ruled his homeland—Franz Neumann detested everything which was empty or false. He was first and above all a critic of established institutions and structures. "A conformist political theory is no theory,"[48] he once declared, and this statement—characteristically brief and cutting—might serve as an epigraph for his entire published work.

In *Behemoth*, the book that first established his reputation, such ruthless incisiveness marked the tempo of both the analysis and the marshaling of fact. Neumann remained faithful to the Marxist tradition in his insistence on "unmasking" as the political scientist's primary concern. "In analyzing the structure and operation of National Socialist economy," he contended, "we must never rest content with the legal and administrative forms. They tell us very little."[49] Yet one could not expose the irrelevance of these forms until one had fully understood their complexities. Thus Neumann felt obliged to plunge his powerful lawyer's mind into a morass of legislation and administrative decrees in which someone less endowed with self-confidence and *Sitzfleisch* would soon have foundered, and he emerged triumphantly with what he regarded as a sure key to the workings of Nazi society.

The key, predictably enough, was economic. This was the first and more compelling of two parallel lines of analysis whose connection was not always apparent. Here Neumann aimed to demolish the facile explanations of Nazism currently in vogue—those which described Hitler's regime in terms of a "managerial" society, or, possibly, as one whose anticapitalist intent was evident in its effort to reconcile class antagonisms—by charting the links between big business and the Nazi leadership. Far from being

48. "The Concept of Political Freedom" (originally published in 1953), *The Democratic and the Authoritarian State: Essays in Political and Legal Theory*, ed. by Herbert Marcuse (Glencoe, Ill., 1957), p. 162.

49. *Behemoth: The Structure and Practice of National Socialism* (New York, 1942), p. 227. The second edition, published in 1944, differs from the first only in including an appendix covering the developments of the two intervening years.

directed against business interests, he maintained, National Socialist economics was "an affirmation of the living force of capitalistic society." But it would be wrong to claim, as doctrinaire Marxists were doing, that the regime was merely a front for monopoly capital. The relationship was more subtle than that: "The German ruling class" in fact consisted of "four distinct groups" whose interests were overlapping and mutually reinforcing—"big industry, the party, the bureaucracy, and the armed forces." And among these the relations between the first two gave the clue to the functioning of the entire system:

> National Socialism could, of course, have nationalized private industry. That, it did not do and did not want to do. Why should it? With regard to imperialist expansion, National Socialism and big business have identical interests. National Socialism pursues glory and the stabilization of its rule, and industry, the full utilization of its capacity and the conquest of foreign markets. German industry was willing to cooperate to the fullest. It had never liked democracy, civil rights, trade unions, and public discussion. National Socialism utilized the daring, the knowledge, the aggressiveness of the industrial leadership, while the industrial leadership utilized the anti-democracy, anti-liberalism and anti-unionism of the National Socialist party, which had fully developed the techniques by which masses can be controlled and dominated. The bureaucracy marched as always with the victorious forces, and for the first time in the history of Germany the army got everything it wanted.[50]

Within the framework thus established, Neumann subjected each aspect of Nazi society to unsparing dissection. He traced the steady advance in the cartelization of German business and how the officially recognized regional or functional groupings had come to be dominated by the large concerns. He exposed the sham of the German Labor Front and the "atomization" of the working classes; in this, the most expert of his individual analyses, he returned to his old profession as labor's advocate, systematically

50. *Ibid.*, pp. 305, 361.

3. *The Critique of Fascism*

dismantling the National Socialist showpiece of class reconciliation. He further demonstrated that the so-called party sector of the economy was the product of little more than legalized "gangsterism" on the part of the Nazi chiefs, and that these latter were more and more entering into a state of symbiosis with the great capitalists themselves. "The practitioners of violence tend to become businessmen," he concluded, "and the businessmen become practitioners of violence."[51] Such was the final shape of the National Socialist ruling class as defeat drew near.

In subsequent years, hasty or hostile readers frequently dismissed Neumann's interpretation as Marxist and simplistic. And it is true that he had occasionally let fall an expression—such as a passing reference to an "iron law of capitalistic concentration"—which showed the hold that his original intellectual allegiance still exerted over his thought.[52] But in fact Neumann's argument was far from simple-minded. It was flexible and often hard to follow, and it spared no variety of Marxist politician—whether Social Democratic or Communist—in its analysis of how Weimar democracy had gone wrong. It never claimed that fascism was the sole or necessary political expression of monopoly capitalism. Moreover, it closely paralleled what Salvemini was simultaneously writing about the fraudulent character of Mussolini's "corporative" institutions. It is curious that Neumann, who certainly knew of Salvemini's work, never referred to it in his *Behemoth*.

However complex his view of Nazi society, Neumann did insist on one clear distinction: that the Soviet Union (even under Stalin) operated on different principles from those of Hitler's Germany, and that to lump them together made only for terminological confusion. It was partly for this reason that he pursued a second line of argument parallel to his major economic and social one. The subsidiary analysis was implicit in the book's title, with its Hobbesian reference to an eschatological monster. It was more formal and legalist than the first—and less relevant to the main matter at hand. In brief, Neumann maintained that Nazi Germany—as opposed, in their different fashions, to both Soviet Russia and Fascist Italy—could no longer be described as a state in

51. *Ibid.* (Appendix to 1944 ed.), p. 633.
52. *Ibid.*, p. 272.

the traditional meaning of the term: it had sunk to a level of ethical and legal dissolution in which the distinction between state and society, along with every other customary norm, had been absorbed in a mass politicization of existence.[53]

Although Neumann admired the author of the *Leviathan* and owed much to his influence, the effort to attach his own work to the Hobbesian inheritance was excessively abstract and in part artificial. Here once again the postwar years revealed the shape of reality, and in this case national and middle-class allegiances proved more tenacious than Neumann had imagined. Along with so many of his counterparts in the emigration, he had been generous to a fault in his judgments on the ordinary German. He had depicted the mass of his former countrymen as pulverized by a combination of economic and psychological pressures and incapable of expressing their sentiments of common decency. He had minimized the strength of popular anti-Semitism and had gone so far as to refer to the German people as "the least Anti-Semitic of all." (Even in the second edition of his book, when Hitler's decision to exterminate the Jews had become known in Washington, he had dealt with the "final solution" only in passing.)[54] In similar vein, Neumann had simultaneously branded racist or "social" imperialism as the "most dangerous formulation of National Socialist ideology" and denied that it had seriously infected the German working classes. As his book drew to its close, it was apparent that for all his hard-headedness and skepticism, he retained a faith in spontaneous indignation, a conviction that in the end the Nazi regime would be overthrown not only by the armed power of the victorious coalition, but by the "conscious political action" of Germany's "oppressed masses."[55]

That this was not the scenario which unrolled in the spring of 1945 was enough in itself to explain Neumann's subsequent disillusionment. Still more, the cement that held German society together through the prostration of the next four years was the traditional middle-class ethos whose dissolution *Behemoth* had announced. After the collapse of Nazism, Neumann had pre-

53. *Ibid.*, pp. vii, 470.
54. *Ibid.*, p. 121 and (Appendix), pp. 551–552.
55. *Ibid.*, pp. 215–217, 476.

dicted, the middle classes would have "ceased to exist as a stratum out of which a democratic society" could "be rebuilt."[56] Yet such a reconstruction was precisely what happened during the era in which the spirit of Konrad Adenauer rather than that of the intellectual emigration presided over Germany's return to the Western community.

If *Behemoth* was mistaken in its specific predictions, the fault may be ascribed to the fact that Neumann's method had been either legalist or economic and had left too little room for emotional considerations. It is in this sense and this alone that the charge of narrow-minded Marxism directed against his work can be accepted. Neumann himself was unquestionably aware of the insufficiencies of his analysis, which he never revised for postwar publication. In his years at Columbia University he began to subject his earlier certainties to critical scrutiny. He expressed a new respect for the achievement of Max Weber.[57] He found intellectual refreshment in studying as unlikely a precursor as Montesquieu. Above all, like Mannheim, he reflected on what it meant for his thought to be a citizen of a country where democracy was a living reality rather than the precarious web of compromise it had been in Weimar Germany. Yet Neumann found no substitute for the faith in Marxism and economic explanation that he had lost. Nor did he succeed in writing the comprehensive study of dictatorship that he had projected. Understandably enough, his postwar output was slight and fragmentary. Neumann's scrupulous and self-tormenting search for a new vision of the social world can be documented in the collection of essays entitled *The Democratic and the Authoritarian State* which Herbert Marcuse, who was Neumann's closest friend and was to marry his widow, edited for publication after his death.

What most clearly distinguished the Neumann of *Behemoth* from the later Neumann of the postwar essays was a new insistence on liberty as the condition *sine qua non* of all rational or humanist action, as of all political theory. Whereas earlier, no

56. *Ibid.* (Appendix), p. 629.
57. "The Social Sciences," *The Cultural Migration*, pp. 21–22.

different from other Germans in the Marxist tradition, he had been concerned with unmasking the pieties of conventional liberalism, he now quite consciously joined the liberal-democratic current stemming from England and France. He wrote a perceptive and laudatory introduction to Montesquieu's *Spirit of the Laws,* locating the crucial distinction in the French theorist's writings in the "sharp dividing line" he drew "between despotism and all other forms of government," while limiting the celebrated theory of the separation of powers to its "irreducible minimum" of an independent judiciary. He similarly associated himself with John Stuart Mill's "classic formulation" of the doctrine of political liberty.[58] These new—or better, rediscovered—ideological affiliations highlight the dilemma with which he was contending in the postwar years: he never found a way to reconcile the passionate devotion to liberty that his belated Anglo-American education had given him, with the harsh Germanic conviction, which he refused to abandon, that most of what passed for liberty in the contemporary world was a disgusting fraud.

Thus Neumann's "Notes on the Theory of Dictatorship" remained an unfinished and disappointing fragment. And in his published writings he felt compelled to argue that constitutional guarantees, however desirable in themselves, were inadequate to check the abuse of political power. Nor did he discover any formula which would clearly define the citizen's right of resistance to tyranny: the decision to disobey constituted authority, he concluded, was one that each man was obliged to make in the loneliness of his own conscience. Moreover, the remedies commonly proposed for the failings of liberal democracy were in themselves of questionable value: "social rights," corporatism, attempts to "spiritualize" labor—all these palliatives failed to take sufficient account of the fact that modern industrialism was "politically ambivalent." Industrial society, Neumann found, simultaneously intensified "two diametrically opposed trends in modern society:

58. "Montesquieu" (originally published in 1949), *Democratic and Authoritarian State,* pp. 126, 142; "Intellectual and Political Freedom" (speech delivered at Bonn in 1954, trans. by Peter Gay), *ibid.,* pp. 208–209.

the trend toward freedom and the trend toward repression."[59] Much as he might have liked to share the faith of a Sorel or a Veblen in industrialism's potential as a liberating force and a school of cooperation, he was far too conscious of its stultifying effects to harbor any comforting conviction that twentieth-century urban culture contained its own built-in correctives.

The dominant trend, Neumann knew, was toward political apathy and acceptance. And this he combated with all the intellectual weapons at his command. But here again he never found a formula which brought him satisfaction. His unremitting attack on the tendency of professors and writers to remain "above" the political battle suggested how sorely he himself was tempted to adopt what he called an "Epicurean" attitude of detachment. Even more strenuously than Weber, he argued the intellectual's moral obligation to take a stand.[60] Yet he could provide neither himself nor his readers with any fully convincing reason for resuming the ideological battles of his youth in the disappointing and ambiguous circumstances of his middle age.

The cold war exacerbated these doubts and scruples. From the beginning of the confrontation between the United States and the Soviet Union until his death, Neumann never ceased protesting against the distortion of intellectual and moral values that had resulted from it. He assailed in turn the newly fashionable Machiavellianism among American sociologists and political scientists, the perversion of independent thought through propaganda and vilification, and the "loyalty" program in Washington, with the irrational fear and distrust it engendered of those defined as ideological enemies.[61] Neumann's own passionate revulsion was clear to those who conversed with him and who could discern the emotion under the surface of his dry, clipped prose. Yet in his public style he remained restrained and judicious. This was not

59. "Approaches to the Study of Political Power" (originally published in 1950), *ibid.*, p. 16; "On the Limits of Justifiable Disobedience" (originally published in 1952), *ibid.*, p. 159; "The Concept of Political Freedom," *ibid.*, pp. 189–193; "Notes on the Theory of Dictatorship," *ibid.*, p. 251.
60. "Intellectual and Political Freedom," *ibid.*, p. 215.
61. See particularly the statements in "The Concept of Political Freedom," *ibid.*, pp. 161–162, 188, 194.

through any shallow conformism or fear of the consequences of speaking out. It was rather a manifestation of the tragic dilemma of American (and émigré) intellectuals in the half-decade from 1948 to 1953 when the cold war was at its height: how was one to perform one's essential role as a critic of Western democracy without playing into the hand of either Stalinism or political reaction, or possibly of both at the same time? In Neumann's case this agonized self-questioning was raised to maximum intensity by his previous experience of Nazism and his total lack of illusion.

Neumann died too early to find a way out of what had become a classic impasse—in the very year when, with the passing of Stalin and the end of the Korean war, a glimmer of hope for the future was appearing. Meantime he had felt obliged to act as the defender of a democracy of whose weakness and degeneration he was fully and unhappily aware. It was fitting, then, that his last major public appearance should have been a lecture on the political implications of anxiety. In the summer of 1954, only a few weeks before his death, the Free University of Berlin, which he had so notably aided, awarded Neumann an honorary doctorate. He took the occasion to outline a new view of politics that had been slowly maturing in his mind. The lecture, subsequently published under the title "Anxiety and Politics," marked the fact that Neumann had at last caught up with Freud and the psychoanalytic current; by the same token it showed how far he had advanced beyond the boundaries of law and economics within which he had earlier confined his thought; and it demonstrated his thorough understanding of the manipulation by despots such as Adolf Hitler or by demagogues such as Joseph McCarthy of the anguish and the sense of guilt that afflicted the contemporary world.[62]

"Anxiety and Politics" revealed that Neumann had finally recognized and rectified the insufficiencies in his earlier writing. But in itself the lecture was not notably original; at fifty-four Neumann was too old and too well fixed in his intellectual patterns to make a major contribution to the psychoanalytic study of politics and history on which so many others, younger and

62. Trans. by Peter Gay for *ibid.*, pp. 270–295.

better qualified than he, were about to enter. It is far from certain that had he lived a decade or two longer, his new interests would have significantly altered the character of his intellectual legacy.

This legacy was at least as much oral as it was written. The great difficulty in arriving at an assessment of Neumann's career is that his published work gives no adequate sense of his range and influence. Like most of the émigrés from Central Europe, he never learned to write English with literary ease; but he wrote clearly and directly and without the Teutonic portentousness which so many of his countrymen carried with them across the Atlantic. The trouble with Neumann's prose was almost the opposite: it was so compact and schematic, it made so few concessions to rhetoric or anecdote, that it conveyed little of its author's personal power. Moreover, it was burdened with scholarly paraphernalia and historical citations which were unnecessary to his argument and foreign to the very special combination of practical-mindedness and abstraction that was his natural temperament. To cite merely one example: although a central contention of his *Behemoth* was that the intellectual rationalizations of National Socialism could be dismissed as "pure eyewash," he nonetheless felt obliged to rehearse them at tedious length.

Those who had never met Neumann in person could scarcely be expected to find the human being behind the aridity of his prose style. Those who knew him well recognized the familiar figure—the bald head, the metallic voice, the hearing aid which he switched off with a beatific smile when he sensed that someone was about to embark on a pompous or boring exposition, the thick, heavy-rimmed glasses framing a face that was both ugly and radiating sexual attraction. One of his younger friends concluded that Neumann's mind was like an incandescent bulb which, although it had burned away his hair, his sight, and his hearing, continued to exert a fascination on all it encountered. And another who saw a great deal of him during his years at Columbia named Neumann without hesitation as his "most extraordinary teacher":

It was not simply that he was a European intellectual on an American campus. He would have had an equally startling impact on a European university, as in fact I saw him have at the Free University. Nor was it simply his erudition, great and varied though it was. What struck all, I think, was that he embodied in his own person the vitality and the drama of intellectual life. . . . He had a dazzling power of incisive analysis and critical judgment, and students were over-whelmed by the rapidity and certainty with which he imposed logical meaning or order onto a set of facts or problems. His habit of subsuming various phenomena under logical or historical categories and of seeing things as orderly and clear where to others they had appeared ambiguous or blurred might have been Hegelian-Marxist in origin and might have been practiced in lawyer's briefs and political arguments, but the results were always new and strikingly unpredictable. . . . By his own intellect he belied any crude notion of the social determinism of ideas; he communicated to his students his interest in the social origins and relevance of ideas, and he surprised students and friends alike by his precise and intimate knowledge of so much of European literature. Finally what impressed his students—because rare in any age—was his simultaneous and reciprocal function as philosopher and political man. . . .

The students' admiration was aroused by more than a brilliant mind. There was something in this seemingly austere man, with his brusque manners and his relentless seriousness, that awed students. He was often hard on them. His critical comments were likely to be curt and devastating, and it took little acumen to realize that he did not suffer fools gladly. But there was a magnetism of character and intellect that many students could not withstand. They became disciples and critics, admirers and rebels by turn. . . .[63]

Neumann's own estimate of his role was more modest. He saw himself in a mediating capacity, on the one hand telling his German friends that they cared too little for empirical research while simultaneously counseling his American colleagues to balance their empiricist enthusiasm with a greater concern for history and theory.[64] Within his chosen discipline of political science,

63. Fritz Stern, in a letter to the author of August 21, 1967.
64. "The Social Sciences," *The Cultural Migration*, p. 25.

Neumann's advice was rarely heeded: the quantitative and behavioral approaches which became so influential in the United States immediately after his death were in large part responsible for the neglect into which his work began to fall. And the excessive legalism of his own method frequently gave it an old-fashioned air. It was on historians, rather than on political scientists, that Neumann's precepts left their most lasting impression.

During his war years with the Office of Strategic Services, Neumann had gathered about him an informal circle of younger men, all American-born, but concerned with German affairs and destined to receive professorships of modern European history at some of America's most influential universities. Later on, at Columbia, he attracted into his orbit the talented sons of émigrés from Germany. Toward his younger associates, Neumann was in turn an ideological mentor, an initiator into the realities of European society, and a friend who never ceased inspiring a certain amount of awe. In the informal seminars he conducted in Washington or New York—and a conversation with Neumann seldom failed to turn into a seminar—he refrained from trying to impose any formal Marxian concepts on his listeners. And none of the young historians closest to him in fact became a Marxist. What Neumann imparted to them was something less specific and more pervasive: a conviction that the study of history must begin with economic and class relationships, and that one understood little of politics or ideology unless one was aware of the pressure of interest groups that lay behind them.

A decade or two later such precepts became the common coin of graduate instruction in history, but when Neumann first made the acquaintance of his young admirers, his point of view was far from being generally accepted. The study of contemporary European affairs was still dominated by Ranke's notion of the "primacy of foreign policy"—a conviction reinforced by the tendency of so many American scholars in the post-Versailles years to focus their attention on diplomatic history. Neumann took up the challenge that the most talented of Social Democratic historians, Eckart Kehr, had thrown down: he asserted the "primacy of domestic policy,"[65] in the sense that foreign affairs should be understood

65. See the references to Kehr in *Behemoth*, pp. 203–204, 206.

not in terms of an abiding and consensual "national interest," but rather as an expression of the economic and ideological forces currently dominant in a given society, and this interpretation his American friends brought with them into the universities at which they subsequently taught. It was characteristic of them that they gave only passing attention to war and diplomacy. What was more surprising—and suggested how much independence they combined with loyalty to Neumann's memory—was that they directed their attention to intellectual rather than to social history. In the way they defined such study, however, the spirit of their mentor was readily apparent: as opposed to the older "history of ideas" which dealt in abstract terms with great thoughts perceived as protagonists in their own right, Neumann's heirs wrote what one of them has called a "social history of ideas," setting those thoughts in the full context of historical circumstance out of which their creators had given them form.[66]

Thus although Neumann himself did not succeed in resolving his perplexities, his grapplings with them had a clarifying effect on the minds of his younger friends. Never having been sectarian Marxists, they were untroubled by feelings of ideological betrayal when they found Marx in error. And as native-born citizens of the United States or as bilingual Americans who had come very young to this country, they saw no contradiction between a nondoctrinaire socialism and the liberal-democratic tradition. For Neumann it had been a wrench to recognize that political power or deeprunning sentiments might on some occasions be divorced from any visible economic base. His young American friends had never been tempted to think otherwise.

Neumann's influence, then, lived on after his death in a diffused form which it was difficult for the noninitiated to recognize. Besides the work of his intellectual heirs, he left behind him a superb series of individual critiques of politics and society. Neumann's "all pervasive conviction," his friend Otto Kirchheimer has written, was that "critical analysis of established social structures and . . . institutions" was "the political scientist's only worthwhile

66. See the preface by Peter Gay to *The Party of Humanity* (New York, 1964), pp. ix–xii, and my own definition in *Consciousness and Society* (New York, 1958), pp. 9–12.

job. . . . His late writings no less than his early ones" were "impregnated with the belief in the rational propensities of man" and in the "feasibility and urgency of a cooperative society."[67] In this sense his work had an underlying unity and coherence. In comparing Neumann's aspirations with his published writings, one might easily conclude that his professional life was a noble failure. But to do so would be to suggest that he eventually succumbed to despair. This Neumann steadfastly resisted. Although the abiding ambiguities in his thought made it harder for him to put his reflections on paper than to deliver them orally, he kept on trying to give rational, persuasive form to what he had understood about modern society. "Throughout Neumann's essays runs the struggle against temptations to surrender; pessimism and Epicureanism were his personal devils."[68] These devils never conquered him.

"There are historical situations," Neumann wrote two years before his death, "where an individual, no matter how honest, intelligent and courageous, is quite powerless to affect the course of history."[69] He might well have been speaking of himself; he could equally well have made reference to Salvemini. Both of the great critics of fascism aspired to play a major role in the public arena; both suffered repeated disappointments; both were ultimately far more influential as students of politics and society than as political activists.

In the precarious equilibrium they maintained between scholarship and polemic—or between Marxism and liberal democracy—Salvemini and Neumann made their lasting contribution as critical writers. And the very fact that their analyses of fascism were at once meticulous and engagé gave their work the ring of profound intellectual responsibility. The affinities between the two were readily apparent; but few readers noticed them—perhaps because Salvemini's and Neumann's temperaments and styles were so very different. Yet it was of crucial importance that without reference

67. "Franz Neumann: An Appreciation," *Dissent*, IV (Autumn 1957), 386.
68. David Kettler in *ibid.*, p. 392.
69. Review of *Am Beispiel Österreichs* by Joseph Buttinger, *Political Science Quarterly*, LXVII (March 1952), 141.

to each other they had discerned the same four groups as the
central contenders for power in the fascist systems—the army, the
civil service, big business, and the party—that they had alike
particularly stressed the relationship between the third and fourth,
and that they had agreed in recognizing that whatever the limita-
tions under which it operated, the party leadership in the end had
the decisive say.

This last consideration should have been enough to give pause
to those who labeled *Behemoth* or *Under the Axe of Fascism* as
mere leftist interpretations. And in Salvemini's case such a reminder usually sufficed; his reading of Italian Fascism met little
serious opposition in the postwar period. Neumann's similar interpretation, however, of the German fascist experience was repeatedly called into question. Subsequent research suggested that
the number of German businessmen who remained free of Nazi
involvement was greater than he had supposed; and this numerical
rectification seemed to cast a retrospective doubt on his whole
enterprise. But the same postwar years in which Neumann's work
came under assault also demonstrated that the major German
capitalists had ridden through the Hitler era virtually unscathed.
And it was difficult to see how they could have accomplished such
a feat in the absence of substantial accommodation with the
regime. This Neumann's critics or the defenders of German big
business never satisfactorily explained.

The most general way in which a Marxist or left interpretation
of the socioeconomic bases of the fascist systems might be phrased
was Max Horkheimer's lapidary formula: "Whoever is unwilling
to speak of capitalism should also keep silent about fascism." Any
such interpretation presumed a significant connection between the
economic structure of the one and the political organization of the
other.[70] But in its notion of the tightness of that connection it
could and did take three distinct forms. The most extreme asserted
that the big businessmen ran the show—that fascist leadership was
no more than a façade for the rule of monopoly capitalism. A

70. See the introduction by Kurt Kliem, Jörg Kammler, and Rüdiger
Griepenburg to the anthology ed. by Wolfgang Abendroth, *Faschismus und
Kapitalismus* (Frankfurt and Vienna, 1967), pp. 5–8.

second and more moderate variant of the thesis argued merely that the system intentionally and systematically worked for the benefit of big business. A corollary of both these variants was that fascism was the appropriate expression of monopoly capitalism and that those major industrial states which had not yet "gone fascist" were in imminent danger of doing so. The third and final variant limited itself to asserting that the big businessmen, after certain initial hesitations, for the most part supported the fascist leaders, once the latter were installed in power, and that they received in return substantial favors from the fascist regimes. This was all that Salvemini ever argued and what Neumann argued *most of the time.*

Neither suggested that fascism was the sole or necessary expression of monopoly capitalism. They simply maintained that in Italy as in Germany big business did very well under fascism, that most of the major capitalists were only too happy to cooperate in fascist rule, that as such regimes went on, there occurred a kind of symbiosis between top leadership in business and top leadership in the party, and that this interaction gave the key to the functioning of the entire system. Thus the greater capitalists—almost alone among their countrymen—were able to ride through the fascist experience virtually unscathed, while the members of the lower middle class who had put their trust in the rhetoric of a Mussolini or a Hitler found themselves sacrificed to the "higher" exigencies of a nation girding for war.

iv. *Hannah Arendt and the "Totalitarian" Threat*

For a half-generation following the end of the Second World War no important general or comparative works on fascism appeared— neither in the former fascist countries themselves nor in the Anglo-American world. At the same time the years 1945–1960 saw the unearthing of a mass of documentation that confirmed or corrected hypotheses at which Salvemini or Neumann had been obliged to guess and the corresponding publication of a host of monographs and articles on individual aspects of the Italian or German experience. Indeed the flood of this material was so great as to daunt scholars from attempting a new synthesis—witness Neumann's inability to revise his *Behemoth* or to write his projected study of dictatorship. In the absence of such a synthesis, the term "fascism" itself began to lapse; the word currently in style among historians and political scientists, as among journalists and makers of public policy, was "totalitarianism."[71]

In retrospect it seems clear that the vogue of "totalitarian" explanations, more particularly in the United States, was a byproduct of the cold war.[72] In the late 1940's and early 1950's, the term served to ease the shock of emotional readjustment for Americans or Englishmen—or émigrés—who had just defeated one enemy and were now called upon by their governments to confront another. If it could be proved that Nazism and Communism were very much the same thing, then the cold war against the late ally could be justified by the rhetoric that had proved so effective against the late enemy. And by the same token Fascist Italy ceased to be of much interest: if it was the comparison between Nazi Germany and the Soviet Union that had now become crucial, Mussolini's looser rule could logically be dismissed as nothing graver than a dramatic manifestation of the already familiar phenomenon of pretotalitarian tyranny. A work such as *Behemoth* did not fit the new intellectual conformism: its line of analysis jarred the comfortable convictions of the cold war at its height. Neumann had in fact used the word "totalitarian"; but he had resorted to it sparingly and only when the context was clear.[73] He never exploited it, as the cold war apologists did, to blur the

71. Ernst Nolte, ed., introduction to the anthology *Theorien über den Faschismus*, 2d ed. (Cologne and Berlin, 1970), p. 65; Wolfgang Sauer, "National Socialism: Totalitarianism or Fascism?" *The American Historical Review*, LXXIII (Dec. 1967), 405–407.

72. In Carl J. Friedrich and Zbigniew K. Brzezinski, *Totalitarian Dictatorship and Autocracy* (Cambridge, Mass., 1956), compare the statement in the original edition (p. 7): "The . . . view, that communist and fascist dictatorships are wholly alike, is presently favored in the United States" with that in the revised edition (1965) (p. 19), where the phrase "is presently favored" has been changed to "was during the cold war demonstrably favored."

73. *Behemoth*, e.g., pp. 49–50, 67, 261.

distinction between fascist and Communist society. This was still another reason for the post-1945 denigration of his work.

Both the most erudite and the most emotionally compelling of the books in the new vein, Hannah Arendt's *The Origins of Totalitarianism*, appeared in early 1951 at the zenith of the cold war. A few weeks earlier, the American and South Korean armies had been hurled back from the Yalu River by the Communist Chinese; Stalin was in the grip of the homicidal madness that Alexander Solzhenitsyn was to depict so chillingly in *The First Circle*; never before—or subsequently—had the United States and the Soviet Union seemed so close to war. It was on such a charged ideological atmosphere that *The Origins of Totalitarianism* impinged. Its author, up to then unknown, soon became an intellectual celebrity. Born in 1906 and a favorite pupil of the philosopher Karl Jaspers, Hannah Arendt brought to the study of twentieth-century tyranny, along with the heavily freighted terminology of existentialism, a tone of ethical revulsion that reached a higher pitch than had been true of any of her predecessors.

Her method of attack was threefold. In the late nineteenth century, she argued, three movements, apparently unrelated, were converging to produce the type of mind and political activity which was to evolve into totalitarianism only after the First World War. What these movements had in common was that they all reflected—and accelerated—the collapse of the European class structure and nation-state concept. Class and nation-state had alone given reality to the rights of man. In their default, these rights were reduced to mere abstractions. With the dissolution of the basic institutions of European society, no barriers remained against what "became this century's curse only because it so terrifyingly took care of its problems."[74]

The first of the preparatory movements was anti-Semitism. Refusing to accept the usual explanation that the Jews served as scapegoats for unscrupulous demagogic agitation, Arendt tried to find reasons why they offered the logical target. It was their intimate connection with the nation-state, she found, that marked the

74. *The Origins of Totalitarianism* (New York, 1951), p. 430.

Jews for destruction. As financiers of the European governments, they had incurred the hatred of the political movements which saw in the state the enemy to be conquered. But the irony of the case was that the real growth of anti-Semitism should have come only after the Jews had ceased to be influential. With the flood tide of imperialism in the late nineteenth century, they had lost their near-monopoly of state business. European Jewry, Arendt surmises, had become "an object of universal hatred because of its useless wealth, and of contempt because of its lack of power."[75]

Meantime the second movement, overseas imperialism, had sapped the foundations of the nation-state. As a doctrine of "expansion for expansion's sake," imperialism brought under the control of the nation-state backward areas that could not be integrated into the European political framework. Moreover, the novel experience of confronting vast assemblages of "primitive" and totally alien human beings taught the Europeans to forget their moral scruples, to indulge with a good conscience in mass murder and unspeakable brutality. For the first time in history, racism attained the status of self-conscious doctrine and practice. And it was racism—with its "contempt for labor, hatred of territorial limitation, general rootlessness, and . . . activistic faith in one's own divine chosenness"—that was most deeply to mark the movements of the future.[76]

Overseas imperialism had one saving grace. It at least drew a sharp line between colonial methods and policy at home. With the third movement—what Arendt called "tribal nationalism"—the line disappeared. In Pan-Germanism and Pan-Slavism, the "concept of cohesive expansion" did not "allow for any geographic distance between the methods and institutions of colony and of nation."[77] Under the ostensible aim of uniting all individuals speaking a common language, this new form of nationalism in fact preached the world supremacy of a master race. To those whose national and personal ambitions had been frustrated, it gave the consoling assurance of their own superiority.

Out of these three movements, Arendt concluded, came totali-

75. *Ibid.*, p. 15.
76. *Ibid.*, pp. 131, 197.
77. *Ibid.*, p. 223.

tarianism—the unprecedented madness of the "mob," the "refuse of all classes," which had coalesced at the turn of the century under the leadership of déclassé intellectuals. With the subsequent declassing of entire categories of the population, the "mob" dissolved into the "masses." The masses—the "superfluous men" of the era—had nothing to lose by following their leaders into the most irrational and reckless of ventures. All they sought was to merge with something larger than themselves, to give up their useless individualities to a movement that in the words of Cecil Rhodes "thought in continents and felt in centuries." And their leaders stood ready to offer them a fictitious world which could "outrageously insult common sense" by imposing its own crazy consistency upon a real world in which common sense had ceased to count.[78]

Overwrought, highly colored, and constantly projecting interpretations too bold for the data to bear, *The Origins of Totalitarianism* recalled Borgese's *Goliath* in its historical amateurishness and its striving for shock effect. Yet the intellectual demands it made were far sterner: Hannah Arendt offered no concessions to her readers; they were obliged either to follow to the end the tortuous but relentlessly consistent line of her thought or to give up the effort entirely.

Those who fought their way through her book might not notice how much they had accepted along the way that was either doubtful or positively mistaken. At the very start, for example, she had assured her readers without proof that the great financiers had served both as the leaders and as the symbols of the European Jewish communities, and on this insecure foundation her entire interpretation of anti-Semitism rested.[79] Similarly she never explained the relevance of dwelling at length on British imperialism, when she herself was quite ready to grant that twentieth-century Britain, even overseas, stood for "moderation in the midst of plain insanity." Gravest of all, however, was her insistence on slurring over or belittling the differences between the Nazi and the Soviet

78. *Ibid.*, pp. 309, 342.
79. Benjamin I. Schwartz, "The Religion of Politics: Reflections on the Thought of Hannah Arendt," *Dissent*, XVII (March–April 1970), 154.

forms of the "totalitarian" phenomenon by treating the two as "essentially identical."[80]

Obviously Arendt knew more about Germany than about Russia, and she frequently seemed to be extrapolating from Hitlerian to Soviet experience. For Nazism she provided a full ideological background; in the case of Bolshevism she jumped over a quarter-century from the agitation of the Pan-Slavists to the triumph of Stalin. She confronted her readers with Soviet Communism as the ideological equivalent of Nazism without any adequate account of how it got to be that way. The fate of classic Marxism in Russia, the complex process by which Pan-Slavist elements fused with it in the Stalinist credo—all this she telescoped into a few sentences. Still more, her basic equation of totalitarianism with madness blinded her to the economic rationale of Communist practice; Soviet realities cut across her generalizations by being at once more rational and more totalitarian than Nazi methods. Thus her account lacked any assessment of the distinctions between the two systems that had given Russian Communism its greater resilience and durability.

The basic difference, of course, lay in economic organization and the power relationships deriving from it on which Salvemini and Neumann had put such stress. Hannah Arendt's account, in line with her previous training, was almost entirely innocent of economics—hence her readiness to dismiss Soviet industrial planning as a further example of "insanity." This, like so much else in her book, bore the imprint of the era in which it was published; and, curiously enough, it dated faster than did the analyses of fascism written closer to the event.

In the preface to her work, Hannah Arendt had herself referred to the circumstances of its composition, to the experience of living "in the anticipation of a third World War between the two remaining world powers."[81] Such a catastrophic assessment was not uncommon around 1950; as little as a half-decade later it was already sounding exaggerated. And in a broader sense the same was true of the entire "totalitarian" interpretation. An "ideal type,"

80. *Origins of Totalitarianism*, pp. 221, 429.
81. *Ibid.*, p. vii.

although one that Weber would have found lamentably imprecise, the term began to dissolve as the 1950's came to a close in an ideological situation whose complexities defied any simple scheme of classification. The notion of a bipolar world lapsed; so too did the clear contrast between freedom and totalitarian rule. By the 1960's it was becoming apparent, particularly with reference to the "Third World," that there were infinite gradations between the two and that it was more illuminating to speak of a continuum extending without sharp breaks all the way from the most authoritarian to the most liberal attitudes and practices.

The "totalitarian" interpretation focused on techniques of control—the horrifying surface of life—rather than on underlying social realities. It took at its face value Hitler's or Stalin's claim to complete power over the lives of his subjects, despite the evidence in the concentration camp literature itself that even within those hellish confines one could discover tiny islands of autonomy.[82] In retrospect totalitarianism loomed as an ideal, an aspiration, and not as a historical reality—witness the fact that the term had been coined by Mussolini to describe a regime which never came close to its attainment. The final irony of the study of totalitarianism was that it led to the neglect of its Italian inventor and of the style of rule which rather more than Hitler's had been admired and imitated in the fascist era.

v. *"Radicalism of the Right"*

In the 1960's a new generation of scholars, unscarred by the ideological battles of their elders, returned to the study of fascism with fresh eyes and a willingness to examine without fixed preconceptions both recently discovered data and old interpretations. They not only rehabilitated the term "fascism" itself; they attempted to redefine it in a fashion that would accommodate national variations while maintaining a minimum of conceptual unity. In the former fascist countries these efforts chiefly took the

82. See, for example, Eugen Kogon, *Der SS-Staat* (Munich, 1946), trans. by Heinz Norden as *The Theory and Practice of Hell* (New York, 1950).

form of anthologies of earlier writings;[83] in Britain and America they resulted in a succession of collaborative volumes to which individual scholars contributed essays on some particular feature of the fascist experience.[84]

It was noteworthy, however, that the one major comparative study—Ernst Nolte's *Three Faces of Fascism*, originally published in Germany in 1963[85]—managed to dominate its material only through an exclusion of much that had seemed of critical importance to the investigators of the 1930's. Still more, the attention it received came to it largely by default: its author had at least mustered the courage to make the attempt before which so many others had faltered. And the way he went about it betrayed the well-nigh insuperable difficulties of the assignment: he chose to follow the safe and traditional German practice of delineating political phenomena in terms of the ideas they embodied.

Thus Nolte's work, no less than Hannah Arendt's, was cast in the form of a vast ideal type. Its central feature was a series of splendidly conceived ideological biographies of the major fascist leaders; in contrast, the sociology of the followers remained on the periphery. Moreover, this ideological emphasis led Nolte to place the eccentric, merely protofascist history of the Action Française on an equal footing with the Italian and German movements. For it was Nolte's contention that fascism needed to be understood as an outgrowth of what in the broadest terms could be called anti-modernism, and the Action Française could serve as the ideological bridge from the nineteenth-century counterrevolutionary currents to the twentieth-century parties launched by Mussolini and Hitler. Without question the antimodernist tendency ranked as one of the major components of fascism; it had already engaged

83. Besides the German anthologies ed. by Abendroth and Nolte already cited, one should note the following Italian works: Costanzo Casucci, ed., *Il Fascismo* (Bologna, 1961), which is limited to Italy, and Renzo De Felice, ed., *Il Fascismo: Le interpretazioni dei contemporanei e degli storici* (Bari, 1970), which includes Germany also.

84. See, for example, Hans Rogger and Eugen Weber, eds., *The European Right: A Historical Profile* (Berkeley and Los Angeles, 1965); *International Fascism 1920–1945* (special no. of the *Journal of Contemporary History*) (I, No. 1, 1966); S. J. Woolf, ed., *European Fascism* (New York, 1968) and *The Nature of Fascism* (New York, 1968).

85. *Der Faschismus in seiner Epoche* (Munich, 1963).

the attention of Mannheim, and it was of particular concern to the specialized students of the phenomenon who dealt with the satellite "fascisms" of southern and eastern Europe. But Nolte's almost exclusive stress upon it meant that his book gave little guide to the concrete workings of fascist institutions. Nor did it distinguish adequately among those who led, those who followed, and those who merely profited from fascist rule. Most particularly, Nolte failed to explain how movements that were by definition antimodernist and antirational could so often have fostered economic concentration and the growth of major industry.[86] The absence of such discriminations among different types of class behavior and of any assessment of fascism's economic base suggested how far Nolte had departed from the tough-mindedness of a Salvemini or a Neumann.

With this gap in the only important work of synthesis, it was left for the authors of monographs and essays to ascertain whether the earlier socioeconomic interpretation stood up when tested against the new data now available. In the case of Italy, Salvemini appeared substantially vindicated. Again and again studies of Fascist society drew attention to the crucial role that economic interest played in winning reliable supporters for the regime from among the propertied classes. In the countryside of the north and center it was clear that this support had rallied early: the Fascists alone could give agrarian proprietors—particularly those enriched by wartime and postwar profits—the protection they required against the militance of the landless laborers; the rural struggles of the years 1920 and 1921 figured in retrospect as pitting the propertied who had benefited from inflation against those whose real wages had fallen.[87] Among the businessmen, as Salvemini had already indicated, the rallying to Fascism proved to have been slower and more cautious; large organized industry did not fully accept the regime until it had been in power for nearly three years. And detailed study of the attitudes of the leading industrialists bore out Salvemini's contention that Mussolini was obliged to act

86. See the critique in Sauer, "National Socialism: Totalitarianism or Fascism?" pp. 413–414, and the more sympathetic review by Klaus Epstein: "A New Study of Fascism," *World Politics*, XVI (Jan. 1964), 302–321.

87. Manlio Rossi-Doria, "L'agricoltura italiana, il dopoguerra e il fascismo" (lecture delivered in 1954), in Casucci, *Il Fascismo*, pp. 308–309.

as mediator in keeping at bay the conflicting pressures impinging upon him, and that among the groups to be placated none demanded greater tact than major industry. Fortunately for the Duce, he and the big businessmen cared about different things: "while to the industrialists economics was everything, to Mussolini everything was politics." Each manipulated the other; "each had something that the other wanted."[88]

Thus the picture which emerged of Italian Fascist rule a quarter-century after the fall of the regime was once again that of an alliance of disparate partners who "were never united by positive affinities." While the industrialists did indeed succeed in taming organized labor and in subverting the corporative institutions from the announced goal of class reconciliation, they never liked or really trusted "the political activists of lower middle class extraction" to whose ultimate authority they were obliged to defer. Yet the balance sheet found Italian capitalism intact and strengthened: as Salvemini had already bitingly observed, even the state intervention of the depression years had "relieved private capital of all responsibility for its unprofitable commitments and left it free to concentrate on the development of profitable investments."[89]

In the case of Germany, the postwar critiques of the socioeconomic interpretation eventually coalesced into at least three rectifications of the earlier view. It now appeared that Hitler's rise to power was only marginally aided by the financial contributions of big business; it was also evident that Nazi rule had brought about more widespread social changes than had occurred in Italy under Fascism; and finally it seemed established that politics and ideological leadership exerted a primacy over economic power in the Reich to an extent that never obtained south of the Alps.[90] These

88. Roland Sarti, *Fascism and the Industrial Leadership in Italy, 1919–1940* (Berkeley and Los Angeles, 1971), pp. 38, 75.

89. *Ibid.*, pp. 95–98, 113, 122.

90. On these three questions (in the above order), see Henry Ashby Turner, Jr., "Big Business and the Rise of Hitler," *The American Historical Review,* LXXV (Oct. 1969), 56–70; David Schoenbaum, *Hitler's Social Revolution* (Garden City, N.Y., 1966); T. W. Mason, "The Primacy of Politics—Politics and Economics in National Socialist Germany," in Woolf, *Nature of Fascism,* pp. 165–195.

modifications taken together—more particularly the second and third—suggested that the wartime imperatives with which Neumann had tried to reckon in the second edition of his work had operated more drastically than the author of *Behemoth* had supposed. The big businessmen, it was true, had held on to their factories and their profits; but the siege conditions of war had narrowed their range of decision and imposed a democratization of personal relations and an increase in social mobility which Neumann had omitted from his account.

Yet even the revisers of Neumann's work alike paid their respects to *Behemoth* and took it as their point of departure.[91] And the way in which they differed with him gave the clue to a major distinction between the Italian and the German varieties of fascism which Neumann had appreciated but which he had expressed clumsily and in his characteristic legalist fashion. In his subsidiary or "Hobbesian" argument, he had drawn attention to the fact that in Italy the theoretical bases of the state had remained unchallenged; nor had there occurred any such dissolution of societal norms as had accompanied the rule of Hitler. Neumann had fastened on matters of particular interest to political theory in formulating his sense that there was something peculiar and extreme about the German fascist experience. If he had shifted the axis of his interpretation to focus rather on the individual, microscopic, but cumulative social change that the war had produced—if he had stressed the aspects of Nazi practice that in fact rather than in ideology had revolutionary implications for the future—it might have been clearer why he, in common with most of his contemporaries, saw Nazism as a special case, while continuing to regard the Italian variant as the "normal" form of fascist rule. Here too, in the renewed interest they directed toward Mussolini's Italy, the writers of the 1960's echoed the verdict of a generation earlier.[92]

91. For example, Mason's statement (p. 166 n.), "*Behemoth* remains the best single work on the Third Reich," and Schoenbaum's (p. 272) that Neumann gave "a generally accurate reflection of the basic social situation."

92. For example, Sauer, in "National Socialism: Totalitarianism or Fascism?" p. 421, speaks of "Mediterranean" fascism as the "original" form and of Nazism as a "special form." A similar emphasis is apparent in Renzo De Felice's brief but comprehensive survey: *Le interpretazioni del fascismo*, 4th ed. (Bari, 1972).

In 1969 *Behemoth* was at last supplanted by another closely packed, single-volume study of the Third Reich which now could draw on the wide range of new literature that the intervening three decades had produced. A skilled historian who had already published a monumental study of Hitler's seizure of power, Karl Dietrich Bracher wrote a very different type of book from Neumann's. It was judicious and nominalist in tone, and it ventured few assertions about the nature of fascism in general. Yet its author apparently regarded the term as still useful, stressing in brief but telling passages the tension between party leaders and businessmen as members of the new Nazi elite. Under Hitler, he concluded, Germany's "economic and social structures" had been "subject to profound political and administrative encroachment," but they had been "neither destroyed nor basically reorganized."[93] In sum, Bracher offered a synthesis of the post-*Behemoth* revisions in the assessment of National Socialism along with a reaffirmation of what Neumann had maintained about the tenacity of Germany's vested interests.

More broadly, a large number of the studies published in the 1960's aimed to bring up to date the analysis of fascism's socioeconomic base that in the previous generation had been nearly monopolized by Marxists or bourgeois radicals. From such studies there began to emerge something resembling a new consensus. It seemed clear that in the case of Italy the revolutionary or anticapitalist rhetoric of Mussolini's movement could be discounted (as Salvemini had long ago contended) or at the very most treated as the faith of a minority of true believers. In the case of Germany, the record looked more mixed; yet even here fascism's revolutionary potential had apparently found its embodiment more in the byproducts of wartime stringencies than in any conscious acts directed against Germany's propertied classes. In both countries, the highly charged, ambivalent relationship between industrial and preindustrial values seemed to give the key to much that was bewildering or contradictory in fascist practice. Perhaps one could

93. Karl Dietrich Bracher, *Die deutsche Diktatur* (Cologne and Berlin, 1969), trans. by Jean Steinberg as *The German Dictatorship* (New York, 1970), p. 331.

say that fascism took hold "where preindustrial traditions were both strongest and most alien to industrialism and, hence, where the rise of the latter caused a major break with the past and substantial losses to the nonindustrial classes."[94] Such a generalization fitted Italy and Germany equally well, pinpointing what two societies that looked so dissimilar in fact had in common.

In this view, fascism was a movement of those who had lost out to industrialism. "An analysis in terms of economic growth" suggested that the degree of their radicalization "must somehow be related to the degree of industrialization. The more highly industrialized a society, the more violent the reaction of the losers. Thus Germany stood at the top, Italy lagged behind, and Spain and others were at the bottom." The fascist "radicalism of the Right" preached the "rottenness" of modern society and a return to "the good old values." It presented "the intriguing paradox of a revolutionary mass movement whose goals were antirevolutionary." Its reactionary stance was "fundamentalist," as Talcott Parsons had phrased it in an essay contemporaneous with the work of Borgese and Mannheim and Fromm.[95] All these, of course, had correctly seen the lower middle classes as the main proponents of "fundamentalism." Yet they had been unable to explain why such reactionary (or, if one prefers, revolutionary) aspirations had been disappointed, why the fascist leaders had been unable to put into practice the ideology they shared with their most loyal followers. If a return to preindustrial values—if a reconciliation of classes in a restored sense of community—had been one of the basic fascist aims, why had its attainment proved impossible?

Here the simple answer, as Salvemini and Neumann had already proposed, was that the power of large industrial capital could not be broken. It might be bent or curbed, as happened in Germany, but its toughness and resiliency astounded friend and foe alike. After all, if the fascist powers were to gird for war, they needed the economic base that heavy industry alone could supply. And the

94. Sauer, "National Socialism: Totalitarianism or Fascism?" pp. 415, 420.
95. *Ibid.*, pp. 417, 419; Talcott Parsons, "Some Sociological Aspects of the Fascist Movements" (originally published in 1942), *Essays in Sociological Theory*, rev. ed. (New York, 1954), p. 137.

major industrialists were well aware of their own indispensability. Military preparation and a return to preindustrial community values were incompatible goals, and Mussolini and Hitler, in terms of their own hierarchy of aims, had no alternative but to choose the former. In this ultimate sense the primacy of politics over economics in the fascist systems had the curious result of preserving the economic status quo, while systematically sacrificing those who put their faith in the political ideology of the movement.

Fascist Italy and Nazi Germany, then, were doomed to remain industrial powers. The process of modernization proved irreversible—indeed it was notably accelerated in the generation following Mussolini's and Hitler's fall. Thus those scholars, notably Mannheim and Neumann, who had broadened their treatment of fascism to include some assessment of contemporary industrial society were amply vindicated. And an analysis in terms of class relationships was correspondingly confirmed when it became clear to the investigators of the 1960's, as it had been to those of the 1930's, that the major social drama of fascism in power had been the muted, unrecognized, but deadly struggle between two segments of the middle class—between the faithful followers from the old lower middle class, whose fidelity for the most part went unrewarded, and the new industrial upper bourgeoisie, which consolidated its holdings and maintained its profits.

Such a class analysis might further suggest that in the long view the antilabor policy that the fascist regimes pursued did not have as fatal consequences as Salvemini and Neumann had supposed. Organized labor, like large capital, was indispensable in advanced industrial society, and its situation of potential strength began to bring results with the onset of prosperity in the 1950's. In this case the error in the "classic" studies of fascism was the reverse of the one usually charged to them: rather than overstressing the economic factor, as their critics maintained, they had not given it sufficient weight. Or, to put the matter in terms of analytical method, far from succumbing to doctrinaire Marxism, they had not been Marxist enough.

On balance, a broadly Marxist canon of interpretation had worked better in the critique of fascism than any alternative

3. *The Critique of Fascism*　　　　　　　　　　　　133

schema. It had adhered more closely to the concrete details of existence under the rule of Mussolini and Hitler than had the method subsequently proposed—the loose ideal type procedure epitomized in the work of Hannah Arendt and Ernst Nolte. Nor had the passion infusing *Behemoth* and *Under the Axe of Fascism* vitiated their conclusions. Since their authors made no claim to being "value-free" and had alerted their readers to their own critical stance, they had given no grounds for a complaint of propagandist distortion. Neither Salvemini nor Neumann ever knowingly juggled his data to fit his argument; both were far too conscientious scholars for that. And the fact that the investigators of a generation later reached conclusions which in so many respects resembled theirs gave further proof that their emotional involvement in their subject matter had not figured as an insuperable handicap.

Yet what there was of Marxism in *Behemoth*—or even more clearly in *Under the Axe of Fascism*—was far from systematic or thoroughgoing. It amounted to little more than a deep-running conviction of the primacy of class and interest-group conflict in modern society. In this working hypothesis the critics of fascism had remained true to the reassessment of the Marxian heritage that had engaged the minds of so many social thinkers, Marxist and non-Marxist alike, at the turn of the century.[96] Subsequently there had come the writings of Lukács and the publication of Marx's own manuscripts of the early 1840's, and with them a new wave of Marxist theory and a reemphasis on the Hegelian concept of alienation. These theoretical rediscoveries had not touched Salvemini at all; they had affected Neumann only marginally through the work of his émigré friends. Both had held to an eclectic and practical definition of social-science method. The neo-Hegelian Marxism of the second quarter of the twentieth century was to put its stamp on the thought of the emigration at a more rarefied level, in a philosophical critique of a phenomenon that was wider and more pervasive than fascism, a critique of what came to be called mass society.

96. See my *Consciousness and Society*, Chapter 3.

CHAPTER

4

The Critique of Mass Society

I N THE COURSE of the 1950's the concept of mass society began to win acceptance among the more speculative American sociologists. The publication of David Riesman's *The Lonely Crowd* at the midcentury had both reflected and stimulated a mood of national soul-searching. What this work and its successors had in common was the effort to locate and define the attributes that distinguished the contemporary United States—and by implication other advanced industrial societies—from the phenomena of fully developed capitalism and clearly drawn class lines that earlier social critics, Marxist and non-Marxist alike, had more or less taken for granted. The American analysis of mass society was not uniformly polemical in intent. Yet the experience of cold war abroad and McCarthyism at home of necessity gave it a tone of moral urgency. At the very least it was prompted by anxiety and a sense of intellectual disorientation.

The term "mass society" was shot through with ambiguities: the ways in which it was used were imprecise, overlapping, and frequently contradictory. Sometimes its emphasis was on undifferentiated numbers, sometimes on mechanization, sometimes on bureaucratic predominance. Yet for all their fuzziness of language, the analysts of mass society agreed on a few defining characteristics: what they saw about them was a situation at once uniform and fluid—a state of social "nakedness" in which the notion of community seemed to be slipping away and the individual lacked a cushion of intermediate groups to protect him against direct and overwhelming pressure from the wielders of political and economic power.[1]

Warnings of the threat from the masses were nothing new in Western social thought. The nineteenth century had seen the forebodings of men as diverse as Burckhardt and Nietzsche, Tocqueville and Henry Adams. The first generation of the twentieth had produced the nostalgic musings of Ortega y Gasset and the more systematic analyses of the Italian trio of Croce and Mosca and Pareto. But these had been aristocrats both in their social position and in their intellectual stance: they had shrunk in fastidious revulsion from the vulgarity or "leveling" of taste and opinion that the enfranchisement of the masses was bringing in its wake. The great novelty in the mid-twentieth-century critique of mass society was its democratic inspiration. Those who wrote of America in the 1950's accepted the transition to highly concentrated industrial conditions as an accomplished fact; they did not suggest that the process of modernization could be either undone or stopped. Their underlying moral purpose was not to preserve what was left of a society based on status and cultural privilege; it was rather to protect the mass men themselves from the fruits of their own liberation by exposing what had been lost in the process.

Such was true for the most part of the native-born Americans. The émigrés were more likely to be skeptical of political democracy—at least in the form in which they saw it around them—and to discover their ideological point of departure in Marxism. But the Marxian doctrine that alone made sense to them was curious in lacking a historical protagonist. It derived instead from a massive disappointment—disappointment in the course of recent history, in the strategy of the political parties that laid claim to the inheritance of Marx, and, most particularly, in the proletariat itself. The class which Engels had celebrated as the "heirs of classical philosophy" had failed to perform in the style expected of

1. Daniel Bell, "America as a Mass Society: A Critique," *The End of Ideology* (Glencoe, Ill., 1960), pp. 21–25; William Kornhauser, *The Politics of Mass Society* (Glencoe, Ill., 1959), pp. 23, 30, 114–115. For a survey of the literature, see also Cesare Mannucci, *La società di massa* (Milan, 1967).

it. It had preferred creature comforts to heroism, and kitsch to the elevation of its intellect.[2]

Thus at the hands of the émigré students of mass society, what had been propounded in the nineteenth century as an *economic* critique of capitalist relationships became transformed into a *cultural* critique of the business civilization that large-scale industry had produced. Implicit in such an analysis was the assumption that mere abundance would never suffice. However close capitalism might come to the century-old socialist aim of eliminating poverty and drudgery—and in the affluent circumstances of 1950 such an eventuality did not yet appear far-fetched—humanity's plight would remain unchanged. As long as men's perceptions of their work (and play) were "alienated" or "reified"—as long as in a world whose quintessence was *Entfremdung* and *Verdinglichung* people acquiesced in their own transmutation into "things"—it was pointless to vest one's hopes in a merely technical shift of ownership in the means of production. The Soviet Union stood as the sobering example: though the critics of mass society offered widely varying interpretations of the realities of contemporary Russian life, they were agreed that the goal of a more authentic human existence was still far from attained.

Some such assessment of the nature of twentieth-century industrial society was presupposed in Franz Neumann's *Behemoth*, more especially in the parts that dealt with the working classes. But Neumann's focus was primarily legal and economic; he touched only tangentially on the issue of mass culture. It remained for men with whom he was once closely associated—Max Horkheimer, Theodor W. Adorno, and Herbert Marcuse—to try to discover the link between technological rationality and the aesthetic and moral values of the contemporary masses. In this latter view, fascism figured not as the polar opposite of liberal democracy but as the "most extreme example" of a trend that was general throughout the industrialized West—a "trend towards irrational

2. Edward Shils, "Daydreams and Nightmares: Reflections on the Criticism of Mass Culture" (first published in slightly different form in *Sewanee Review*, LXV [1957]), *The Intellectuals and the Powers and Other Essays* (Chicago, 1972), pp. 249–252.

domination."[3] As Adorno was to put it, "In the body movements that machines" demanded "of those who served them," there could already be detected what was violent and incessant and unrelenting in "fascist abuse."[4]

Adorno, Horkheimer, Marcuse, and their like had been disturbed by the cultural corollaries of a machine civilization long before their emigration from Germany. But it was the move to America that gave these concerns an immediate relevance. If there was indeed an underlying cultural uniformity in which all the advanced industrial nations shared, how did the democratic United States differ in its essentials from the authoritarian National Socialist Reich? If ideological ignorance and apathy, stereotyped thinking and the cult of "personality," were the predestined political manifestations of mass society, what would prevent the Americans from following where the Germans had pointed the way? Was it possible—even probable—that the same threatening forces which had driven the émigrés from their homeland were now confronting them in a more subdued and disguised form in their country of refuge? These agonizing questions led naturally to an exploration of the features of American society that appeared to hold a "fascist potential"—the blander varieties of social coercion which figured as the functional equivalents of what the Nazis had accomplished through terror and violence. The behavior that Riesman was subsequently to identify as "other direction" could be observed under ideal conditions in the United States. And in California, where Adorno and Horkheimer eventually chose to settle, the practice of taking one's cue from the subtle but overpowering pressure of one's fellow citizens was daily displayed with the naïveté of people who found in it nothing to be ashamed of.

All this would have been enough in itself to give the émigrés pause. To it was added a sense of intense personal exposure. In Europe it had been possible for intellectuals to protect their own

3. Martin Jay, *The Dialectical Imagination: A History of the Frankfurt School and the Institute of Social Research 1923–1950* (Boston, 1973), p. 166.
4. *Minima Moralia: Reflexionen aus dem beschädigten Leben* (Frankfurt, 1951), p. 60.

lives from the inroads of popular culture. Shielded by the ramparts of traditional status and respect, they had been able to keep at a safe distance the grosser and more offensive manifestations of mass taste. With the move to America, these walls collapsed: a flood of vulgarity struck the new arrivals in the face. And correspondingly their mood became more embattled: what in Europe had been no more than "vague disdain" in the United States turned into an "elaborate loathing."[5]

Yet in this respect, as in so many others, Adorno and his friends viewed the combat they were waging as an ambiguous two-front struggle. In the task of subjecting to unsparing criticism the tastes and attitudes of the masses, they found it patently insufficient merely to defend the values of traditional "high culture." For one thing, it was not really the masses' fault if they behaved so disappointingly. It was rather the fault of the economic relationships that dominated their existence or, in more personal terms, of those who systematically manipulated the lives of others. Perhaps it was for this reason that Adorno and Horkheimer did not use the term "mass society"; they preferred to speak of the *verwaltete Welt*— "the world of the administered life." Within such a world, they thought, it would be reactionary to join the run of critics whose conservatism expressed itself in a frantic attempt to cling to bits and pieces of the cultural values of the past. Unaware of the social processes from which true culture sprang, critics of this sort were guilty of a special and insidious kind of "fetishizing": in handling art and literature as prized "goods," they tore them from their spontaneous context and rendered them lifeless. Under such circumstances, the authentic and fully conscious critic could not side with those who made a cult of the mind or spirit. Nor could he enroll in the far more crowded ranks of the enemies of traditional civilized values. Still more, it was questionable whether there was any high culture left to defend: its purveyors had so dressed it up and "neutralized" it as to reduce it to "trash." "Self-sufficient contemplation" would not do; even to speak of what had gone wrong ran the risk of degenerating into mere chatter; "after

5. Shils, "Daydreams and Nightmares," p. 258.

Auschwitz," Adorno concluded, in his most poignant cry of despair, it was "barbaric" to go on writing poetry.[6]

1. *The Return to Hegel*

The major presupposition behind the émigré critique of mass society was a view of the world that to Americans was alien and virtually unknown—a Marxist doctrine renewed by a return to its Hegelian source. Beginning with the appearance of Lukács's *History and Class Consciousness* in 1923, there had occurred within the "ancient Central European heartland of the Marxist tradition" a "revival of metaphysical idealism." Communist party discipline had forced Lukács to repudiate his youthful aberrations. For all practical purposes he had subscribed to the "orthodox" view of dialectical materialism as the mechanical working out of fixed economic laws.[7] But he could not prevent his writings from leading a life of their own; the underground reputation of *History and Class Consciousness* continued to grow; and the publication in the early 1930's of the *Economic and Philosophical Manuscripts* in which the young Marx had gropingly formulated his original conception of human society had given Lukács a retrospective validation—it was now apparent that the Hungarian literary critic turned revolutionary had divined by a process of sympathetic reconstruction what his ideological master had written nearly eighty years before.[8]

Adorno and Horkheimer referred only rarely to Marx's Paris manuscripts. Their relations with Lukács were distant and for the most part hostile. They also denied that they were idealists. Despite their disclaimers, a wider view of their work suggests that

6. "Kulturkritik und Gesellschaft" (originally published in 1951), *Prismen* (Frankfurt, 1955), trans. by Samuel and Shierry Weber as *Prisms* (London, 1967), pp. 22–23, 33–34.

7. See the qualified retraction of his original retraction in the preface to the new edition (1967) of *Geschichte und Klassenbewusstsein*, on which the English translation (Cambridge, Mass., 1971) is based.

8. On this whole topic, see George Lichtheim, *From Marx to Hegel* (New York, 1971), pp. 2, 19–21, 38.

they too exemplified the subjectivist reinterpretation of Marxism which in the four decades from the 1920's to the 1960's gave that doctrine a new and enhanced philosophical standing. In such a view, Antonio Gramsci ranks as an isolated Italian precursor and Maurice Merleau-Ponty as a belated and quasi-liberal French propagator of twentieth-century neo-Marxism—a Marxism stripped of its late-nineteenth-century scientific pretenses and thrown back on its early-nineteenth-century Hegelian base. For ideologists of this stamp, the concept of alienation offered the key to social analysis. It was the guiding term which bound together the most diverse thinkers. (The discussion of alienated labor was after all the centerpiece of Marx's own early manuscripts.) Originally employed by Hegel, with its range expanded through the work of Nietzsche and Freud, the word "alienation" eventually took on universal connotations as an overarching characterization of contemporary existence. It carried the promise that those who had been reduced from "ends" to "means," who had even lost all feeling for the wrong that had been done them, could be restored to full humanity through a laborious process of bringing into consciousness the dismal contrast between men's current behavior and the potentialities that lay within them unused.

Max Horkheimer was the dominating figure in the Institut für Sozialforschung (Institute for Social Research) founded in Frankfurt in 1923. Privately endowed and loosely affiliated with the city's university, which was itself less than a decade old, the Institut insisted on and managed to maintain its intellectual and ideological independence. Marxism—variously understood—was the common denominator that linked the Institut's associates. Indeed, it was for reasons of prudence alone that the word was not included in its title. As the Institut's researches developed, however, and competing intellectual influences impinged upon it, this original identification was to become ever more nuanced.[9]

A second point of common experience was Jewish origin. Nearly all the Institut's leading members came from prosperous, assimi-

9. The early history of the Institut and the biographies of Horkheimer and Adorno are fully detailed in Jay, *Dialectical Imagination*, Chapter 1.

lated Jewish families. Yet as was so often the case with German Jews, they preferred most of the time not to speak of the matter or to speak of it with a certain embarrassment. Not until the advent of Hitler and the Institut's move to America did the question of anti-Semitism come to rank high among their concerns. Meantime they were distinguished as particularly outspoken representatives of the cosmopolitan and freethinking minority within the German academic community—a minority whose tendency to look to France for inspiration dated back to Heine and to Marx himself.

The beginnings of the extraordinary collaboration between Horkheimer and Adorno are difficult to establish with precision. They made each other's acquaintance in 1922—the year before the Institut was founded—but it was not until a decade and a half later that Adorno became formally associated with that body. The coalescence of their minds seems to have been a gradual process which eventually reached a point of such fusion that Horkheimer could flatly refer to their philosophies as "one."[10] A symbiosis of this sort is extremely rare in intellectual history: the parallels that most readily spring to mind are the collaboration between Tocqueville and Beaumont and that between Marx and Engels. But in these earlier cases it was apparent who was the junior partner: both at the time and in the view of posterity one mind clearly dominated the other. Adorno and Horkheimer's relationship was less simple: while the former wrote much more and became far better-known, the latter was the man who organized their common projects and the one to whom his partner deferred. The secret of their untroubled friendship—which went as deep personally as it did in the intellectual sphere—apparently lay in a happy contrast of temperaments and a largely fortuitous division of responsibilities.

Horkheimer was eight years Adorno's senior. Born in 1895, the son of a prosperous Stuttgart manufacturer, he had just completed his graduate studies in philosophy when he served as one of the Institut's founding associates. Hence his whole mature life was bound up with that body, and the history of its migrations was identical with his own. It was not until 1930, however, when he

10. Preface to *Eclipse of Reason* (New York, 1947), p. vii.

became its director and was named to a new chair in "social philosophy," that Horkheimer took his place as the Institut's tenured representative on the University of Frankfurt faculty and the leading spirit within the Institut itself. As the title of his professorship suggested, his understanding of philosophy was broad and unconventional. It also involved a passionate commitment to social change. Although Horkheimer lost his ideological model with the murder of Rosa Luxemburg in 1919 and never discovered another political leader toward whom he could feel entire sympathy, his adherence to a Marxist interpretation of events and a Marxist stress on the unity of theory and practice remained unwavering.

As a young man, Horkheimer seems to have been moody and diffident. By the 1930's he had gained a self-confidence which apparently got sturdier as his life went on. Perhaps the change was associated with a brief but apparently helpful psychoanalysis that he underwent in 1928–1929. In any case the personality which came to the fore in exile was that of a strong and even ruthless organizer—what in the United States would be called a promoter—with something of a Mephistophelean manner. As he gained in personal force, however, the matter of putting his thoughts on paper, which had never been easy for him, grew still more troublesome. Thus it was that he increasingly served as the protector and fosterer of the cherished friend who by the same token became the one who usually gave the final form to what they had talked out in common.

"Teddie" Adorno has been described by a younger associate as an "unguarded" human being who was constantly in need of human shelter. "Unguarded," that is, in the sense of never learning to play the game of being an adult and never seeing through the petty stratagems by which others lived and took advantage of him. He joined the Institut late and stayed clear of its organizational struggles. When at the end of his life he became a professor, he did not behave in the accepted academic fashion and seemed ill at ease in his new role. Although he achieved eminence in at least four fields—philosophy, musicology, literary criticism, and sociology—it was only in the last of these that he received full recognition by the professional guild. (When as an elderly man he was chosen president of the German Sociological Association, he was overcome by a childlike joy.) Throughout his career Adorno figured as an "eccentric," on the margin of corporate intellectual endeavor.[11]

In his writings from exile, Adorno more than once referred to the "damaged" (*beschädigtes*) life. But it was not necessarily his own that he had in mind. The offspring of wealthy parents—his father was a Frankfurt wine merchant—he had had a happy childhood and youth in which his every taste was indulged. Music and cosmopolitanism were in the air he breathed. (He was eventually to prefer his mother's exotic-sounding name, that of a Corsican-French army officer who had married a German singer, to his paternal name of Wiesengrund.) Having already studied composition at home and taken his doctorate in philosophy, he was turning twenty-two when he went to Vienna in 1925 to work under Arnold Schönberg's disciple Alban Berg. There he frequented the circle around Schönberg, with whom he was to renew his acquaintance in California many years later. Although Adorno returned in 1928 to Frankfurt and to philosophy, he remained, as had been true of Nietzsche, a philosopher whose life was suffused by music. In this sense the damage wrought him by external events could always find an inner compensation. Never lacking for money, enclosed by the devotion of his great friend and his utterly loyal wife, Adorno managed to live a rare and uncompromisingly intellectual existence right up to the bizarre tragedy with which his life ended.

Horkheimer and Adorno described their work as "critical theory." By this they meant a style of thought that proceeded from negation to negation until its subject matter had been bounded or pierced by a series of devastating cross-fires. Unsystematic by definition and practice (Horkheimer almost invariably preferred the essay form to the organized treatise, and Adorno did so most of the time), critical theory was necessarily hostile to every sort of closed philosophical structure. Thus its debt to Hegel lay more in its method of attack than in its ultimate development. Like most twentieth-century neo-Hegelians, Adorno and Horkheimer

11. Jürgen Habermas in *Die Zeit*, September 12, 1969.

esteemed the author of the youthful, intellectually open, and potentially revolutionary *Phenomenology of Mind* rather than the established Berlin professor who had composed *The Philosophy of Right* and *The Philosophy of History*. In thus discriminating between the early and the later Hegel, they were following in the path of the original Left Hegelians and of Marx himself. But they were not returning simply to the idea-world of the 1840's. Too much, both in social change and in the history of ideas, had happened in the meantime. The moment of consciousness of the European proletariat had come and gone, and a host of new philosophies had crowded Hegel from his erstwhile lonely eminence. Horkheimer's earliest philosophical enthusiasm had been for Hegel's deadly enemy Schopenhauer, whom he was to celebrate nearly a half-century later as the unsparing destroyer of human illusions and the ancestor of psychoanalytic theory. And of course beyond Schopenhauer lay not only Freud but Dilthey and Weber and Mannheim, the whole new German intellectual pantheon, most of whom had had little use for Hegel.[12]

Critical theory, then, found itself obliged to integrate with the Hegelian inheritance the social thought of the succeeding century. In its unremitting process of negation, it was led to employ "the Hegelian method beyond and against Hegel's own system." The result was a new type of dialectic, methodologically still more subversive than that of Marx, a "dialectic without synthesis."[13] In common with Marx, Adorno and Horkheimer detested the abstractions in which German metaphysics and philosophical idealism had veiled the real world; they similarly reproached Hegel with the primacy he had conferred on the thinking subject. But they refused to fall into what they regarded as the opposite error of vulgar materialism or pseudoscience. Their theory hung precariously between a down-to-earth insistence that "things" took priority over one's perception of them and a rarefied form of expression

12. Jay, *Dialectical Imagination*, pp. 41–44; Max Horkheimer, "Die Aktualität Schopenhauers" (originally published in 1962), trans. for *The Critical Spirit: Essays in Honor of Herbert Marcuse*, ed. by Kurt H. Wolff and Barrington Moore, Jr. (Boston, 1967), pp. 64, 71.
13. George Lichtheim, "Adorno" (originally published in *The Times Literary Supplement*, LXVI [Sept. 28, 1967]), *From Marx to Hegel*, p. 140; Gian Enrico Rusconi, *La teoria critica della società* (Bologna, 1968), p. 245.

which was itself abstract in the extreme. In this latter sense they remained in the idealist and metaphysical mold. Moreover, in maintaining even more rigorously than Hegel that nothing could be known directly, that everything in the natural or human universe was "mediated" by something else, critical theory was as many-sided, as elusive, and as bewildering as the thought of the late Wittgenstein.

The two key terms—one favorable and one pejorative—which regularly recurred throughout Horkheimer and Adorno's writings were "reason" and "positivism." The former carried the traditional Hegelian meaning of a quality that subject and object potentially had in common: "a principle inherent in reality"; the latter served as a catch-all for a number of intellectual tendencies which critical theory opposed. If the social thinkers of the turn of the century had already been inclined to lump their dislikes under the word "positivism," Adorno and Horkheimer's usage was looser still. The two Frankfurt philosophers not only dismissed as positivist the materialism and "scientism" that had been the particular targets of the critique of the 1890's;[14] they included along with them the whole nominalist, empiricist tradition. Thus at their hands the logical positivism or logical empiricism of the 1920's and 1930's fared no better than the cruder forms of such doctrines whose errors these twentieth-century philosophies had tried to correct: all figured alike as enemies of "reason," since all of them had reduced it to a merely "subjective faculty of the mind."[15]

Frank irrationalism, one scarcely needs add, stood condemned before critical theory as worse still. And where the self-declared foes of reason had come to power—notably in Nazi Germany—Adorno and Horkheimer's attitude was necessarily one of passionate revulsion. Here once more they found themselves in a war on two fronts: German "thinking with the blood" they loathed with a hatred even mightier than that they directed against Anglo-American empiricism. At the same time they suspected that these two views of the world were not in as total contradiction as was commonly assumed. One was perhaps the historical result of the other. The most original and jarring feature of Adorno and

14. See my *Consciousness and Society* (New York, 1958), Chapter 2.
15. Horkheimer, *Eclipse of Reason*, p. 5.

Horkheimer's thought was the conviction which gradually settled upon them that twentieth-century neobarbarism was the direct heir of the eighteenth-century Enlightenment.

All the foregoing figured in embryo in a programmatic essay entitled "Traditional and Critical Theory" that Horkheimer published in 1937. Here the word "traditional" did service in much the same inclusive fashion in which "positivism" usually made its appearance. In the study of society, Horkheimer explained, empiricists and traditional theorists were only superficially at odds: basically they held to the same theoretical model—a model derived from natural science and primarily from mathematics. This "eternal Logos" determined the way they conducted their own work; they isolated themselves from the life about them, parceling out their investigations as the specialized division of labor dictated. Critical theory, in contrast, tried to understand the human universe "in the context of real social processes"; it was "dominated at every turn by a concern for reasonable (*vernünftig*) conditions of life."[16]

As opposed to the "aimless intellectual game, half conceptual poetry, half impotent expression of states of mind"—which was all that in Horkheimer's view traditional social theory amounted to— he urged his fellow intellectuals to direct their thought toward the emancipation of mankind and "an alteration of society as a whole." "Reason," he explained, could not "become transparent to itself" as long as men acted "as members of an organism" that was lacking in reason. Thus, in terms of critical theory, the distinction between the scholar's "scientific" role and his role as citizen on which Weber had insisted so strenuously made no sense at all. It sundered the human unity of intellectual labor: "in genuinely critical thought," research and value, knowledge and action, were inextricably entangled; here explanation signified "not only a logical process but a concrete historical one as well. In the course of it both . . . social structure . . . and the relation of the theo-

---

16. "Traditionelle und kritische Theorie" (originally published in *Zeitschrift für Sozialforschung*, VI [1937]), *Kritische Theorie*, II (Frankfurt, 1968), trans. by Matthew J. O'Connell for *Critical Theory* (New York, 1972), pp. 191, 194, 197–199. The translated volume is a selection from Horkheimer's two-volume collected essays.

retician to society" underwent alteration; the explainer changed along with the matter he was explaining.[17]

In another essay published earlier in the same year, Horkheimer had stressed more bluntly the interconnectedness of the thinker's two roles:

> When an active individual of sound common sense perceives the sordid state of the world, desire to change it becomes the guiding principle by which he organizes given facts and shapes them into a theory. The methods and categories as well as the transformations of the theory can be understood only in connection with his taking of sides. This, in turn, discloses both his sound common sense and the character of the world. Right thinking depends as much on right willing as right willing on right thinking.[18]

This activist definition of the intellectual's task condemned as an "evasion of theoretical effort" the sentimental leftism which was "satisfied to proclaim with reverent admiration the creative strength of the proletariat." A "professional optimism," a "happy feeling" of finding oneself "linked with an immense force," might well turn to despair in "periods of crushing defeat" such as that in which Horkheimer himself was writing. It was better for the social critic to face being thrown "back upon himself" in ideological isolation. Nor should the thought which derived from a withdrawal into theory be confused with "an abstract utopia." Whatever it might have "in common with fantasy," it rested on the bedrock conviction that there was "only one truth" and that "the positive attributes of honesty, internal consistency, reasonableness, and striving for peace, freedom, and happiness" could not be ascribed "in the same sense to any other theory and practice."[19]

Such a conviction, Horkheimer recognized, meant that to an important extent mind (*Geist*) was "not liberal." The fact that it was "not cut loose from the life of society," that it did "not hang

17. *Ibid.*, pp. 208–211.
18. "Der neueste Angriff auf die Metaphysik" (originally published in *Zeitschrift für Sozialforschung*, VI [1937]), *Kritische Theorie*, II, trans. for *Critical Theory*, p. 162.
19. *Ibid.*, pp. 214, 219–220, 222.

suspended over it," precluded the notion, dear to the "liberalist intelligentsia," of a "detached" (*freischwebend*) role. The mediating function which Mannheim had assigned to social thought was patently incompatible with the formulations of critical theory. At the same time Horkheimer was prepared to say that mind was indeed liberal in the sense of tolerating "no external coercion, no revamping of its results to suit the will of one or another power."[20] Throughout the next three decades of their intellectual labors he and Adorno were to wrestle with the dialectical relationship between the liberal and the illiberal aspects of their thought, as they stoically accepted the isolation which events forced upon them.

II. *Max Horkheimer and Theodor W. Adorno: The Years in America*

When these preliminary definitions of critical theory were elaborated, the Frankfurt philosophers had already been four years in exile. The advent of Hitler had doomed the Institut für Sozialforschung: as a Marxist-oriented body, consisting almost entirely of scholars of Jewish origin, it was doubly anathema to the Nazis. In March 1933 its activities in Germany came to an end; Horkheimer escaped to Switzerland; and in the following month his name appeared among the first batch of university professors whom the new regime had dismissed from their posts.

After a brief sojourn in Geneva, the Institut moved in 1934 to the United States, where Columbia University had offered it hospitality. Here Adorno—who had spent a half-decade in Oxford and London—officially joined its ranks in 1938. The fact that the Institut had its own private endowment (prudently transferred abroad in time to escape seizure by the Nazis) gave it a mobility which comparable organizations lacked. But this ease of travel did not mean a corresponding adaptability to a new environment. On Morningside Heights Horkheimer and his associates remained stubbornly European; indeed a number of the latter tarried across

20. *Ibid.*, pp. 223–224.

the Atlantic until the last possible moment. A branch office continued to exist in Paris, and it was from there that the Institut's publications—still in German—regularly appeared.

The fall of France in 1940 and America's entrance into the war a year and a half later changed all that. Now that the tie with Europe had been severed, Horkheimer and his colleagues reluctantly decided to publish in English. Shortly thereafter the Institut underwent a series of internal crises. High costs and unsuccessful new investments forced it to cut its staff and curtail its activities. Fortunately, the American government's wartime need for expertise on Germany helped to solve the Institut's personnel difficulties. A number of its members left for Washington, first among them Franz Neumann, who had joined the group in the mid-1930's. Although the author of *Behemoth* was a new recruit, he had apparently soon taken a leading role in its discussions. As a man of forceful temperament who differed with Horkheimer in his interpretation of Nazism, Neumann had almost inevitably become the director's ideological and organizational rival. His departure for Washington served to head off the clash of two indomitable personalities.

Meantime Horkheimer himself had felt obliged to leave New York. Persuaded by a heart condition to seek a milder climate, he had moved in 1941 to southern California—more precisely to Pacific Palisades, where Thomas Mann had just settled. Here Adorno loyally followed him, as the rump of the Institut which remained on Morningside Heights slowly withered and died.[21] Hence it was in California, where German culture in exile established its most substantial beachhead, that Horkheimer and Adorno were to write the works for which they would be chiefly remembered.

In view of the tenacity with which they clung to their European inheritance and the virulence with which they assailed American mass culture, one might be tempted to conclude that they regarded their experience in the United States as totally negative. Yet such was not Adorno's final judgment. In a reminiscence

21. On all the foregoing, see Jay, *Dialectical Imagination*, pp. 29–31, 37–40, 113–114, 167–169, 172.

published a year before his death—perhaps tempered by the passage of time—he stressed the things he had learned from his hosts that had corrected an imbalance in his intellectual preparation. Although he had arrived, he recalled, "free from nationalism and cultural arrogance," his previous work had been "thoroughly speculative"—directed exclusively toward interpretation. In America he found that people kept asking him for "the evidence" for what he said, and he in turn began to acquire greater respect for empirical methods. Still more, the first assignment that came his way was a study of jazz which was quite at variance with his own intensely cultivated musical tastes. From it, however, he was able to derive such concepts as "pseudo-individualism" and spurious "personalization" that were later to take a prominent place in his social theory. More broadly he discovered—and here his view paralleled Neumann's—that in the United States, as opposed to Weimar Germany, "democratic forms" had "penetrated the whole of life." Beyond that recognition, he naturally questioned the extent to which these forms mirrored the underlying realities—and this was to be the central concern of his years in exile. Yet when all the negative features had been noted, the intellectual debt remained: it was "scarcely an exaggeration to say that any contemporary consciousness" which had not "appropriated the American experience, even if in opposition," had "something reactionary about it."[22]

The book in which these new concerns surfaced was *The Authoritarian Personality*. Although it was the last in point of composition of Adorno and Horkheimer's major writings in exile, it was the first to come to the attention of the wider American public. It was also the one that clashed least with the American intellectual tradition. Thus it makes sense to analyze these writings in reverse order and to work only gradually toward their most challenging formulations.

22. "Scientific Experiences of a European Scholar in America," *The Intellectual Migration: Europe and America*, 1930–1960, ed. by Donald Fleming and Bernard Bailyn (Cambridge, Mass., 1969), pp. 339–340, 351, 367, 369–370.

Launched in 1944 and published in 1950, *The Authoritarian Personality* formed part of a wider collaborative project entitled "Studies in Prejudice." This sort of venture was already familiar to the Institut's associates: its single largest effort in the 1930's had been a series of extended essays on problems of authority and the family. What was new about *The Authoritarian Personality* was its juxtaposition of American and émigré authorship and of empirical and speculative method. While Horkheimer had been its original moving spirit, he did not participate in the actual research and writing; this devolved, for the quantitative analysis of test and interview material, on a team of native-born psychologists based in Berkeley, California, and, for the "qualitative" interpretation, on Adorno himself. Adorno was later to recall that the "cooperation in a democratic spirit" which characterized the work, "in contrast to the academic tradition in Europe," had been "the most fruitful thing" he had experienced in America, and he paid particular tribute to one of his collaborators, R. Nevitt Sanford, who had painstakingly edited his own English prose.[23]

The basic assumption behind *The Authoritarian Personality* was that there existed in the United States—and presumably throughout the Western world—a "fascist potential" which could be isolated in specific individuals. Such men and women manifested what might be called in psychoanalytic terms an "authoritarian syndrome." Deriving from a "sadomasochistic resolution of the Oedipus complex," this syndrome betrayed an unconscious "hatred against the father . . . transformed . . . into love" for those perceived as the strong and directed against the weak and defenseless. In its psychic economy, the Jew frequently became "a substitute for the hated father." And so, predictably, anti-Semitism figured as its key symptom. Among the others was a tendency to think in stereotypes and to be taken in by the facile "personalizing" of public rhetoric, whether in politics or in advertising, along with a stubborn rejection of any utopian vision.[24]

23. *Ibid.*, p. 358.
24. T. W. Adorno, Else Frenkel-Brunswik, Daniel J. Levinson, R. Nevitt Sanford, *The Authoritarian Personality* (New York, 1950), pp. 1, 664–665, 695, 759–760.

The Authoritarian Personality was widely read and commented upon by the American social-science community.[25] Even those who found fault with its methods and conclusions acknowledged its suggestive power. Yet there was something bewildering about the book that eluded nearly all its readers. It had been six years in the making—and it might have taken still longer had Adorno not decided to return to Germany and thereby obliged his colleagues to hurry it to completion without the overhaul and shortening by which it could have profited. In a quieter period, such a lapse of time would have made little difference. In this case, the book was published in an ideological atmosphere sharply at variance with the one in which it had been projected. As David Riesman complained, it addressed itself to the problem of twenty years ago. Anti-Semitism was no longer the issue. Although *The Authoritarian Personality* appeared in the very year in which Joseph McCarthy launched his campaign of defamation, it dealt only tangentially with the mass fears on which the Senator played with consummate skill: its frame of reference was still a European-style fascism markedly different from what was currently threatening the United States.[26]

From the methodological standpoint critics noted mistakes that the authors had made in sampling techniques, their tendency to disregard the educational level and social situation of those they interviewed or tested, and a certain arbitrariness in the handling of qualitative material. The more discerning surmised that these failings derived at least in part from the "marriage" of two disparate research styles. Although a common allegiance to Freudian categories bound together the émigrés and the native-born who collaborated on *The Authoritarian Personality*, it had not sufficed to close the gap between data gathering and speculation. In the end, Adorno stood out as the intellectual virtuoso of the team. "Quantitative statistical method" was "all too often cast in the

25. See, in particular, Richard Christie and Marie Jahoda, eds., *Studies in the Scope and Method of "The Authoritarian Personality"* (Glencoe, Ill., 1954).
26. David Riesman, *Individualism Reconsidered* (Glencoe, Ill., 1954), pp. 476–477.

4. The Critique of Mass Society

role of the stodgy husband" answering " 'Yes, dear' to . . . the
bright suggestions made by the wife."[27]

Underlying and overlapping this imperfect fusion of method
was an unrecognized divergence in ideology. *The Authoritarian
Personality* used the word "democratic" as the antithesis to "fascist"; such presumably was the spontaneous vocabulary of its
American-born authors. But the term did not come so naturally to
Adorno: he would more likely have spoken of "socialist" or
"revolutionary." The Institut für Sozialforschung had always been
sparing in its reliance on Marxian expressions. After its transfer to
the United States, its tendency to write in "Aesopian" language
became even more marked.[28] Impelled by what seems in retrospect an excessive caution, Adorno and Horkheimer and their
colleagues tried to conceal their true ideological affiliation. No
wonder that American readers found the implicit argument of *The
Authoritarian Personality* confusing and had trouble in detecting
its latent drift.

The clue, of course, lay in the works in German on which
Adorno had been simultaneously working. There was also one
other book in English that might have dispelled some of the misunderstanding. In 1947 Horkheimer published under the title
Eclipse of Reason a revised version of a series of lectures he had
given at Columbia University three years earlier. *Eclipse of Reason*
went over much of the same ground that its author had covered in
his major essays of 1937. But it did so in a flatter and less arresting
manner: in passing from German to English, Horkheimer's style
lost its verve and its polemical force. *Eclipse of Reason* impressed
neither the critics nor the public; its effect on American intellectuals was almost nil.

Perhaps with his new audience in mind, Horkheimer concentrated his fire on those targets which were particularly prominent
in the United States. Warning of "the tendency of liberalism to

27. Herbert H. Hyman and Paul B. Sheatsley, "A Methodological Critique," *Studies in the Scope and Method of "The Authoritarian Personality*,"
pp. 69–71, 91, 102–104, 114–115.
28. Jay, *Dialectical Imagination*, pp. 226–227.

tilt over into fascism and of the intellectual and political representatives of liberalism to make their peace with its opposites," he
noted that a merely "formal" or "subjectivist" view of reason
could be of no "help in determining the desirability of any goal."
The liberal empiricist, he argued, was at sea in dealing with the
problem of values; under contemporary conditions, people were
"living on the residue of . . . ideas" which had once embodied
"elements of truth" but which were now "gradually losing their
power of conviction." From assertions such as these it was only a
short step to a full-scale assault on pragmatism, America's sole
home-grown philosophy. Pragmatism, Horkheimer alleged, tried
"to model all spheres of intellectual life" on "the techniques of
the laboratory"; it was "the counterpart of modern industrialism,
for which the factory" offered "the prototype of human existence." As the American variant of the pervasive positivist outlook,
it gave "a censorial power" to science, transferring "the principle
of the closed shop to the world of ideas." The open-mindedness
on which it prided itself proved in practice to be no different from
the intellectual absolutism of other positivist philosophies: "in a
way, even the irrational dogmatism of the church" was "more
rational than a rationalism so ardent" that it overshot "its own
rationality."[29]

Thus in its current guise positivism figured rather as a symptom
than as a corrective in a general cultural "failure of nerve." The
"objective mind"—the spirit pervading "social life in all its
branches"—worshiped "industry, technology, and nationality
without a principle that could give sense to these categories"; it
betokened "the pressure of an economic system" that admitted of
"no reprieve or escape." Still more, the world of nature itself was
becoming "the object of total exploitation" which had "no aim set
by reason, and therefore no limit." This emphasis on conflict
between man and nature—on the unprecedented domination of
one species over all the others—was a new element in Horkheimer
and Adorno's thought, an element that suffused much of their
work in America and that received a triumphant vindication two

29. *Eclipse of Reason*, pp. 7, 20, 34, 50, 71, 77–79.

decades later with the widespread awakening to the ecological facts of life toward the end of the 1960's.[30]

Meantime Adorno had been sporadically at work on a book which led an even more obscure existence. Composed in fragments over the years 1944–1947, *Minima Moralia* was to see the light only in 1951—and then only in German. Adorno's immediate occasion for putting his private reflections into some tentative order was Horkheimer's fiftieth birthday and the accompanying realization that their labors in common had been broken off by his friend's organizational responsibility for "Studies in Prejudice." And so it was to Max—using only his first name—that Adorno dedicated his book in "gratitude" and "fidelity." *Minima Moralia* he characterized as a *dialogue intérieur:* the French expressions scattered through it suggested its debt to the Gallic tradition of the short essay or aphorism on which Nietzsche had also drawn. If it had a central theme, it was the "damaged" life referred to in its subtitle. Of this, Adorno explained, the intellectual émigré possessed a knowledge that was peculiarly painful. Whether he knew it or not, every such émigré was damaged and would do well to recognize the fact himself before being taught it "cruelly behind the tight-shut doors of his self respect." However he might come to feel at home in his professional guild or in driving a car, he would always go astray. His sole source of help lay in a "steadfast diagnosis of himself and others"—an analysis that could at least save him from "blindness" to his misfortune. "Where everything is bad," Adorno quoted the English Hegelian F. H. Bradley, "it must be good to know the worst."[31]

As he plumbed the depths of his anguish, a new word had crept into Adorno's vocabulary: "redemption" (*Erlösung*), which carried Christian overtones. It had been prefigured at the very start of *Minima Moralia*, where the author had announced his intention of exploring what had once been the true sphere of philosophy but had since fallen into "disregard" and "forgetfulness," the precepts of "right living." Year after year his search for such precepts had led him through the twisted, broken, and overgrown paths of his

30. *Ibid.*, pp. 85, 108–109, 154; Jay, *Dialectical Imagination*, pp. 256–257.
31. *Minima Moralia*, pp. 14, 44–45, 145.

own inner reflections. In the end he had emerged with the conviction that in the face of despair, it was the responsibility of philosophy to present matters "from the standpoint of redemption"—and that in this light "the question of the reality or unreality" of redemption was "almost immaterial."[32]

The task which Adorno and Horkheimer had shared before their conflicting responsibilities separated them was the work entitled *Dialectic of Enlightenment*. Begun in 1941, with their move to California, and substantially completed in 1944, it marked the climax of their intellectual collaboration. No other of their books gave so clear a notion of the farthest reaches of their thought: picking up where their essays of the 1930's had left off, *Dialectic of Enlightenment* mercilessly spelled out the half-concealed assumptions underlying *The Authoritarian Personality* and *Eclipse of Reason*, finally providing the key to what its authors really meant. Yet for the first decade and a half of its existence, the book was known only to small circles of specialists and enthusiasts. Originally published in German in Amsterdam in 1947, it did not become widely available in Germany until its reissue in 1969, and in the United States until an English translation appeared three years later.

From the text itself it was impossible to tell which parts each author had composed. According to their own account, Horkheimer and Adorno "jointly dictated lengthy sections" of it. Yet readers might guess that where the prose came in hammer blows, it was the work of the older man, and where it was more nuanced and involuted, it bore the mark of Adorno's discriminating intelligence. The book's organization suggested a series of linked essays —first a treatment of the concept of enlightenment itself, then an "excursus" on Homer and another on the Marquis de Sade, followed by the detailed examples of the main theme that the "culture industry" and anti-Semitism provided, the whole concluded by a set of "notes and drafts" which might well have found a place in *Minima Moralia*. The argument, while sometimes repetitive, was continuous and cumulative. The authors' view of

32. *Ibid.*, pp. 7, 480–481.

the Jewish question—highly idiosyncratic and the explanation for much that was puzzling about *The Authoritarian Personality*—could be appreciated only in the light of the reasoning which had gone before.

Horkheimer and Adorno's aim was to discover "why mankind, instead of entering into a truly human condition," was "sinking into a new kind of barbarism." More specifically it was to determine why enlightenment had succumbed to "self-destruction." In employing this term, the authors meant something wider than the progressive thought of the eighteenth century: they meant the whole process of rationalization or "disenchantment" in the modern world which Weber had defined in classic fashion. The enlightenment, Horkheimer and Adorno argued, had striven to shatter myths; in the course of so doing, it had in turn become a myth—the myth of "false clarity." "The only kind of thinking . . . sufficiently hard" to break the hold of superstition was ultimately led to direct its weapons against itself. Thus it was incumbent on the contemporary intellectual, if men were "not to be wholly betrayed," to *redeem* "the hopes of the past," through rethinking the concept of enlightenment.[33]

Considered in its broadest contemporary manifestations, enlightenment proved to be the equivalent of manipulation. According to the scientific-positivist vocabulary, knowledge meant the power to manipulate things; in the course of understanding them, "abstraction, the tool of enlightenment," liquidated its objects. Its simple, harsh terminology expressed the realities of domination; it converted the world into "a gigantic analytic judgment," in which the "brute facts" constituted a "sacred . . . preserve" impervious to criticism.[34]

All this could be found elsewhere in the writings of Horkheimer and Adorno. But never before or subsequently was it expressed with greater intransigence. Moreover, the two digressions that immediately followed the introductory statements gave them the living actuality which critical theory so often lacked. The first

33. *Dialektik der Aufklärung,* new ed. (Frankfurt, 1969), trans. by John Cumming as *Dialectic of Enlightenment* (New York, 1972), pp. ix, xi, xiii–xv, 4.
34. *Ibid.,* pp. 9, 13, 27–28.

excursus retold the story of Odysseus sailing past the island of the sirens. At Horkheimer and Adorno's hands, the Homeric legend became a prophetic "allegory of the dialectic of enlightenment." Odysseus, well aware that the charm of the sirens' song was irresistible but wanting to hear it nonetheless, had had himself bound to the mast of his ship; his oarsmen—his "pliable proletarians"— with "stopped ears" and all unknowing had doggedly rowed past the danger. And so it had been in the subsequent experience of humanity: the majority of mankind had been denied the knowledge of beauty and love; the minority who had won the right to leadership had gained it "at the price of the abasement and mortification of the instinct for complete, universal, and undivided happiness." The history of civilization was the history of "man's domination over himself," a "history of renunciation."[35] What Weber had accepted with stoic resignation, what Freud in his *Civilization and Its Discontents* had reckoned as the inevitable cost of curbing men's destructive drives, Horkheimer and Adorno were determined to protest with all the dialectical skill they could muster.

The second excursus introduced the Marquis de Sade, not, as Albert Camus was to do a few years later, in the guise of prefiguring the world of concentration camp torture, but in a more provocative incarnation as "the bourgeois individual freed from tutelage." The eighteenth-century Enlightenment, Horkheimer and Adorno maintained, had been incapable of finding a basis for ethical judgment; while its overall theory might be "firm and consistent," when it came to formulate "moral doctrines," it succumbed to propaganda and sentimentality. Kant himself, despite the care with which he had approached his task and the "sublime and paradoxical" nature of his results, had failed in his effort "to derive the duty of mutual respect from a law of reason." He and his fellow rationalists had bequeathed to the nineteenth-century bourgeois order no ethical sanction beyond convention and fact. This Nietzsche had revealed: he had "trumpeted far and wide the impossibility" of basing on reason as his contemporaries understood it "any fundamental argument against murder." And with it

35. *Ibid.*, pp. 34–36, 54–57.

he had rejected the facile moral optimism of the bourgeoisie, the "assurance" that sought "only to console." Whatever else Horkheimer and Adorno might mean by "redemption"—and the term remained shrouded in obscurity—it was apparent that consolation formed no part of it: they preferred the "merciless doctrines" which proclaimed the "identity" of domination and enlightenment.[36]

After this second excursus had probed the relationship between enlightenment and morality, the main argument resumed with a discussion of the "culture industry" in which enlightenment manifested itself as "mass deception." Horkheimer and Adorno quite consciously chose to speak of mass culture as an industry in order to suggest that what was popular about it was spurious and contrived.[37] Far from being democratic, it too expressed the realities of domination. While the great art of the past had embodied "a negative truth"—while even classical music tested the dictates of a "flawless and perfect style"—the contemporary culture industry reduced art to "absolute . . . imitation." It impressed "the same stamp on everything"; it provided for everyone, discarding tragedy and purveying in "fun" a "self-derision of man" or "parody of humanity."[38] It was here that the mark of their residence in America showed most clearly in Horkheimer and Adorno's work. When they wrote *Dialectic of Enlightenment*, they were living close to Hollywood and associating with fellow émigrés from Germany who had ties to the entertainment industry. In these circumstances, it was only natural that the cinema should offer them their finest examples of the covert coercion which underlay "the world of the administered life."

If the culture industry demonstrated how enlightenment had turned to deception, anti-Semitism betrayed its limits. Horkheimer and Adorno's treatment of this subject was both the most subtle and the most shocking to come out of the emigration; it surpassed even that of Hannah Arendt in its challenge to the comfortable convictions of the liberal intelligentsia. For the Frankfurt philosophers argued in effect that the conventional bourgeois had

36. *Ibid.*, pp. 85–86, 118–119.
37. Jay, *Dialectical Imagination*, p. 216.
38. *Dialectic of Enlightenment*, pp. 120, 130–131, 141, 149, 153.

"good," if unacknowledged, reasons to hate the Jew. By his mere existence the Jew reminded his fellow citizens of what they had lost in the act of self-domination; by his ambiguous marginal status he recalled the possibilities which had been cut off when men had renounced their claim on happiness. "Liberalism had allowed the Jews property, but no power to command." In place of authority it had left them free to indulge the "expressiveness" that others had curbed—"the painful echo of a superior power . . . voiced in a complaint." The Jew's eternal lamentation was like a woman's: as those who had not ruled "for thousands of years," women and Jews, out of "their fear and weakness," had retained an "affinity to nature which perennial oppression" had granted them. They had kept alive the memory of "happiness without power." And to those who were neither Jews nor women the thought of such "true happiness" was "unbearable." Thus when the Nazi derisively mimicked the Jew, he was in fact projecting upon his imagined enemy the longing for a more natural and expressive life that he had tried to stifle in his own soul.[39]

Anti-Semitism, then, was simply the most readily identifiable manifestation of the dehumanizing ideology into which enlightenment had degenerated. It suggested obedience to "social mechanisms in which the experiences of individual persons with individual Jews" played no part. In their all-or-nothing quality, anti-Semitic judgments had regularly "borne witness to stereotyped thought." And herewith came at last the explanation for why hatred of the Jews had figured so prominently in *The Authoritarian Personality*. Anti-Semitism, Horkheimer and Adorno had discovered, offered the clearest possible evidence of the "ticket" behavior—the inclination to accept a program in toto—which characterized not merely those of authoritarian bent but even the ordinary victims of the administered life. Yet the very fact that it occurred "only as part of an interchangeable program" gave "sure hope" that it would "one day . . . die out."[40] It was on this unanticipated note of optimism that *Dialectic of Enlightenment* closed.

39. *Ibid.*, pp. 112, 172, 182, 187.
40. *Ibid.*, pp. 200–201, 207.

When it was republished in 1969, its authors could perhaps have said that they had been right in predicting a waning of anti-Semitism. More broadly they claimed that their "prognosis of the . . . conversion of enlightenment into positivism" and the accompanying "identification of intellect" with what was "inimical to the spirit" had been "overwhelmingly confirmed." Faced with the apparently irresistible "advance toward an administered world," Horkheimer and Adorno could only demand "support for the residues of freedom," even if these seemed "powerless in regard to the main course of history."[41]

III. *Max Horkheimer and Theodor W. Adorno:*
The Postwar Polemic

Despite their hostility to American mass culture and the depth of their European allegiance, Horkheimer and Adorno's decision to return to Germany after the war was not as easy as might be supposed. Their work on "Studies in Prejudice" had finally given them a stake in American-style research, and it proved hard to disentangle themselves from this commitment. Three years passed before Horkheimer made his first postwar visit to his native land. The centennial of the 1848 Frankfurt Parliament provided the occasion: the director of the Institut für Sozialforschung received a warm reception and an invitation from the University of Frankfurt to move that body back to the city in which it had been founded a quarter-century earlier. Besides this official recognition, the new generation of students seemed eager to learn about critical theory: the imaginary audience for which Horkheimer and Adorno had continued to write in German had at last become a reality. In 1949 Horkheimer's university chair was restored to him; his lectures quickly became a thunderous success. A year later the Institut—the "Café Max," as the students nicknamed it—reopened in Frankfurt, with Adorno now in the position of assistant director and subsequently professor of philosophy and sociology. Although during the next decade the two friends returned at

41. *Ibid.*, preface to the new ed., pp. ix–x.

intervals to the United States, their center of gravity had definitively shifted back across the Atlantic. Their Institut had successfully accomplished what no other organized German intellectual group had managed to do—to bridge the gap of exile between the culture of Weimar and the new post-Nazi culture that was beginning to unfold.[42]

In 1951, Horkheimer was chosen rector of Frankfurt University, the first Jew ever to have been elevated to such a position. His election by his colleagues signified something more than a decline in anti-Semitism. It underlined Horkheimer and Adorno's new position as "official" ornaments of culture in a Federal Republic which could as yet boast of few intellectual luminaries. As the cold war passed its height, their critics found evidence of an unwonted ideological caution in the critical tone that the Frankfurt philosophers adopted toward the Soviet Union and China. But this was no real novelty: Horkheimer and Adorno had never equated Stalinist or Maoist despotism with their notion of Marxist practice and had long denounced Communist terror in the name of freedom. What was actually new about their writings of the 1950's and 1960's was that they now focused their generic antipositivism on specific, concrete problems of social-science method.[43]

Adorno and Horkheimer had always thought of their work as at the very least a two-front combat. After the midcentury, however, they began to reckon with a shift in the opposing forces. Abstract idealism was no longer a potent foe. In the intellectual void left by the discrediting of conventional German thought, the Frankfurt philosophers were in an optimum position to teach their postwar students what they had learned of empirical social science in the United States. Yet only up to a point—as American techniques caught on and threatened to sweep the field, Horkheimer and Adorno found it necessary to call a halt. They felt it incumbent on them to restate more fully the basic precepts of critical theory and to delimit the respects in which it was compatible with other types of social thought and the respects in which it was not. The task

42. For full particulars, see Jay, *Dialectical Imagination*, pp. 281–282, 285–288, 298.
43. Rusconi, *Teoria critica*, pp. 207–208.

devolved mainly on Adorno: with Horkheimer engrossed in administrative responsibilities and writing even less than before, the younger man was obliged to speak for both of them. And in so doing he became the most prestigious intellectual on the German scene. This last phase of Adorno's life—his two decades of postwar polemic—falls outside the scope of the present study. But a summary treatment of its main features is essential to an assessment of critical theory as it emerged from its period of intellectual obscurity and ideological concealment in the United States.

In 1966 Adorno published what many took to be his philosophical summa—a substantial volume entitled *Negative Dialectics*. But far from being a systematic treatise, it developed once again as a succession of extended essays. It embodied Adorno's final reckoning with his philosophical predecessors and more particularly with the idealist tradition which he had assailed all his life while remaining true to its metaphysical rhetoric and arcane form of expression. Indeed, from the standpoint of style, *Negative Dialectics* was as difficult a book as Adorno had ever written. Its argument did not unfold: it was "hurled at the reader in an unbroken sequence of staccato affirmations whose precise and lucid phrasing" failed to "make up for the absence of a discernible logical skeleton."[44] It offered, Adorno announced, on the model of the "anti-drama" or "anti-hero" of contemporary literature, an "anti-system" that with the "strength" of the subjective itself would "break through the fallacy of . . . subjectivity."[45]

"Philosophy, which once seemed obsolete," lived on, "because the moment to realize it was missed." With these words Adorno said the farewell to Marxist practice that had been in the making ever since the great disappointments of the 1930's. The proletariat had not reaped the inheritance of classical philosophy which Marx and Engels had promised it; what had happened instead had been the advent of the administered life. Thus philosophy was still needed—but a philosophy that would "disenchant" the whole

44. Lichtheim, "Adorno," *From Marx to Hegel*, p. 141.
45. *Negative Dialektik* (Frankfurt, 1966), trans. by E. B. Ashton as *Negative Dialectics* (New York, 1973), p. xx.

process of conceptual thinking. Nor—despite its total lack of fixed concepts—would it resemble the sociological relativism of a Mannheim or the desperate plea for "engagement" of a Sartre. Relativism Adorno dismissed as a "popularized" form of materialist thought. Existentialism in its French guise he found—as Sartre himself had eventually recognized—still "in idealistic bonds." The author of *Being and Nothingness,* in propounding the notion of absolute freedom of choice, had against his own intention condemned his philosophy to irrationality: the Sartrean individual was obliged to make a choice without knowing the reason which determined that choice. It was to Sartre's honor, Adorno added, that in the plays which were supposed to embody his formal philosophy the protagonists behaved not as free subjects but as though they were in chains.[46]

The existentialists, of course, in common with Adorno, had gone back to Hegel, and by preference to the Hegel of the *Phenomenology.* In this last assessment of the Hegelian legacy, Adorno did not repudiate his philosophical debt; but he underscored those aspects of it which confined rather than inspired the course of the dialectic. These he discovered more especially in Hegel's notion of a world-spirit and the "mythical," if secularized, teaching of an immanent "logic of things" that accompanied it. The result, Adorno contended, had been a stress on the general at the expense of the particular—an overemphasis which was eventually to lead to the worship of society itself. By reasoning in similar fashion a positivist such as Durkheim could "overtrump" Hegel in substituting for the metaphysics of the world-spirit the spirit of the human collectivity. The author of the *Phenomenology* had "abhored . . . insipid edification"; but in his *Philosophy of History* he had lapsed into precisely what he had earlier condemned. Through his insistence on the independent status of a "people's spirit" (*Volksgeist*), he had legitimized despotism over individual human beings—just as Durkheim was later to do with his notion of "collective norms" and Spengler with his theory of the "souls" of different cultures. Hegel, in short, had fought the historiographic battle on the side of what was immutable and identical in

46. *Ibid.,* pp. 3, 13, 36, 49–50.

its action, a "totality" in which he had found salvation. For this he stood accused of having fabricated a "mythology of history."[47]

Yet Adorno did not deny that history had a course which the philosophic mind could discern. He simply maintained that Hegel had used categories such as freedom and justice in a generic and potentially reactionary fashion. A speculative philosophy of history Adorno apparently considered an intellectual enterprise worth attempting, but with results quite different from what Hegel had imagined. In a passionate outburst in one of the drafts appended to *Dialectic of Enlightenment*, he and Horkheimer had in fact sketched their own vision of past and future.

> In the sense of . . . serious history, all ideas, prohibitions, religions, and political faiths are interesting only in so far as they increase or reduce the natural prospects of the human race on earth or in the universe. . . . Reason plays the part of an instrument of adaptation. . . . Its cunning consists of turning men into animals with more and more far-reaching powers, and not in establishing the identity between subject and object.
>
> A philosophical interpretation of world history would have to show how the rational domination of nature comes increasingly to win the day, in spite of all deviations and resistance, and integrates all human characteristics. . . . Either men will tear each other to pieces or they will take all the flora and fauna of the earth with them; and if the earth is then still young enough, the whole thing will have to be started again at a much lower stage.[48]

When these words were written, the first atomic weapon had not yet been exploded and the public consciousness of ecological peril was still more than two decades away.

Besides putting his formal philosophy in final order, Adorno also found it necessary to defend and explain his critical theory in the new professional guise of sociologist he had acquired in America.

47. *Ibid.*, pp. 316, 319, 326 n., 337–338, 357. I have altered the translation slightly.
48. *Dialectic of Enlightenment*, pp. 222–224.

His sense of intellectual responsibility led him into the sort of elaborately arranged confrontations that German scholarship delighted in—notably with the philosopher and social-science methodologist Karl Popper—and into assessments of such eminent "positivists" as Weber and Wittgenstein. Adorno's lofty and intensely committed polemic can be followed in a series of essays on the theory of society extending over the years 1955–1969 and published shortly after his death.[49] Here the traces of his stay in the United States were everywhere apparent—and not least of all in the Anglicisms or Americanisms with which his prose was strewn.[50]

It was only natural that positivism, as in the past, should figure as the chief target of Adorno's polemic. But in this respect too, the decade spent across the Atlantic had left its mark: in these essays of the 1950's and 1960's the judgments on individual figures were more nuanced than had been true of the Frankfurt philosophers' earlier programmatic pronouncements. Thus a new respect for Weber accompanied the reiteration of a profound disagreement on the problem of values. The notion of ethical or aesthetic value, Adorno pointedly observed, was modeled on an economic exchange rate. The whole problem could be dismissed as useless "ballast" which sociology had been dragging along with it; the "dichotomy of is and ought" was as "false" as it was "historically constraining"; a judgment about something was "always . . . prescribed" by that thing and did not "exhaust itself in a subjectively irrational decision" as Weber had imagined. The abstract knowledge of society, Adorno predictably added, could "crystallize . . . only around a conception" of what "a correctly-constituted society" might be; it arose from criticism, "from a social conscious-

---

49. *Aufsätze zur Gesellschaftstheorie und Methodologie* (Frankfurt, 1970). These essays were subsequently republished in Adorno's *Gesammelte Schriften*, VIII (*Soziologische Schriften* I) (Frankfurt, 1972). For the context of the polemic, see George Lichtheim, "Marx or Weber: Dialectical Methodology" (originally published in *The Times Literary Supplement*, LXIX [March 12, 1970]), *From Marx to Hegel*, pp. 200–218.

50. A cursory inspection turns up the following: "healthy sex life," "some fun," "go-getters," "social research," "team," "middle range theory," "trial and error," "administrative research," "common sense," "fact finding," "statement of fact," "case studies," "facts and figures," "nose counting," "likes and dislikes."

ness of contradiction and necessity." Yet despite these strictures, he was ready to grant that when one looked at Weber's own writings, the "disjunction of objectivity and value" appeared "more qualified" than the sociologist's "battle-cry" might "lead one to expect" and that they could serve as a starting point for rethinking categories which had hardened into dogmas.[51]

Similarly in regard to Wittgenstein, Adorno recognized the "pain" that the Viennese philosopher had experienced in trying to meditate on logic with the intellectual tools which logic itself provided. This "most reflective of positivists" had demonstrated his superiority over those of the Vienna Circle by becoming "aware of the limits of logic"—and therewith had reached "the threshold of a dialectical consciousness." What he had not seen, Adorno maintained, was that everything which went beyond pure sense experience had "an aura of indeterminacy," that "no abstraction" was "ever entirely clear," and that every such abstraction was "indistinct . . . through the multiplicity of its possible content."[52] But this last was precisely the purport of Wittgenstein's *Philosophical Investigations*, a work which Adorno apparently never read; the references in his essays clearly indicate that he knew only the early Wittgenstein of the *Tractatus*. If Adorno could speak with such respect of a book which its own author had half-repudiated, how would he have written if he had been familiar with the later works in which so much that was dogmatic or limited in the *Tractatus* was refined and put into a new context? One may conclude that in Adorno's failure to come to grips with the *Philosophical Investigations*, an enormous intellectual opportunity was missed—the chance to associate two of the finest intelligences of the century in the enterprise of bridging philosophical traditions which Wittgenstein's death had cut off in midcourse.

In the absence of a full reckoning with the author of the *Philosophical Investigations*, Adorno was thrown back on the dialectical base that he had maintained intact during his years in America.

51. "Zur Logik der Sozialwissenschaften" (originally published in *Kölner Zeitschrift für Soziologie und Sozialpsychologie*, XIV [1962]), *Aufsätze zur Gesellschaftstheorie*, pp. 122–124.
52. "Der Positivismusstreit in der deutschen Soziologie" (originally published in 1969 as an introduction to a volume with the same title), *ibid.*, pp. 169, 189–190, 228.

Idealism, he explained, "which once glorified speculation," might have "passed away," but the speculative "moment" that critical theory exemplified remained "indispensable." Curiously enough, although it was the positivists who believed they had done the job of discrediting the idealist way of thinking, in their stress on the "perceiving subject" these same positivists remained far closer to idealism than was true of critical theory. His own position, Adorno kept insisting, had a concreteness that the conventional sociology of the midcentury lacked. Its very cast of sentences suggested it: in place of the usual scientific formulation of a law in terms of an eternal "whenever—then," dialectical thinking spoke in historically specific terms which could be expressed as "after this happens—that must follow." Even the critical theorist's stubborn conviction that beneath "appearance" (which was all that positivism recognized) there lay something else which could be called "essence" (*Wesen*)—even this apparently most traditional and abstract category betokened an effort to reach the concrete reality below or beyond the world of surface manifestations. It made a difference, Adorno explained, whether one subsumed human phenomena (as in the sociological tradition stemming from Weber) under such words as "prestige" and "status," or whether one sought as he himself did "to derive them from objective relationships of domination." An ostensibly "value free" debate over selecting a "system of coordinates" in fact went to the heart of conflicting concepts of society: within the "logical-scientific" style of thought, the real social antagonisms could not become visible. As had always been true of Adorno and Horkheimer's polemic, the Hegelian-Marxist notion of a potential truth embedded in the data of economic existence had the last word: "the idea of scientific truth" was "not to be split off from that of a true society."[53]

In 1958 Max Horkheimer retired as director of the Institut für Sozialforschung, thereafter to spend most of his time in Italian Switzerland in a house overlooking Lake Lugano until his death in 1973. Adorno naturally succeeded him—and at a most difficult

53. "Zur Logik der Sozialwissenschaften," *ibid.*, p. 118; "Der Positivismus-streit," *ibid.*, pp. 172, 175, 179, 197–198, 214.

moment when pressure from the German radical left was mounting. The newest student generation had no use and even less understanding for the Frankfurt philosopher's upper-bourgeois fastidiousness and intellectual discrimination. After repeatedly occupying the building of the Institut, in April 1969 the young militants invaded Adorno's classroom; three girl students bared their breasts and mockingly overwhelmed him with flowers and kisses. Thereupon, with characteristic cruelty, they declared him dead "as an institution." For one so vulnerable, the experience must have come as a fearful shock; apparently he never fully recovered. Five months later he died of heart failure.[54]

Not until he was gone did the wider public outside Germany begin to appreciate the loss that Western intellectual life had sustained. And this was in part Adorno's own fault in insisting on a mode of expression which was "mannered, hermetic and remote from ordinary discourse." It was not merely that the Gallicisms of his early work and the Americanisms of his postexile writings raised special linguistic hurdles. It was that he consciously chose "a style refined and formalized to the point of complete artificiality." At least one critic has found in this "density" a necessary expression of Adorno's intellectual "intransigence," characterizing "the bristling mass of abstractions and cross-references" as "precisely intended to be read . . . against the cheap facility" of its surroundings and as "a warning to the reader of the price" he had "to pay for genuine thinking." More commonly, even sympathetic commentators have noted a contradiction in the fact that so musically inclined a philosopher should have written a prose so lacking in music. They have similarly remarked on the discrepancy between Adorno's championship of the ordinary suffering human being and "his inability to cast off a stylistic armature impenetrable to all but an elite of readers." This "discordance between the medium and the message" was the first of two baffling problems that Adorno left behind him.[55]

The second—and here he shared responsibility with Hork-

54. Martin Jay, "The Permanent Exile of Theodor W. Adorno," *Midstream*, XV (Dec. 1969), 66–67.
55. Lichtheim, "Adorno," *From Marx to Hegel*, pp. 132, 137; Fredric Jameson, *Marxism and Form* (Princeton, N.J., 1971), p. xiii.

heimer—concerned the extent to which the Frankfurt philosophers still adhered to the Hegelian style. In their vocabulary and cast of sentences, they unquestionably remained rooted in the Hegelian tradition. Moreover, they drew on the best of that tradition in passing effortlessly back and forth from philosophy to history or aesthetics—while adding to them a more than respectable competence in such newer disciplines as psychology and sociology. Only in economics did the writings of Adorno and Horkheimer betray a certain amateurishness. Moreover, in their application of the dialectical method the Frankfurt philosophers had tried to cast off what was stiff and schematic in the way it was conventionally understood. Scarcely less conscientiously than Wittgenstein, they had striven to think in terms of a universe of fluid relationships. Yet once more only up to a point. Despite all that they had renounced in the Hegelian or Marxist tradition— despite the intricate many-sidedness of their perceptions—one aspect of their philosophical inheritance they steadfastly refused to give up: "the conviction that an all-embracing or fundamental structure of being could be discovered."[56]

This conviction was held even more strenuously by their former associate Herbert Marcuse, who had made the opposite choice from theirs in staying after the war in the United States. Whereas Adorno was utterly serious and uncompromisingly intellectual in nearly everything he wrote, Marcuse preferred to indulge a playfulness of manner. He also stuck more closely than Adorno to strict Hegelian categories. The question of Adorno and Horkheimer's Marxist-Hegelian allegiance can be further illuminated by considering the work of a man whose ideological origins were almost identical with theirs but who diverged increasingly from them as his life went on.

IV. *Herbert Marcuse's Vision of Happiness*

Born in Berlin in 1898 and thus between Horkheimer and Adorno in age, Marcuse came as they did from a well-to-do, assimilated Jewish family. He too had sympathized with the left wing of the

56. Horkheimer, *Eclipse of Reason*, p. 12.

Social Democratic party, from which he had resigned in 1919 following the assassination of Rosa Luxemburg. Thereafter he remained a critic outside the ranks of organized German socialism, in notable contrast to the course pursued by Franz Neumann, who tried to change Social Democracy from within and who in the years of exile was to become Marcuse's closest friend.

When Marcuse joined the Institut für Sozialforschung in 1933 —which by this time meant assignment to its Geneva office—he had behind him more than three years of formal philosophical study at Freiburg with Husserl and Heidegger. The latter in particular seems to have exerted a strong influence on Marcuse's thought, and it was under his guidance that the young philosopher produced his first book, a study of Hegel's ontology. Indeed, it may have been to Heidegger that Marcuse owed his ineradicable hostility to modern technology.[57] But by 1932, with his mentor moving toward collaboration with the Nazis, whose accession to power was now looming, Freiburg no longer afforded Marcuse a congenial intellectual environment. In this precarious situation, the Institut offered a welcome haven.

Marcuse brought into its ranks, besides his exposure to phenomenology and existentialism and a Hegelian expertise surpassing that of any of his colleagues, a difference of temperament which was to become more marked with each passing decade. He took his stand far closer to both utopia and anarchism than did either Horkheimer or Adorno; he tried to envision, as they did not, what the new postrevolutionary society would actually look like. And in so doing he made it his particular province to give substance to the notion of personal happiness—to define what Stendhal and Nietzsche had meant in referring to beauty as *une promesse de bonheur*, a theme to which his co-workers constantly returned but which they preferred to leave in a state of misty abstraction.

In the summer of 1934 Marcuse was among the first of the Institut's members to reach its new headquarters in New York. From here he published—in Paris and in the German language—a series of major essays that remained almost totally unknown to

57. Martin Jay, "Metapolitics of Utopianism," *Dissent* XVII (July–Aug. 1970), 343.

American readers until their translation into English a full generation later. These essays staked out the lines of thought which were to bring Marcuse fame in the quasi-revolutionary atmosphere of the late 1960's; they anticipated most of the argument subsequently developed in *One-Dimensional Man*. But they did so in a less uncompromising form and in a style inaccessible to the ordinary reader. As their author himself remarked, in restrospect they struck him as perhaps "not radical enough."[58]

Most of their themes paralleled what Horkheimer and Adorno were simultaneously writing—the link between liberal society and the advent of fascist rule, the alienation of humanity under the capitalist system, the intellectual deceptions of an ostensibly "presuppositionless" positivism, the status of the dialectic as a privileged mode of thought. Where Marcuse sounded a new note was in the last essay of the series, "On Hedonism," which appeared in 1938. In this reassessment of a philosophical tradition dating back to classical antiquity, he discriminated between hedonist ethics, which he found frequently mistaken, and the liberating aspect of hedonist teaching. The criterion of pleasure seeking, he maintained, had been "right precisely in its falsehood," since it had "preserved the demand for happiness against every idealization of unhappiness." It had acted as a counterweight to the "devaluation of enjoyment," whether through the cult of work or through the celebration of an "affirmative culture" that transformed beauty into disembodied consolation. More particularly hedonism served as a reminder of the sacrifice of sexual happiness which humanity had endured in the reduction of sex to a matter of duty, habit, or emotional hygiene; it contained an unsuspected revolutionary potential which might one day break loose upon a startled world:

> The unpurified, unrationalized release of sexual relationships would be the strongest release of enjoyment as such and

58. Foreword to *Negations: Essays in Critical Theory* (Boston, 1968), p. xvii. This volume includes translations by Jeremy J. Shapiro of the following essays originally published in the *Zeitschrift für Sozialforschung:* "Der Kampf gegen den Liberalismus in der totalitären Staatsauffassung," III (1934); "Zum Begriff des Wesens," V (1936); "Über den affirmativen Charakter der Kultur," VI (1937); "Philosophie und kritische Theorie," VI (1937); "Zur Kritik des Hedonismus," VII (1938).

the total devaluation of labor for its own sake. No human being could tolerate the tension between labor as valuable in itself and . . . freedom of enjoyment. The dreariness and injustice of work conditions would penetrate explosively the consciousness of individuals and make impossible their peaceful subordination to the social system of the bourgeois world.[59]

This was a motif that Horkheimer and Adorno were to touch on a few years later when they inserted in *Dialectic of Enlightenment* their excursus on Odysseus and his "proletarian" oarsmen. Characteristically they left it on the level of metaphor and platonic protest. Equally characteristically Marcuse was eventually to pursue it into a full-scale critique of Freud's *Civilization and Its Discontents*. But that was to wait for nearly two more decades. In the meantime Marcuse was only beginning his education in psychoanalytic theory; he still owed an almost exclusive allegiance to Hegel and to Marx; and in the mature writings of these two the goal of personal happiness was mediated through so much else as to be barely perceptible.

It is curious that Marcuse's essay on hedonism should have come just before his work on Hegel entitled *Reason and Revolution,* the major achievement of his early period in America and the first book that he, or indeed any other leading member of the Institut für Sozialforschung, was to publish in English. When it appeared in 1941, it created little stir. With the United States girding for war, its only immediate relevance seemed to be its defense of Hegel against the accusation of having served as one of the remote progenitors of Nazism. But the fashion in which Marcuse undertook this defense both summed up what he had written before and anticipated his work of the 1950's. In effect, he discovered in Hegel the insight which Marx in his Paris manuscripts had derived from the same source; Marcuse argued that Hegel's use of the term "alienation" was virtually identical to the understanding to which Marx had fought his way in what he believed to be an act of independence from his philosophical master. In thus converting Hegel into a revolutionary, Marcuse was following a tactic similar to the one he was later to pursue in

59. *Ibid.*, pp. 118–119, 162, 173, 186–187.

the case of Freud. "With both he attempted to make his case by disregarding their explicit political pronouncements and turning instead to an analysis of their basic philosophical or psychological conceptions. . . . And in both instances the result was to uncover beneath an apparently conservative veneer the same critical impetus which achieved explicit formulation in the writings of Karl Marx."[60]

Reason and Revolution closed the first phase of Marcuse's intellectual life. The year following its publication, he went to Washington, where he accompanied Franz Neumann into the newly founded Office of Strategic Services. Therewith began a decade of government service, which marks a strange hiatus in his biography. To those who have written on his thought, this second phase has sometimes seemed a "moratorium," in the psychological sense with which Erik H. Erikson was subsequently to invest the word. Alternatively it has figured as a plunge underground in a period of maximum stress, both personal and ideological. Perhaps it can best be viewed in terms of the Freudian concept of latency: the ideas that came to the surface once more in *Eros and Civilization* might be much the same as those Marcuse had expressed in his essay on hedonism, but in the interval between the two they had acquired the explosive force of a long-delayed intellectual maturation.

Again it is curious that during his years in Washington Marcuse should have moved into Neumann's orbit and away from Horkheimer and Adorno, with whom he apparently had so much more in common. Physical distance, of course, played a part: in wartime it was not easy to travel between California and the national capital. But there was also the matter of Neumann's personal magnetism: a diffident Marcuse allowed himself to be dominated by his overpowering friend. In this case once more the man who in the end was to emerge as the better-known of the two began the association in the role of junior partner.

The anomalies of Marcuse's position as a civil servant, which during the war had been papered over by the prevailing mood of solidarity in the struggle against Nazism, became less tolerable

60. Paul A. Robinson, *The Freudian Left: Wilhelm Reich, Geza Roheim, Herbert Marcuse* (New York, 1969), p. 156.

when the conflict ended. Moving, again with Neumann, into the Department of State, he shared the latter's research responsibilities as an expert on Germany. In retrospect—particularly after Neumann's departure for Columbia—it has seemed deliciously incongruous that at the end of the 1940's, with an official purge of real or suspected leftists in full swing, the State Department's leading authority on Central Europe should have been a revolutionary socialist who hated the cold war and all its works. No doubt Marcuse would have left the government much sooner if a suitable professorship had offered itself; denied this option, he stayed on desolately in Washington, as though paralyzed by the painful, lingering death of his first wife and apparently disinclined to return to Germany.

Besides the composition of a number of classified memoranda—which notably simplified his English style—Marcuse produced in these years only one bit of published work, a review of Sartre's *Being and Nothingness*. Most of what he wrote about it was negative: as Adorno was subsequently to do, Marcuse rejected the book's concept of freedom as "idealist" and remote from human reality. Ironically enough, Sartre himself by 1960 was to come around to the same opinion, a fact which Marcuse duly noted when his review finally appeared in German translation; the author of *Being and Nothingness* now received congratulations for his conversion to Marxism and his militant stand in support of revolution in the colonial world. Even the earlier version, however, had had words of praise for Sartre's explicit discussion of the ontological meaning of "the flesh" and the sexual caress—an intimation that Marcuse's essay on hedonism would one day find a sequel.[61]

With Neumann's death, his own remarriage, and his entry into the American academic world, the third and major phase of Marcuse's intellectual life began. After a transition period at Columbia's Russian Institute, during which he lived in Neu-

61. "Existentialism: Remarks on Jean-Paul Sartre's *L'être et le néant*," *Philosophy and Phenomenological Research*, VIII (March 1948), 322, 327–328; Marcuse's revised opinion may be found in the collection of essays entitled *Kultur und Gesellschaft*, II (Frankfurt, 1965), 83–84.

mann's house, Marcuse moved in 1954 to the Boston suburbs and began teaching at Brandeis University, where an attractive professorship had at long last materialized. Not until his mid-fifties, then, did he become a professor, and only then did he acquire the self-confidence that enabled him to speak out after his protracted silence.

A year later there appeared the book—*Eros and Civilization*—which first brought Marcuse to general attention. Subtitled "a philosophical inquiry into Freud," it was the fruit of a decade and a half of pondering on psychoanalytic theory. In it Marcuse undertook to unravel the social riddle that Freud's metapsychology had passed on to his successors—the problem of how Eros, "the builder of culture," could also be the force which needed to be curbed and weakened, through "continuous sublimation," in order for culture to survive. Most readers of *Civilization and Its Discontents* had taken Freud at his word, concluding with him that renunciation, guilt, and self-punishment were and would remain the inevitable emotional cost of life in civilized society. Marcuse refused to leave it at that: he dug below Freud's pessimistic pronouncements about the impossibility of a "nonrepressive" civilization and emerged with "elements" that he believed could "shatter the predominant tradition of Western thought and even suggest its reversal." Freud's work, Marcuse explained, was

> characterized by an uncompromising insistence on showing up the repressive content of the highest values and achievements of culture. In so far as he does this, he denies the equation of reason with repression on which the ideology of culture is built. Freud's metapsychology is an ever-renewed attempt to uncover, and to question, the terrible necessity of the inner connection between civilization and barbarism, progress and suffering, freedom and unhappiness—a connection which reveals itself ultimately as that between Eros and Thanatos.

Marcuse did not argue, however, that Freud himself had shown humanity the way out of its self-imposed imprisonment. On the contrary, in "extrapolating" from what the founder of psychoanalysis had actually said, Marcuse felt obliged to introduce two new terms into the psychoanalytic armory—"surplus repression" and the "performance principle." The first he distinguished as the restrictions required by "social domination," over and above the "basic . . . 'modifications' of the instincts necessary for the perpetuation of the human race in civilization." The second he defined as the "prevailing historical" guise of Freud's reality principle—the injunction to *perform* according to society's expectations, whether on the assembly line or in the marriage bed.[62]

Marcuse's use of the word "surplus" was already a tip to the alert reader that Marx was lurking in the background. In thus combining Marxist with Freudian categories, Marcuse put on a spectacular intellectual performance of his own—more particularly since Marx's name never appeared in his pages. The idea of surplus repression enabled him to graft onto Freud's instinctual-biological trunk of theory a devastating socioeconomic critique of modern industrial society. The performance principle similarly extended Marx's concepts of alienation and reification into the sexual realm. This principle, Marcuse maintained, had instituted a "genital supremacy"; it had concentrated libido "in one part of the body, leaving most of the rest free for use as the instrument of labor." Hence the way to human fulfillment lay through a re-sexualization of the body; the tyranny of the merely genital or procreative must and could be broken by a rehabilitation of the so-called perversions, the "polymorphous-perverse" inclinations of original undifferentiated sexuality, which, Marcuse suspected, offered a *promesse de bonheur* greater than that bestowed by what society conventionally sanctioned as normal.[63]

A program breathtaking in its utopian sweep—but, as a French critic soberly pointed out, one that circumvented Freud's basic categories. Whatever Marcuse might have done to Marx (on which it was difficult to be precise, since a Marxian ghost alone was present), in the case of psychoanalytic theory he drew the extreme implications from Freud's boldest speculative flights with no attention to the clinical "soil" from which these latter had sprung. Thus when he ran up against such a triad of coupled terms as id-unconscious, instinct-drive, repression-suppression, Marcuse

---

62. *Eros and Civilization* (Boston, 1955), pp. 17, 35, 83.
63. *Ibid.*, pp. 48–49; Robinson, *Freudian Left*, pp. 204–207.

invariably settled on the first of each pair; the second failed to figure in his line of thought. In a treatment dealing almost exclusively with the instincts and their repression, the absence of any clear delineation of the unconscious made it impossible to situate Marcuse's work unambiguously within the context of psychoanalytic speculation.[64]

All this notwithstanding, *Eros and Civilization* ranked as the most original and important of Marcuse's books. It accomplished the incredible feat of fully accepting the pessimistic aspects of Freud's metapsychology—the predominance of sexuality, the determination of future behavior in the emotional events of early childhood, the death instinct (Thanatos), and all the rest—while turning them toward even more "positive" conclusions about human fulfillment than was true of Freud's most optimistic heirs.[65] It likewise reversed the classic psychoanalytic conviction about man's destructiveness by arguing that the release of sexuality rather than its denial was the way to tame humanity and pacify the world. In brief *Eros and Civilization* managed to convert Freud into a still more revolutionary figure than Marx by ascribing to him a sense of cosmic injustice in the thwarting of instinct—an injustice which cried out for radical, but unspecified, social changes.

The process of thinking through these changes was to occupy Marcuse for the next decade. At its end he was to endorse as his own, in the 1966 reissue of *Eros and Civilization*, the slogan of the young militants "Make love, not war" which gave the book a clear political thrust. The faint beginnings of such a shift were already apparent in two lectures he delivered in Germany at a commemoration that Horkheimer and Adorno had organized for the centennial of Freud's birth in 1956. Coming only a year after *Eros and Civilization*, these lectures made more explicit the notion of "domination" as the guiding reality in contemporary society. "In acknowledging it," Marcuse observed, Freud was "at one with idealistic ethics and with liberal-bourgeois politics." The founder

64. Jean Laplanche, "Notes sur Marcuse et la psychanalyse," *Marcuse cet inconnu* (special no. of the review *La Nef*, XXVI [Jan.–March 1969]), 115–116, 126, 128.

65. Robinson, *Freudian Left*, p. 201.

of psychoanalysis, he added, felt justified in combating "the integral claim of the pleasure principle," the organism's constitutional bent toward "fulfillment, gratification, peace."[66] Once Marcuse turned, then, toward specifying the contours of a non-repressive existence, the image of Freud the revolutionary began to recede. By 1963 he had reached the conviction that the Freudian concept of man was "obsolescent" in its emphasis on "private autonomy and rationality." In the contemporary world the best that could be said for psychoanalysis was that it might enable one "to live in refusal and opposition to the Establishment," that it invoked "not only a past left behind but . . . a future to be recaptured."[67]

In the meantime Marcuse had at last come to the point where he could offer his own picture of human happiness:

a state in which there is no productivity resulting from and conditioning renunciation and no alienated labor: a state in which the growing mechanization of labor enables an ever larger part of . . . instinctual energy . . . to return to its original form, . . . to be changed back into energy of the life instincts. It would no longer be the case that time spent in alienated labor occupied the major portion of life and the free time left to the individual for the gratification of his own needs was a mere remainder. Instead, alienated labor time would not only be reduced to a minimum but would disappear and life would consist of free time.[68]

Some such vision of man's potentialities had hovered on the utopian wing of socialism ever since the young Marx had speculated that in the remote future people might "hunt in the morning, fish in the afternoon, rear cattle in the evening, criticize after dinner," as their inclination might prompt.[69] But Marcuse was

66. "Trieblehre und Freiheit," *Freud in der Gegenwart*, ed. by Theodor W. Adorno and Walter Dirks (Frankfurt, 1957), trans. by Jeremy J. Shapiro and Shierry M. Weber for Marcuse's *Five Lectures* (Boston, 1970), p. 11.
67. "The Obsolescence of the Freudian Concept of Man," *Five Lectures*, pp. 60–61.
68. "Die Idee des Fortschritts im Lichte der Psychoanalyse" (originally published in *Freud in der Gegenwart*), *ibid.*, p. 39.
69. *The German Ideology*, International Publishers ed., p. 22.

almost unique in bringing this vision down to earth and in arguing
for its contemporary feasibility.

With the publication of *One-Dimensional Man* in 1964, Marcuse's decade-long evolution toward ideological explicitness—and
from Freud back to Marx—was virtually completed. This book
reintroduced Marx under his own colors; it also further extended
the circle of Marcuse's readers. For here the revolutionary message
which had previously remained clouded by its Hegelian wrappings
found a clear target in the society of the author's adopted country.
By the early 1960's American minds were ready for a work that
opened vistas of liberating social change; the terrors of McCarthyism lay in the past, and the civil divisions with which the decade
closed were still in the future. On such an atmosphere, *One-
Dimensional Man* could impinge with optimum effect; and it
came as more of a novelty than would have been the case if
Horkheimer and Adorno's *Dialectic of Enlightenment* had already
been in translation.

Marcuse discerned in the United States—as the farthest point
that advanced industrial civilization had reached—"a comfortable,
smooth, reasonable, democratic unfreedom" where technology had
triumphed all along the line; where the "Welfare State" and the
"Warfare State" coexisted in apparently untroubled harmony;
where a universal "flattening out" of values meant that the citizenry failed to notice its lack of any real choice; where the same
people did not believe—or did not care sufficiently to disbelieve—
what their rulers told them, yet acted "accordingly"; where fascism
was no longer required for social discipline, since the status quo
defied "all transcendence"; where Marxism, although still theoretically valid, lacked historical agents; and where one's sole faint hope
for the future must be vested in the anger and the aspiration for a
decent life among the "substratum of the outcasts and outsiders."[70]
Marcuse's catalog of horrors did not go perceptibly beyond the
analysis of society that American-born critics were simultaneously
producing. What gave his work a different and arresting tone was

70. *One-Dimensional Man* (Boston, 1964), pp. 1, 17, 19, 57, 103, 256–
257.

his insistence, in common with Horkheimer and Adorno, that in the culture of the midcentury language and thought were losing their evocative character and becoming, like the reality they reflected, "one-dimensional."

Hence, as Horkheimer had done in *Eclipse of Reason*, Marcuse coupled his social critique with a renewed attack on "positivism"—and this time specifically in the sphere of language. Anglo-American linguistic philosophy naturally offered him a prime target; so too did the later works of Wittgenstein. Marcuse had read the *Philosophical Investigations*, as Adorno had not. But quite evidently he had misunderstood them: by citing the less significant passages in one of the key sections of Wittgenstein's work, he dismissed the matter as a succession of trivia.[71] Marcuse's misreading of the *Philosophical Investigations* put off many Americans who would have been ready to accept the main lines of his social analysis. It also epitomized the curiously bifurcated character of a book that both closed his four decades of philosophical speculation and inaugurated a new phase of political activism.

This last phase of Marcuse's endeavors lies beyond the present inquiry. Stimulated by a combination of outrage at the Vietnam war and friendly contact with the German student movement, it gave to the work he published from 1967 on a sharply polemical character.[72] In the year following the appearance of *One-Dimensional Man*, Marcuse had gone from Brandeis to the University of California at San Diego, and it was there that he assumed his new role as the philosophical idol of militant youth. For a thinker who had lived the greater part of his mature life in almost total obscurity—and who had been known in intellectual circles for scarcely more than ten years—the sudden transition to international fame might well have been disorienting. Marcuse carried it off gracefully: his success did not change him; he could administer

71. *Ibid.*, pp. 173–179 (the part of the *Philosophical Investigations* is ‖ 97–124).
72. One may note an abrupt shift in tone in the *Five Lectures* between the third, dating from 1963, and the fourth and fifth, which were delivered in 1967.

a rebuke to the young when he felt they deserved it, while remaining true as an old man to the ideological faith he had embraced a half-century earlier.

"Pleasure is, so to speak, nature's vengeance. In pleasure men disavow thought and escape civilization."[73] This aphorism of Horkheimer and Adorno epitomizes their abiding difference from Marcuse. It was not merely that they became more conservative—and in particular more skeptical about revolutionary practice—as they grew older, whereas Marcuse moved even further to the left than he had been before. It was also that despite their yearning for personal happiness, Horkheimer and Adorno retained Freud's original sense of the fateful paradox of civilization—of the inescapable anguish inherent in the clash between men's desire for pleasure and their deeply seated need to build a viable culture or society. Adorno never resolved the dilemma: he remained torn and perplexed—and in deadly earnest—until the end. Marcuse tried to rescue what he could of the element of play that mankind had sacrificed, while insisting on its compatibility with a life of thought.

In so insisting, Marcuse resembled the Young or Left Hegelians rather more than he did the mature Marx. His stress on the alienation of men from their own sexuality and his endeavor to restore to them an assurance of primeval innocence recalled such immediate precursors of Marx as Ludwig Feuerbach.[74] This Left Hegelian—or possibly even Romantic—aspect of Marcuse's writings goes far to explain their popularity in the effervescent atmosphere of the late 1960's. It also suggests the extent to which, despite his transplantation to the United States, he remained rooted in the idea-world of early-nineteenth-century Germany.

The vast majority of his American readers had no inkling of the cultural inheritance that lay behind Marcuse's strictures on con-

73. *Dialectic of Enlightenment*, p. 105.
74. This is the contention of Alasdair Macintyre, *Herbert Marcuse: An Exposition and a Polemic* (New York, 1970), pp. 18–19, 41, 58. On Feuerbach and the rest, see the unpublished Ph.D. thesis by John Edward Toews, "The Innocence of the Self: Cultural Disinheritance and Cultural Liberation in the Experience and Thought of the Young Germans and Young Hegelians" (Cambridge, Mass., 1973).

temporary industrial society. Nor—since their own intellectual preparation was for the most part modest—did they feel obliged to explain the ambivalence in Marcuse's writings between his refined appreciation of literature and the arts and his assaults on traditional or "affirmative" culture. One contradiction, however, could not escape the least attentive: the discrepancy between the activist role he eventually assumed and his passive, nonstriving, tactile-sensuous conception of happiness. Marcuse himself recognized that his "non-repressive . . . order of values" was "in a fundamental sense conservative." He also expressed his dissent from Sartre's notion of human existence as "an eternal 'project'" which never reached "fulfillment, plenitude, rest."[75] There was in Marcuse's life and work an apparently congenital element of passivity—witness the number of years that passed before he resolved to enter the public arena. The fact that he finally did so gave evidence of a quite extraordinary civic courage, since it went against his own inclination.[76]

A hale, elderly man with a puckish grin, looking far younger than his years, his white hair blowing on some sun-drenched beach—such was the picture of Marcuse that lingered with those who knew and loved him. Even the friends who could not follow him into his last phase of activism cherished his mordant turn of phrase, his abounding love of life, and his indomitable independence.

v. *From Marx to Freud and Back*

"In psychoanalysis nothing is true except its exaggerations."[77] In this case an aphorism of Adorno suggests the common element in what he and Marcuse discovered in Freud. Both fastened on the shocking and the culturally subversive. Both tried to determine the ground on which psychoanalytic insight could broaden the range of the philosophical and sociological categories they had derived

75. *Five Lectures*, pp. 23, 41.
76. This courage is stressed in the basically critical analysis by Pierre Masset, *La pensée de Herbert Marcuse* (Toulouse, 1969), p. 183.
77. *Minima Moralia*, p. 78.

from Marx. But the way they went about the job of integration once again betrayed their temperamental differences: Marcuse built an entire theoretical book upon a couple of risky extrapolations; Adorno delivered his opinions in the form of casual comparisons and obiter dicta—plus, of course, his collaboration in *The Authoritarian Personality*.

From the very foundation of the Institut für Sozialforschung, Horkheimer and his associates had been concerned with Freud. They maintained cordial relations with the Frankfurt Psychoanalytic Institute, and a number of their early studies drew heavily on psychoanalytic material. Among them Erich Fromm, the future author of *Escape from Freedom*, was the most knowledgeable; but by the time he wrote his psychological interpretation of Nazism, he had taken leave both of the Institut and of Freudian orthodoxy.[78] Thereafter psychoanalysis seldom emerged very far into the foreground of critical theory: it remained a reference point, a set of injunctions that the social thinker could disregard only at his peril, and, above all, a bulwark against any teaching that aimed to "console" mankind or to reconcile it to its contemporary fate.

Six years after the Institut's return to Germany, the Freudian centennial gave Horkheimer and Adorno an opportunity to specify their own debt to the founder of psychoanalysis. Besides Marcuse, the roster of invited speakers included Erik H. Erikson and representatives of both the "revisionist" and the "existential" wings of psychoanalytic thinking. While these gave regular lectures, the Frankfurt philosophers limited themselves to brief statements designed to situate the centennial in its wider intellectual context. Most obviously they felt it urgent to reintroduce Freud to a German academic public which a half-generation of Nazi rule had denied knowledge of his writings and which even after 1945 had not seemed much inclined to restore those writings to honor. Perhaps it was with his conservative colleagues in mind that Horkheimer referred to Freud as an "enlightenment figure" (*Aufklärer*), using the term for once in a favorable sense, and that he and Adorno sharply rejected the notion that psychoanalytic theory could be dismissed as "out of date." Quite the contrary, they

78. Jay, *Dialectical Imagination*, pp. 88, 98, 101–105.

asserted, Freud's legacy needed to be rescued from those who had embraced it with shallow enthusiasm as "cultural goods" or who had reduced it to a "trivial psychology"; it needed to be viewed once more in the "youthful style" of its "most sublime discoveries."

Yet to see Freud intact meant to see him in dialectical terms. It meant to stress above all the economic pressure that Freud had recognized in the form of *Lebensnot*, or the bitter necessity of life.[79] Hence Horkheimer and Adorno's assessment of Freud's abiding validity was bound to cut both ways: while giving their full endorsement to his unsparing critical acumen, they felt obliged to warn against the undercurrent of resigned acceptance in his writings. Such a warning, they thought, would be particularly salutary when applied to those who attempted facile syntheses between psychoanalysis and Marxism or between the disciplines of psychology and sociology. In an essay prepared for Horkheimer's sixtieth birthday—one year before the Freud centennial—Adorno characterized as an "expression of helplessness" the "war-cry" of intellectual integration. One would succumb to "false consciousness," he explained, if one tried to separate the psyche from the society that conditioned it: it would be equally false, he added, to fail to recognize the difference between one's inner and one's outer life. "The divergence of the individual and society" was "essentially of social origin," was "perpetuated by society," and was "first of all to be explained in social terms." Only in this fashion could one comprehend how under contemporary conditions what pointed to a "higher condition" for mankind was always the "damaged" and not the "more harmonious." And only thus could it be made clear that even a successful psychoanalytic treatment bore the "stigma" of emotional damage and of "fruitless . . . adaptation."

Psychoanalytic therapy, Adorno concluded, in its very origins and not merely in its decline on the intellectual marketplace, fitted the dominant mode of "reification."[80] A decade later, he had not

79. *Freud in der Gegenwart*, pp. ix, xi, 33–34.
80. "Zum Verhältnis von Soziologie und Psychologie" (originally published in *Aufsätze, Max Horkheimer zum 60. Geburtstag gewidmet* [Frankfurt, 1955]), *Aufsätze zur Gesellschaftstheorie*, pp. 10, 16–17, 23, 34, 53.

changed his mind: even more strenuously than before he insisted that while one should "hold fast" to Freud's "strict sexual theory" against the "obscurantism" which was still trying to suppress it, one should also recognize that a therapy which was "installed" in the social mechanism itself strengthened "the functional capacities of human beings within a functional society." The author of *Civilization and Its Discontents*, Adorno added, might not have been fully aware of the ravages that his reality principle inflicted on his fellow men. But it was time to admit the harm that the psychoanalytic "contempt for humanity" could do to a living individual. What Freud had called anxiety and what the existentialists had "ennobled" with the same term was in fact a sense of "claustrophobia in the world." It betokened the chill that had descended on human relations. "In the universal coldness" of contemporary society, anxiety was "the necessary form of the curse" that hung over mankind.[81]

With Adorno and Horkheimer, then, as with Marcuse, the original allegiance to Marx in the end predominated over an infusion of psychoanalytic thinking which was never entirely assimilated. Yet the Marxism of the Frankfurt philosophers was more nuanced and skeptical than Marcuse's and became even further attenuated as their lives went on. Some critics have suggested that after their return to Germany they could be called Marxists no longer. Or perhaps one could say of them—as Merleau-Ponty implied of his own late writings—that the question of whether they were or were not Marxists was simply pointless. That, however, would be a patent exaggeration: virtually all the concrete examples in Adorno's postwar methodological essays derived from the economic substructure of society or the pressure of economic interests and were phrased in the terminology of dialectical materialism. When the Frankfurt philosophers got down to cases, they returned to Marx for inspiration.

This abiding allegiance goes far to explain the curious alternation in their writings—more especially in those of Adorno—between rarefied complexity and brutal assertion. It also helps us to

81. *Ibid.* (postscript of 1966), pp. 58–59; *Negative Dialectics*, pp. 346–347, 351–352 (I have altered the translation slightly).

understand their ineradicable hostility to "positivism" and their bludgeoning use of the term. It finally suggests why their receptivity to intellectual stimulus or their readiness to alter their ideas during their stay in the United States always ran up against impassable if not fully specified limits. It was not merely that they were reluctant to write in English and that they recoiled from the kitsch or middle-brow aspects of American life. It was that their philosophical set remained fixed, that beneath the dazzling variety of their cultural attainments lay a residue of dogmatism of which the casual reader might be totally unaware.

Scarcely less than Marcuse, Adorno and Horkheimer dwelt in the spiritual universe of preindustrial Germany. Despite their efforts to keep up with the contemporary avant-garde, at the deeper levels of their being they felt more at home in the world of Hegel or of Beethoven. The early, the Hegelian Marx was the one they really understood: their passionate protest against the works of capitalism had little of Marx's own subsequent appreciation of capitalist rationality as a necessary stage in the advance of society toward a socialist future; to them the process of economic rationalization figured above all as the overriding (and most grievous) symptom of the degeneration of the enlightenment into manipulation. To a surprising extent, Adorno and Horkheimer echoed the "other" Germany of their ideological enemies—the anachronistic, romanticized Germany of those who preached rural values and community solidarity—an echo epitomized by their longing for a society of warm, direct human relationships and an "organic," shared understanding of high culture and refined taste in literature and the arts.

Yet this nostalgic element in their thought did not necessarily invalidate what they wrote about mass society. It might be responsible for the imprecision and the emotional tone of their strictures on contemporary urban life—as it was for their disorienting blend of revolutionary indignation and intellectual snobbery. It might make them leap to the conclusion that America's "culture industry" was the functional equivalent of fascist terror. But it got to the heart of the quiet, uncomplaining desperation of the midcentury; it articulated what lurked just below the threshold of consciousness among millions of ordinary citizens. And in so doing it kept alive the notion of transcendence in an era when most social scientists—particularly in the United States—were settling for acceptance of the status quo. Adorno and Horkheimer's forebodings about the fascist potential in their host country proved (for the time at least!) excessively alarmist: their delineation of the "administered life" was increasingly borne out by the facts. Still more, in the late 1960's, the smoldering discontent with this kind of existence was to erupt in sterile, uncoordinated violence—and to claim Adorno himself as one of its victims. The wave of interest in Adorno's writings which followed almost immediately upon his death suggested that the "administered life" had been experienced as a clear and present reality by those who labored to decipher them. And by the same token it served notice on the sociologies and psychologies which traveled under the banner of adjustment or adaptation that they had a new and unexpected force to reckon with.

CHAPTER

5

The Advent of Ego Psychology

I suspect that Freud's contempt for men is nothing but an expression of such hopeless love as may be the only expression of hope still permitted to us."[1] Thus Theodor W. Adorno tried to embrace in one convoluted formula his full ambivalence toward the founder of psychoanalysis. Love and contempt, he surmised, might be two sides of the same coin: Freud's lack of illusions about humanity anticipated what Adorno himself had learned in the isolation of exile. Far more than one might suppose, the Frankfurt philosopher accepted the bleakness of the Freudian perspective on mankind; the two had in common a hatred of sentimentality and an insistence on integrity in personal relations as in intellectual pursuits. Where Adorno drew the line was at Freud's Olympian detachment from politics and his "skepticism about all ideologies except those of the private life."[2] And he argued that the founder's original error in developing a therapy of social "adaptation" had been compounded by followers who had steadily "watered down" the basic distinction between consciousness and the unconscious.

In protesting against the practice he saw about him of convert-

1. Paper delivered in Los Angeles in April 1946 entitled "Social Science and Sociological Tendencies in Psychoanalysis," cited in Martin Jay, *The Dialectical Imagination: A History of the Frankfurt School and the Institute of Social Research 1923–1950* (Boston, 1973), p. 105.
2. Philip Rieff, *Freud: The Mind of the Moralist*, Anchor paperback ed. (Garden City, N.Y., 1961), p. 278.

ing psychoanalysis into "a superficial ego psychology," Adorno
lumped together two distinct tendencies—the revisionism of the
"neo-Freudians" and the current closer to psychoanalytic orthodoxy exemplified by the founder's daughter Anna and by Heinz
Hartmann. He accused both these tendencies of distortion in
interpreting psychologically what was social in origin, although he
granted that Hartmann had delineated with greater insight than
the revisionists the way in which a given social structure selected
out the emotional attitudes which fitted it best. Both, he argued,
established an illusionary "harmony between the reality principle
and the pleasure principle." Both underestimated the ego's regres-
sive dependence on the primary id and failed to differentiate
between the functions of the ego that were individual in origin
and those that embodied the claims of society.[3]

Adorno's difficulty in situating the post-Freudian schools was a
common experience in the quarter-century following the founder's
death. After 1939, there had emerged no uncontested heir to
psychoanalytic leadership, although Hartmann came closer than
anyone else to that position. Moreover, the Freudian legacy itself
was sufficiently rich and bewildering to leave doubt as to where the
course of orthodoxy lay—let alone the path of creative renewal. In
its completed form, psychoanalytic terminology crisscrossed and
overlapped: to the original threefold system of classification within
his theory—topographical, dynamic, and economic—Freud had
subsequently added the "structural" distinctions among id, ego,
and superego, which, as Adorno observed, became the main
ground of contention among his heirs.

The status of these four modes of "metapsychological" description varied widely within the practice of psychoanalysis. Nearly all
its adepts accepted the structural triad, while reserving the right to
reinterpret the three components. Similarly the topographical
distinction between the conscious and the unconscious remained
the bedrock of theory. But the precise fit of topography to structure was subject to debate: if the id could clearly be located in the

3. "Zum Verhältnis von Soziologie und Psychologie" (originally published
in *Aufsätze, Max Horkheimer zum 60. Geburtstag gewidmet* [Frankfurt,
1955]), *Aufsätze zur Gesellschaftstheorie und Methodologie* (Frankfurt,
1970), pp. 25, 39, 42, 49.

unconscious, it was not equally correct to assign the ego to consciousness; indeed, the unconscious aspects of the ego presented a particularly knotty theoretical problem. As for the dynamic category of explanation—the terminology of "drives" (*Triebe*) and the ego's defenses against them—here once more an apparent consensus concealed deep-seated theoretical divergences. While people could agree that it was a vulgar error to confuse a drive with a merely biological instinct, and while virtually everyone granted the usefulness of such words as repression and rationalization, projection, sublimation, or identification, the same people were at odds over whether the dynamics of the mind should be depicted primarily in terms of conflict, as Freud had done, or whether the emphasis should be shifted toward equilibrium and reconciliation.

Freud himself had specified as the minimum tenets of orthodoxy his own earliest discoveries: the primacy of the unconscious and infantile sexuality (plus the Oedipus complex that went along with it). At the very least, then, a topographical and a dynamic way of looking at things constituted a prerequisite for belonging to the psychoanalytic movement at all. The same was not true of the other original explanatory mode—the "economic" terminology which spoke of the storing and spending of psychic energies. This had long ranked as the most doubtful and dated of Freud's interpretative schemata; it had borne most clearly the stamp of mechanistic nineteenth-century assumptions. It was to a large extent responsible for the positivist tone that infused his work; it gave a determinist cast to statements that in fact derived from an elaborately nuanced approach to the limits of mental and emotional freedom. By the end of his life Freud had long outgrown his mechanistic vocabulary; it had become increasingly inappropriate to his later speculative writings. But Freud himself seemed uncertain as to whether he considered these works his crowning achievement or a series of mental lapses. What was undeniable was his inclination to tinker with his own theoretical results as he constantly extended the reach of his metapsychological system.[4]

4. On this whole subject, see my *Consciousness and Society* (New York, 1958), Chapter 4, III.

Perhaps Freud could properly be described as a positivist in his tendency to write as though the mind "really" operated as he had explained it. In his casual remarks on methodology he had sometimes implied that one might treat his terms more modestly as metaphors or heuristic devices. But most of his followers had not thought in this fashion: at their hands psychoanalytic concepts had hardened into a set of unquestioned dicta. The displacement of the movement's center to the United States had encouraged this tendency: American Freudians, like the run of their countrymen, were impatient with epistemological hairsplitting. If the shift across the Atlantic, with the vastly enlarged opportunities it opened up, finally gave psychoanalysis a chance to become the "general" psychology at which the founder had aimed, it also threatened to restrict the movement's philosophical range and depth. Those among the émigrés who continued to explore the status of the abstractions that Freud had left behind him were out of step with the practical-mindedness of their new associates.

The refugees and the native-born could agree, however, on the crucial importance of one problem at least in the Freudian legacy: the individual's relationship to society, and more particularly his vicissitudes in adapting to the circumstances of his group life. While Freud's own therapeutic and theoretical work had concentrated on the individual, it had not totally neglected the social dimension. Less than a decade after the publication of *The Interpretation of Dreams*, he was beginning to speculate on the emotional consequences of a rigidly imposed sexual morality. By 1921, in *Group Psychology and the Analysis of the Ego*, he was trying to define in erotic terms the tie that bound human beings together and led them to identify with a beloved leader. But these speculations never got much beyond the stage of tantalizing suggestions which subsequent commentators have endeavored to piece together.[5] They merely hinted at the possible application of psychoanalytic insight to the study of history or group relations. It was left to Freud's heirs to pick up where he had left off and to develop as best they could a coherent social theory. And the way in

5. Besides Rieff's *Freud* and my *Consciousness and Society* (Chapter 4, IV), see Paul Roazen, *Freud: Political and Social Thought* (New York, 1968).

which they carried out this assignment served to delineate, perhaps more than any other single issue, the conflicting tendencies that separated them.

1. *The Freudian "Left," "Right," and "Center"*

Compared with the clamorous secessions of Jung and Adler before the First World War, the quarrels within the psychoanalytic movement in the 1930's and 1940's were polite and muted. The original dissenters had been sufficiently close to Freud in age—Adler was fourteen years younger, and Jung nineteen—to approach him as a near-contemporary, and their rupture with orthodox psychoanalysis, in particular that of Jung, had left correspondingly deep scars. The subsequent contestants stood in a quite different relationship to the founder. Born for the most part in the 1890's, they were clearly of a different generation. Those who were personally acquainted with Freud knew him only as an old man wracked by illness. A few had had their psychoanalytic training with him; the majority had trained with one of his older followers. In the generational succession of the movement, they ranked somewhere between Freud's "sons" and "grandsons."

A neat, if perhaps arbitrary way to classify them—with special reference to their social philosophies—is in the classic political terms of Left, Right, and Center. In such a schematization, Marcuse unquestionably belonged on the left. But Marcuse figured as an unusual case: without psychoanalytic training himself and in no position to draw on clinical experience, he simply speculated on the implications of the therapy that Freud had devised. Two others, however, both trained clinicians, shared Marcuse's radicalism and engendered an embryo left wing within psychoanalysis itself—Wilhelm Reich and Geza Roheim. In their case, as in Marcuse's, the radicalism was threefold: sexual, political, and stylistic. To an "enthusiasm for sex" and a belief that sexual pleasure was "the ultimate measure of human happiness," they joined the conviction that politics and sexuality were closely linked, that the repression of instinct functioned as a major weapon of political domination. And in stylistic terms, all three indulged in extreme statement, pursuing a given line of argument to its farthest reaches.[6]

Reich, Roheim, and Marcuse worked independently of one another. The same was not true of the neo-Freudian revisionists, who for the most part were bound together by professional ties and were frequently perceived as a constituted school. Here too the interpretation of sexuality was central to the group's definition. If the "Left" went beyond Freud himself in stressing the primacy of sex, the "neos" tried to modify the founder's more categorical statements on the subject and to suggest that nonsexual elements should receive greater recognition in psychoanalytic theory. It is primarily in this sense that they can be classified as a Freudian "Right."

From the political standpoint, however, they were not uniformly conservative. The remote progenitor of the revisionist tendency, Alfred Adler, had regarded himself as just the opposite and had adhered, as had most of his immediate followers, to his own brand of socialism. But the neo-Freudians refused to acknowledge him as their ancestor: one of the most curious chapters of psychoanalytic history is the stubborn denial on the part of men and women whose theories bore the strongest resemblance to Adler's that he had exerted any influence at all upon their work.[7] Adler had stressed the imperatives of the communal life; he had urged the therapist to turn the neurotic back toward human society; and in so doing he had reintroduced a "surface" moralizing which Freud had endeavored to banish forever from psychoanalytic practice. All this the revisionists echoed, but in a blander tone and in a language that stuck closer than Adler's to Freud's original terminology.

The native-born American members of the school, notably Harry Stack Sullivan, entertained few doubts about the society in which they lived. While they sought out, as Adler had, the social origins of individual neuroses, they were more inclined than he had been to suggest adjustment to a milieu they thought of as on

6. Paul A. Robinson, *The Freudian Left: Wilhelm Reich, Geza Roheim, Herbert Marcuse* (New York, 1969), pp. 4–6.

7. Henri F. Ellenberger, *The Discovery of the Unconscious: The History and Evolution of Dynamic Psychiatry* (New York, 1970), pp. 638, 645.

the whole beneficent. The émigrés were less sure: their recent experiences in Berlin or Vienna had not encouraged them to take a favorable view of the political status quo, and they shared some of Adorno and Horkheimer's anxiety about the direction in which their host country might be heading. But most of these too eventually accepted the tenets and practices of American democracy as presuppositions of their psychoanalytic labors. Here once more we may find evidence of a drift toward conservatism.

In a broader sense, the psychoanalytic émigrés' uncompromising rejection of Nazism as irredeemably evil entailed a critique of ethical relativism: in discovering what they were against, they almost found out what they were for. Psychoanalysis, of course, was not necessarily relativist; Freud himself had upheld the sternest standards of personal conduct. But in philosophical terms it had suspended judgment on questions of morality and been skeptical of mankind's capacities for improvement. For a resolute minority among the émigrés, this disabused stance no longer sufficed; in the ideologically open and welcoming atmosphere of the United States, they became militant optimists. Emotional suffering, they began to imply, was not integral to the human condition; beyond Freud's modest goal of alleviating psychic misery gleamed the vision of maximizing man's potentialities in a reordered society.

The most persuasive and popular advocate of such optimism was Erich Fromm. Already in *Escape from Freedom* he had rebuked Freud for accepting the conventional Judeo-Christian view of the human propensity toward antisocial behavior. Six years later he was ready for a full-scale assault on the citadels of psychoanalytic orthodoxy. In *Man for Himself* Fromm undertook a task that Freud had barely sketched out and that Weber and Moore and Wittgenstein had dismissed as impossible of accomplishment —to build an ethical world view on a theory laying claim to the status of science. *Man for Himself* aimed to unite psychoanalysis with the major secular tradition of humanist ethics; it reached back for intellectual support to Plato and Aristotle, to Spinoza and Goethe. "In many instances," Fromm argued, "a neurotic symptom" was "the specific expression of moral conflict" and demanded to be resolved in moral terms. But what Freud, no less than Jung, had offered in response had been the unacceptable alternatives of ethical agnosticism or religious faith. A third path—the path of human values expressed in exclusively human terms—they had left unexplored. So Fromm set out to inquire into the nature of man, and more particularly into man's chances for "productive" living—by which he meant self-love, a sense of plenitude and autonomy, and the unfolding of human powers, as opposed to the altruism and self-denial that religion had taught—in brief, what was "good for man" without any element of transcendence.

In trying to delineate humanity's full potential, Fromm made a number of telling observations. He found a covert puritanism in the near-obsession of classic psychoanalysis with the sexual drive. He followed—and expanded—Max Weber's concept of inner-worldly asceticism in showing how the modern capitalist's ostensible ethic of self-interest in fact amounted to an ethic of self-denial as punishing as anything that religion had devised.[8] Fromm's critique of the cult of work and of the anxiety and insecurity which a highly competitive society had created recalled his early association with the Institut für Sozialforschung. But there remained little in it of Adorno and Horkheimer's—and Freud's—tragic sense of humanity's emotional entrapment. Fromm patently overestimated man's capacity for autonomy, just as he underrated the devastating force of sexual and destructive urges. As *Man for Himself* begot sequel after sequel, Fromm's theoretical substance grew ever thinner and his reliance on ethical abstractions more intrusive. In the end—to use Marcuse's term—the "affirmative" elements in his writing submerged its critical content.

Thus although Fromm, in common with Adler, considered himself a socialist, his emphasis on productive living gradually eroded his points of difference with his American-born colleagues. Like them, he moved away from Freud's fundamental conviction about the primacy of the unconscious. Like them, he perceived among his patients and among humanity at large an unmistakable "capacity for psychic growth" and "drive toward mental health." Like them, he diverted psychoanalysis toward a celebration of the

8. *Man for Himself* (New York, 1947), pp. vii–ix, 6–7, 20, 45, 135.

humane, libertarian values of the civilized West. "Positive freedom," he had asserted in his first book, consisted of "the spontaneous activity of the total, integrated personality."[9] When these
words were written, they stood for an aspiration toward the far
future; as the years went by, they sounded more and more like a
description of what had already occurred or at the very least was
possible of attainment.

The dissatisfaction with a simple schema of primitive drives
extended beyond the ranks of neo-Freudian revisionism. More
generally the younger analysts in the 1930's and 1940's found it
reductive and began to work their way toward a more complex
theory of motivation. By the 1950's there had emerged something
of a consensus: the dominant tendency was now to speak of a
hierarchy of motives that could account for a "progressive taming"
of the drives and to adopt "a view of personality functioning" that
included "its steady, stable, ordinary, organized, enduring patterns
of behavior and thinking."[10] To do all this while remaining true
to basic Freudian principles required a high degree of theoretical
dexterity. The trick was to hold fast to the unconscious while
elaborating above it a sophisticated explanatory structure—to jettison reductionism while making sure that one did not throw the
baby out with the bath. So much for a brief initial definition of
the Freudian "Center."

Fortunately for the psychoanalytic movement the founder himself had suggested what might be done. Freud had a way of
putting theoretical heresies to good use at the very time he was
casting the heretics themselves into outer darkness. Just as he had
drawn on Jung's anthropological insights to launch his own such
speculations with *Totem and Taboo*, so a few years later he exploited the work of Adler in focusing his mind on the ego.[11] In

9. Martin Birnbach, *Neo-Freudian Social Philosophy* (Stanford, Calif.,
1961), pp. 213, 218; Erich Fromm, *Escape from Freedom* (New York,
1941), p. 258.
10. Merton Gill, "The Present State of Psychoanalytic Theory," *The Journal of Abnormal and Social Psychology*, LVIII (Jan. 1959), 1, 3, 5.
11. Roazen, *Freud*, p. 224; Abram Kardiner, Aaron Karush, and Lionel
Ovesey, "A Methodological Study of Freudian Theory: III. Narcissism, Bi-
sexuality and the Dual Instinct Theory," *The Journal of Nervous and Mental
Disease*, CXXIX (Sept. 1959), 207.

his earlier writings Freud had frequently mentioned the ego's role in psychic conflict. But he disliked the metaphysical overtones with which German idealism had associated the term, and he wanted to be sure that he had nailed down his epoch-making original discoveries about dreams, familiar slips, and their relation to the unconscious before exploring systematically the more conventional realm of self-consciousness. Heinz Hartmann was to see in this "retardation of Freud's interest in the ego . . . a rather fortunate event." "The great superiority of his later ego psychology," Hartmann found, lay "to a considerable extent in the very fact that his work on the unconscious mind and on the drives, and his insights into human development, had preceded it."[12] When in 1923, in *The Ego and the Id*, Freud finally enunciated his structural triad, he assumed a previous knowledge (and acceptance) of psychoanalytic fundamentals on the part of his readers and described the structural hypothesis as a completion rather than a basic modification of what he had written before.

In fact matters were not that simple. In ascribing to the ego an organizing function—or better, system of functions—Freud was running the risk that his followers might interpret this change as an authorization to displace the unconscious id from its original position of primacy. Still more, just three years before unveiling his threefold structure, he had found it necessary to embark on a parallel elaboration of his theory of drives. *Beyond the Pleasure Principle* of 1920, perhaps the most tentative of Freud's theoretical works, had added a new and perplexing element to both the dynamic and the economic modes: in trying to account for the repetition compulsion he had found among his patients—a compulsion that struck him as more elementary and primitive than the impulse toward pleasure itself—Freud guessed at a basic drive toward the restoration of an earlier state, a state in which life did not yet exist. Such was the genesis of the notion of "death instinct," whose lack of clinical confirmation was to plague Freud's successors at least as sorely as any of his feats of theoretical acrobatics. (It was characteristic of Marcuse that he was among

12. "The Development of the Ego Concept in Freud's Work" (originally published in 1956), *Essays on Ego Psychology: Selected Problems in Psychoanalytic Theory* (New York, 1964), pp. 280–282.

the few to find merit in the idea.) And to confuse the outlook further, Freud virtually equated the death instinct with hate or aggressiveness as the polar opposite of Eros, while failing to specify the ends toward which aggression might be directed.[13]

Thus the three works of the early 1920's with which Freud rounded out his theory raised new problems even as they put old ones to rest. If *The Ego and the Id* flashed a permissive signal to the psychoanalytic "Center," *Group Psychology* and *Beyond the Pleasure Principle,* in tantalizingly casual or even playful fashion, drew attention to the booby traps with which the promised path was strewn. Those who ventured on it needed to keep their wits about them; after all, they were writing with a glance over the shoulder to catch the reaction of the aging master. They felt obliged to choose their words with care and to weigh with precision every minute shift in emphasis. To this day it has remained debatable to what extent they were correct in laying claim to the title of Freud's lineal heirs or whether they were subverting his theory without ever quite admitting what they had done.

"Gentlemen, I think we are committing an injustice." The girlish voice that rang out in the stormy international psychoanalytic congress of 1927 was that of Freud's daughter Anna, his youngest child and the only one to work professionally with him. The subject at issue was laden with portents for the future—coercion of the American minority on the question of lay analysis— and the fact that Anna, although only just over thirty, was listened to suggested that she had already won the respect of her father's colleagues.[14] Nine years later she was to emerge as a major and once again a conciliatory force in the psychoanalytic movement.

By the mid-1930's the evidence was mounting that some of Freud's closest followers were ready to take the decisive step toward the ego psychology which their master had sketched out. Although the innovators included several men who were destined to make influential contributions to psychoanalytic theory—

13. Kardiner, Karush, Ovesey, "Methodological Study of Freudian Theory: III," pp. 217–218.

14. Ernest Jones, *The Life and Work of Sigmund Freud,* III: *The Last Phase* 1919–1939 (New York, 1957), pp. 295–296.

notably Edward Bibring, Otto Fenichel, and Hartmann's future collaborator Ernst Kris—it was left to Freud's own daughter to produce the work that was to figure in retrospect as the founding document of the new interpretation. The circumstances could scarcely have been more dramatic: the setting was Vienna itself, the world capital of psychoanalysis, living out its half-decade of precarious independence between the advent of Hitler and Austria's annexation to the Nazi Reich; the protagonists were members of Freud's "family," a child and a cherished pupil; the founder himself, stoically enduring his daily round of pain and apparently too sick to say much about what the younger generation was writing, had only three more years to live; sixteen months before his death he was to be driven into the exile that gave his movement a new language and a new home. The founding of ego psychology ranked, then, as the last great event in the history of psychoanalysis in its original Central European incarnation.

Anna Freud's *The Ego and the Mechanisms of Defense*, published in 1936, had about it a disarming air of simplicity. Its style was flat and direct, with none of the literary turns of phrase in which her father had delighted, and its argument proceeded with the clarity of the self-evident. The study of the ego, Anna Freud explained, far from being the "beginning of apostasy from psychoanalysis" that the orthodox feared, should be thought of rather as an essential further exploration. For if, as now seemed apparent, "large portions of the ego institutions" were "themselves unconscious," an inquiry into the workings of the ego did not entail abandoning fundamental convictions about unconscious processes. Quite the contrary: the only way to "reconstruct the transformations . . . undergone" by the basic drives was to analyze the ego's "defensive operations," most of which lay below the threshold of consciousness.[15]

Having skillfully inserted the thin entering wedge of the ego's protection against self-knowledge, Anna Freud went on to specify the roster of such defenses, some of which, like "identification with the aggressor," were themselves to become classic in psycho-

15. *Das Ich und die Abwehrmechanismen* (Vienna, 1936), trans. by Cecil Baines as *The Ego and the Mechanisms of Defense*, rev. ed. (*The Writings of Anna Freud*, II) (New York, 1966), pp. 3, 25–26.

analytic theory. Gently, persuasively she moved from the unconscious to the conscious level, even venturing along the way the suggestion that her father had overestimated the importance of the superego.[16] As the skilled therapist she was, she kept offering reassurance to her skittish colleagues. She defined her subject narrowly and dutifully cited the approved texts. Her method, as she frankly recognized, was cautious and even conventional. It lacked the "revolutionary" potential she attributed to a man who had entered the Vienna Psychoanalytic Society almost simultaneously with herself and whom she regarded in professional terms as her "slightly elder brother, or half brother," since in this respect they "shared the same father." For three decades Anna Freud and Heinz Hartmann were to advance along parallel tracks, each "immersed" in his or her special field, "respecting each other, quoting each other, but not in active interchange." Indeed Hartmann on occasion suspected that the founder's daughter should be reckoned his "silent critic." That this was far from true was to emerge at last in the mid-1960's, when Anna Freud, joining in the tributes which showered on Hartmann for his seventieth birthday, unequivocally ranked herself as his "eloquent supporter."[17]

II. *Heinz Hartmann and the "Conflict-Free Sphere"*

The theoretician who was to make the critical leap beyond the ego's defenses to an assertion of its substantial autonomy was as authentic a Viennese and as respectful a disciple of Freud as one could ask for. In his family origins Hartmann was the most illustrious of the Central European converts to psychoanalysis, and throughout his life he carried himself with an air of effortless inborn distinction. His paternal grandfather had been both a prolific writer and a deputy to the Frankfurt Assembly of 1848. His father, a historian of Rome and professor at the University of Vienna, served as Austria's ambassador in Berlin after the First

16. *Ibid.*, pp. 57, 116.
17. Anna Freud, "Links between Hartmann's Ego Psychology and the Child Analyst's Thinking," *Psychoanalysis—A General Psychology: Essays in Honor of Heinz Hartmann*, ed. by Rudolph M. Loewenstein et al. (New York, 1966), pp. 18, 26–27.

World War. His maternal grandfather had been called by Freud "the most eminent of all our Vienna physicians," and Hartmann himself was to marry a pediatrician from a leading medical family. Even the tutor who supervised his early education, Karl Seitz, was later to win fame as Social Democratic mayor of Vienna. To his more discerning friends, Hartmann seemed a man "whose major challenge in life must have been to protect his integrity and creativeness against an overflow of good fortune."[18]

Born in 1894, Hartmann grew up without religion or even a sense of its loss. (The Jewish origins that his name suggests evidently lay buried in the past.) This lack of a religious problem—or of the moral torments springing from it—sharply distinguished his adolescent development from Wittgenstein's, whose social and cultural milieu in other respects so much resembled his own. Like Wittgenstein, Hartmann breathed from childhood an atmosphere in which artistic attainments were the stuff of life itself; like the future philosopher, who was five years his senior, he became an accomplished musician and learned through early acquaintance with his parents' prominent friends not to be dazzled by public reputations or to seek such prominence for himself.

After Hartmann settled on psychiatry as a career, he continued to cultivate a wide range of interests. In the spring of 1918 he attended the university lectures in Vienna with which Max Weber resumed teaching after more than a decade and a half of silence; in his subsequent writings Hartmann was to return repeatedly to Weber as a methodological guide. A few years later, a stint of service in his father's embassy gave him a chance to observe politics at first hand. He was also unique among the Austrian psychoanalysts in maintaining contact with the Vienna Circle of philosophers. Even within his profession, he refused to limit himself to one branch or school. Having begun his work under the tutelage of conservative, experimentally oriented clinicians, he did

18. Marie Jahoda, "The Migration of Psychoanalysis: Its Impact on American Psychology," *The Intellectual Migration: Europe and America 1930–1960*, ed. by Donald Fleming and Bernard Bailyn (Cambridge, Mass., 1969), p. 430. The best source for details on Hartmann's life is the "Biographical Sketch" by Ruth S. and K. R. Eissler in *Psychoanalysis—A General Psychology*, pp. 3–15.

not encounter psychoanalysis directly until the mid-1920's, when he underwent a training analysis in Berlin. Meantime, however, he had published an influential paper on the experimental validation of Freudian theory and begun to write a book on psychoanalytic fundamentals, which appeared in 1927. The clue to the respect that Hartmann had already won for himself as a young man lay in his unrivaled combination of rigorous training in experimental psychology, close study of psychoanalytic theory, varied clinical experience, and an ingrained concern for the arts, for social science, and for public affairs.

Such was the man who as he was turning forty received the honor (shared apparently by only one other) of being asked by Freud to undertake a second training analysis with the master himself. By 1934 the founder of psychoanalysis had become too weak to maintain a regular relationship with more than a few carefully selected individuals. His choice of Hartmann proved fortunate: the older man found a superbly qualified successor, the younger a chance to complete his intellectual and emotional preparation at the highest source. During his years with Freud, Hartmann pondered, and published nothing.

This period of turning inward came to an end in 1937 with his reading of the paper entitled "Ego Psychology and the Problem of Adaptation" which little by little was to win its place as the most influential single post-Freudian piece of writing. The audience of analysts who originally heard it has been described as both "stunned" and unaware of its full implications. For Hartmann's presentation was so low-keyed and meticulous as to anticipate the objections of the theoretically inclined and to leave the rest at a loss. His purpose, he announced, was nothing less than to stake out the "*general* psychology," the "*general* theory of mental life," the promised land into which Freud himself, now engaged in his final meditation on the mission of Moses, had been unable to lead his followers.

The basis for such an intellectual program, Hartmann explained, the "meeting ground with nonanalytic psychology," was the ego psychology that the old master and his daughter had already been formulating. But Hartmann ventured far beyond them in the role he ascribed to the ego. In expanding what Freud had called its "organizing" system of functions and in characterizing its work of adaptation as "reality mastery," he markedly reduced the classic psychoanalytic emphasis on inner conflict. "Not every adaptation to the environment," Hartmann argued, "or every learning and maturation process" needed to be thought of as conflict-derived. A host of processes in the development of the individual—"perception, intention, object comprehension," and the like—went on in what he designated the ego's "conflict-free sphere." This sphere constituted the particular domain of "ego strength"—and in speaking of such strength in the traditional moral terms of "character" and "will" Hartmann came perilously close to revisionist vocabulary.[19]

Beyond defining the conflict-free sphere, Hartmann added the hope that its study would "open up the no-man's land between sociology and psychoanalysis and thus extend the contribution of psychoanalysis to the social sciences." But he was not yet ready to specify what that contribution might be. He confined himself to speculating on the "hierarchies of values" which every social structure dictated to the individuals within it and on the ways in which psychoanalysis could help people sort out their relationship to those values. While "the deepening of a man's knowledge," he explained, might "change his valuations" by making him see where his true allegiances lay, it could not lead to an assertion of value itself. It was an illusion to think that such understanding could "provide the goals of action." In vigorously denying the existence of "a 'natural' value hierarchy" applicable to all men, and in rejecting the view that values could be "*derived* from psychoanalytic knowledge," Hartmann unequivocally aligned himself with Weber.[20]

The same held true in delineating the bounds of rationality. "The realm of strictly rational action," Hartmann granted, had proved "rather narrower than some of us would expect." But like Weber he refused all "traffic" with those who bemoaned "the

19. "Ich-Psychologie und Anpassungsproblem," *Internationale Zeitschrift für Psychoanalyse und Imago*, XXIV (1939), trans. by David Rapaport as *Ego Psychology and the Problem of Adaptation* (New York, 1958), pp. 4, 6, 8, 15–16, 22, 69.
20. *Ibid.*, pp. 21, 76, 83–84.

mind as the 'adversary of the soul.' " The current task, he suggested, with a bow to Mannheim, was rather to put into perspective the concept of rationality while adhering to rational method: "the tendency of psychoanalysis to enlighten must of necessity relativize the rationalistic doctrine of enlightenment."[21] Hartmann was far from sharing Horkheimer and Adorno's despair of enlightenment itself. Yet he saw as they did that its claims must be tailored to the bitter ideological realities of the 1930's.

In the year which intervened between the reading of Hartmann's paper and its publication in more extended form, the tide of irrationality engulfed his homeland. The annexation of Austria obliged Hartmann, no less than Freud and his daughter, to leave their native city. But Hartmann hesitated longer than most of his colleagues to seek refuge in the English-speaking world. It was only after spending three more years in Paris and Switzerland that he finally reached New York in 1941.

Here he established himself both in private practice and in theoretical work with the ease which came naturally to him. Without striving for primacy, he found it devolving upon him: his personal enemies were few, and his admirers legion. Apparently his associates did not hold against him his aristocratic demeanor or his formidable cultural equipment; they regularly elected him to all the high offices in the international psychoanalytic movement in which he would consent to serve. One explanation for this lack of professional jealousy was his courteous, unpolemical manner of speaking and writing. Another was the fact that he remained unknown to the general public; in contrast to the fame which Fromm or Erikson enjoyed, Hartmann's circle of readers reached scarcely beyond the psychoanalytic community itself.

The three decades between his arrival in the United States and his death in 1970 might strike the casual observer as eventless. Indeed his shift of scene marked no break in his thought, which in its classic abstraction and conciseness passed easily across the Atlantic and from German into English. Yet it was in America and more particularly during his early and mid-fifties that Hartmann's powers of synthesis reached their full development.

21. *Ibid.*, pp. 65, 67–68, 70–72.

Around 1950 he published a cluster of papers—some of them in collaboration with his friends Ernst Kris and Rudolph M. Loewenstein—which together constitute the basic theoretical corpus of ego psychology.

These essays explored three matters that his original paper composed in Vienna had left tentative or uncertain: they spelled out the functions of the ego; they tried to fit Freud's terminology to the new material which the emphasis on the ego had opened up; and they provided at last some specification as to how the findings of psychoanalysis might illuminate the study of society.

The term "ego," Hartmann explained, was "often used in a highly ambiguous way, even among analysts." Hence it could best be defined in negative terms, to distinguish its psychoanalytic meaning from the various other meanings it had acquired in popular or philosophical usage. Viewed from the standpoint of Freudian therapy, it was "not synonymous with 'personality' or with 'individual,'" it did "not coincide with the 'subject' as opposed to the 'object' of experience," and it was "by no means only the 'awareness' or the 'feeling' of one's own self." In analysis, the ego figured as "a concept of quite a different order." It was "a substructure of personality" and was "defined by its functions." These functions were far too numerous to catalog—more numerous than those of the id or the superego. But among the most important one could mention adaptation to reality, action, thinking, and the defenses which Anna Freud had studied. Beyond and less tangible than these lay the set of functions commonly called "a person's character." And at a still further remove from the observable data of experience one could speak of the work of psychic "synthesis" or "organization."[22]

The heterogeneity of these functions already threatened to land Hartmann in multiple complexities: as he listed them, the activities of the ego went on at levels of specificity so different as to be barely comparable one with another. Moreover, he compounded his problem by adopting from one of Freud's last theoretical essays the notion of a congenital element in the ego, the guess that it, no less than the id, had emerged from "the matrix of animal in-

22. "Comments on the Psychoanalytic Theory of the Ego" (originally read in 1949 and published in 1950), *Essays on Ego Psychology*, pp. 114–115.

stinct." To ascribe to the ego so remote and basic a pedigree helped to buttress the newly won conviction of its autonomy. But by the same token it entailed a ramifying definition of its development as the "result of three sets of factors: inherited ego characteristics (and their interaction), influences of the instinctual drives, and influences of outer reality."

> Contrasts in the ego there are many: the ego has from its start the tendency to oppose the drives, but one of its main functions is also to help them toward gratification; it is a place where insight is gained, but also of rationalization; it promotes objective knowledge of reality, but at the same time, by way of identification and social adjustment, takes over in the course of its development the conventional prejudices of the environment; it pursues its independent aims, but it is also characteristic of it to consider the demands of the other substructures of personality. . . .

Such apparent contradictions, Hartmann insisted, became more manageable when regarded "from an intrasystemic point of view."[23] By this he evidently meant to suggest that the ego's widely varying aims derived from its separate functions and that these latter could be seen as fitting together provided one considered them on a sufficiently high plane of abstraction. For those who had learned in elemental Freudian terms to think of the ego as an embattled contestant in its daily struggle for survival against the superego and the id, such a rarefied explanation might offer little more than semantic deliverance.

To enhance still further the ego's newly won status, Hartmann urged his readers to assume that it disposed of "independent psychic energy." Earlier he had taken pains to point out that the energy in question—at least as revealed in analysis—had nothing in common with a "metaphysical" Bergsonian élan vital; it was "rather an operational concept, devised to coordinate observational data." Yet it was also apparent that the whole notion of energy, as a physical term, led ultimately back to biology. And with this recognition, Hartmann found himself in the most doubtful realm of Freud's theory—the question of drives and their

23. *Ibid.*, pp. 119–120, 138–139.

crucial situation at the meeting point of his dynamic and economic modes of explanation. Here Hartmann frankly confessed his puzzlement. Aside from lamenting the fact that Freud's English translators had not seen fit to maintain the distinction between instinct and drive and had used the first expression indiscriminately for both, he treated the whole matter with extreme caution. He refused to "enter into a discussion of Freud's biological speculation." "Assumptions concerning . . . drives toward life or death," he added, facilitated "neither the 'fitting together' of existent propositions, nor the formulation of new ones," if one limited oneself, as he and his closest collaborators did, to hypotheses that could "now or in the foreseeable future be checked against empirical evidence, against data of clinical observation, developmental studies, or experimentation in normal or abnormal psychology."[24] The clear implication was that it was safer to stick with a phenomenon such as sexuality whose reality and force were undeniable.

Yet there was one of Freud's late additions to his energetic theory which Hartmann welcomed in elucidating the ego. The delineation of aggression as an independent drive Hartmann found indispensable to the work of the contemporary analyst. Having separated it out from the "death instinct" with which Freud had left it entangled, he felt free to devote some of his most meticulous pages to elaborating its aims, its derivatives, and its substitutes. For Hartmann the concept of aggression remained among the fundamentals of theory; Freud's duality of sex and aggressiveness passed over intact into his thought.

Hence it was logical that he should reject the course which had been proposed by a number of his colleagues "to confer emeritus status on Freud's concept of instinctual drives, to pay respect to it" in the history of psychoanalysis, "but not to entrust it any longer with active duty in psychoanalytic theory." Hartmann described himself as "in sharpest opposition" to the assertion that the

24. *Ibid.*, p. 130; "Comments on the Psychoanalytic Theory of Instinctual Drives" (originally published in 1948), *Essays on Ego Psychology*, pp. 74, 79; Heinz Hartmann, Ernst Kris, and Rudolph M. Loewenstein, "Notes on the Theory of Aggression" (originally published in 1949), *Papers on Psychoanalytic Psychology* (New York, 1964), pp. 58, 60.

concept in question was "no longer useful."[25] This fidelity to the founder's legacy was central to Hartmann's view of his own professional integrity. It suffused his discussion of the second major issue that he treated in his essays of the 1940's and 1950's—the extent to which orthodox theory still conformed to the findings of ego psychology.

His own starting point, he explained, was to accept "the complexity of psychoanalytic propositions" as Freud had left them—and, he might have added, as he himself had further complicated them. Such complexity, he argued, was "not accidental but necessary." The very term "psychoanalysis" referred to "a set of propositions" that were "internally cohesive, elaborated in some detail, and allowing for predictions of human behavior." Its "validation" constituted "a gradual and slow process" in which one assessed insights derived from many sources and in which multiple types of evidence had "to be taken into account, foremost among them clinical experiences and the study of child development" that Anna Freud had pioneered. "Under these conditions neatness in theorizing" (an apt self-characterization!) figured among the prime qualifications for undertaking to expand or refine the psychoanalytic corpus.

Against the theoretically tidy stood those whom Hartmann viewed, to borrow Jacob Burckhardt's expression, as "terrible simplifiers." Although he himself would never have spoken so categorically, the force of his scorn pierced through the measured politeness of his condemnation. For Hartmann the notion of "dissent" did not depend simply on the extent of agreement of new ideas "with similar ones proposed by Freud" or his heirs. It derived also from the fact that the self-styled innovators forgot that the propositions of psychoanalytic theory were arranged in a hierarchical order and that to disturb this order could lead to impoverishing the entire structure. The dissenters tended "to fragmentize . . . theory, to stress one set of propositions and to neglect others." The result was a "simplified version, reduced to fewer factors, based on fewer concepts," which far from improving that theory put it "in danger of becoming atrophied."

25. Hartmann, Kris, Loewenstein, "The Function of Theory in Psychoanalysis" (originally published in 1953), *ibid.*, pp. 140–141.

Prominent among the abbreviators figured certain well-known students of culture and personality. It was characteristic of them, Hartmann maintained, to fail to reckon with the whole range of psychoanalytic thinking, "to polemicize with insistence against views contained in the earlier writings of Freud and his collaborators" while ignoring the subsequent "reformulations" that ego psychology had devised. This neglect, he thought, was particularly unfortunate in separating natural allies. For ego psychology might "well suggest the most fruitful and pertinent propositions for interdisciplinary cooperation."[26] Such cooperation was already implicit in Hartmann's call to make psychoanalytic theory "general" in its scope. It stimulated his observations on the third problem which his work in Vienna had left unresolved—the relation of psychoanalysis to the study of society.

Rather early in his explorations—as early as 1944—it became apparent to him that anthropology offered a more promising field for cooperative endeavor than either sociology or history. Much of what sociology studied in statistical or quantitative fashion, Hartmann had found, stemmed "from those layers of the personality" which were "not in the center of analytic interest and research." It was above all in explaining "human conflicts" that psychoanalysis could contribute to sociological knowledge. As for history, the full application of Freudian theory could begin only when the historians themselves turned their attention to those "spheres of life" which the analysts regarded as primary. And this sort of data gathering as yet barely existed. Up to now, Hartmann lamented, echoing all-unknowing a plea that Lucien Febvre had made just three years earlier in the silence of occupied France, historical research had unearthed very little about "how, in the Middle Ages, the Renaissance, or the eighteenth century, . . . the feeding, weaning, and toilet training of the infant was managed, or in what way the parents . . . handled the child's sexual and aggressive drives."

With these matters, of course, the anthropologists were already familiar. They were the ones most expert in delimiting "the

26. Ibid., pp. 134–135; Hartmann, Kris, Loewenstein, "Some Psychoanalytic Comments on 'Culture and Personality' " (originally published in 1951), *ibid.*, pp. 88–89.

plasticity of the infantile situation"—the degree to which one culture or another could mold a young personality to its own requirements. Such "social compliance," Hartmann observed, helped to
determine both the "mobility of the ego" and the "severity of the
superego," along with the life roles that individuals fitted themselves to assume.[27] Seven years after this tentative assessment, he
was as convinced as ever that "reports on child care and child
rearing" constituted "the most fruitful and the most suggestive
contact between psychoanalysis and anthropology." But he was
becoming more wary of the anthropologists' relativist attitude
toward cultural norms and less willing to remain the humble
learner.

In his fullest statement on the subject—this time, as so often in
his major theoretical essays, writing in collaboration with Kris and
Loewenstein—he challenged the anthropologists' assumption that
the cultural bent which derived from "institutional regulation"
was necessarily primary to both the observer and the people
observed. In the observer, he argued, at least in the analytic situation, cultural background might be "of comparatively minor relevance"; it was far from true that an analyst reared and trained in
the West was incapable of understanding the emotional disorders
of a patient from another culture. For the analyst was "likely to be
less impressed by the . . . range of differences in everyday behavior than the anthropologist" and more inclined to view such
differences as of diminishing importance as the psychic exploration
moved "from the periphery to the center." Beyond that, Hartmann thought it inadvisable to draw sweeping conclusions from
evidence on child rearing: "similar experiences in childhood," he
had discovered, tended "to produce the most varied results." The
social or familial pressures acting upon the child were no more
than "initial links in a chain of influences." And among those
influences "a decisive point had been insufficiently taken into
account: the mother's personal attitude," much of it unconscious,
toward her offspring and the fact of her own motherhood.[28]

27. "Psychoanalysis and Sociology" (originally published in 1944), *Essays on Ego Psychology*, pp. 24–25, 27, 32, 35–36.
28. Hartmann, Kris, Loewenstein, " 'Culture and Personality,' " *Papers on Psychoanalytic Psychology*, pp. 102, 105, 107, 109–111.

Thus while still respectful and cooperative in his view of anthropology, Hartmann insisted on two crucial divergences in emphasis. In nominalist vein, he drew attention once more to the uniqueness of individual experience; as a universalist, he stressed what was common to the human condition and transcended the barriers of culture. "Under the impact of cultural anthropology," he observed, "the question how man" behaved "under any given set of circumstances" tended "to be neglected in favor of the question how a member of a specific culture" behaved. The contradiction between Hartmann's two points of difference was only apparent: both derived from his deepest professional and personal conviction. The "autonomy of the ego"—its nurture and its strengthening—united them in an aim that was alike particular to the individual and universal in range. And it was, Hartmann surmised, less esteemed in the "primitive" societies which the anthropologists preferred to call "preliterate" than in a society such as his own in which scientific thinking had for centuries combated the remnants of "magical attitudes."[29]

Hartmann's reflections on anthropology had already led him deep into the problem of values. This problem—which had lurked in the back of his mind for a quarter-century—he finally undertook to unravel in his last sustained piece of writing, a lecture on psychoanalysis and ethics delivered in 1959 and published in extended form in 1960.

With Weber, Hartmann had all along insisted that the notion of reason involved no more than the weighing of means against ends, or of ends against their consequences, and was incapable of establishing the rationality of any particular human goal.[30] If, then, psychoanalysis, as a technique of reason in action, debarred itself from providing "ultimate moral aims or general moral imperatives," if it treated such matters simply as "psychological givens," was there no way in which the theorist or the therapist could offer ethical assistance? Into this treacherous terrain, Hartmann advanced with his characteristic prudence. He rejected most

29. *Ibid.*, pp. 95, 115.
30. "On Rational and Irrational Action" (originally published in 1947), *Essays on Ego Psychology*, pp. 49–50.

of what passed for psychiatric counsel among the uninitiated and the methodologically sloppy: he refused to speak of social or cultural systems as "healthy" or "sick," adding that even the concept of "maturity" had been frequently abused. Yet he did not throw up his hands in despair; he surmised that there were a few things that psychoanalysis could venture to say, and in specifying what these might be he turned once more to the congenial field of anthropology.

With the passage of time he had come to the conclusion that the anthropologists might not be such thoroughgoing relativists as they themselves conventionally supposed. "Common elements shared by different moral systems" had recently begun to appear in their work:

> . . . Murder, unlimited lying and stealing are everywhere valued negatively; also something like a principle of "reciprocity" is recognized everywhere. . . . Some incest regulations are universal; nowhere is cannibalism regular practice. Also, the duty of the adults to take care of the children is generally accepted; a certain respect for private property is, too, and so is respect for the dead of one's own group. The analyst will be ready to accept, he will indeed expect, that there are such commonalities.

Since human beings in all cultures went through comparable experiences in growing up—and more especially in the formation of their superegos—it was only natural that the anthropologist or the analyst should encounter a few virtually universal ethical valuations.[31]

Beyond the common condition of mankind, Hartmann speculated that psychoanalysis itself might offer elements of a moral code. In its attitude toward the two basic human drives, he found it drawing a significant practical distinction: "full discharge of the sexual drives" it considered "rarely as damaging to society" as people had "assumed in the past; the same" could not "be said of the full discharge of aggression." In his relatively "relaxed" stand toward sexuality and in his concern for the social dangers of

31. *Psychoanalysis and Moral Values* (New York, 1960), pp. 60, 73, 78–79, 82–83.

aggressive behavior, Hartmann's view of psychoanalysis recalled what Fromm had argued a decade earlier about its place in the tradition of humanist ethics. But unlike Fromm, Hartmann refrained from spelling out the implications of his moral obiter dicta. He refused to formulate a world view; he recoiled from the role of the psychoanalyst as preacher. Following the example of his master Freud, he kept his own high personal standards to himself. Here once again one can discriminate the nuanced position of the psychoanalytic Center as against the moralizing of the Right wing and the ultrapermissiveness of the Left.

Hartmann similarly cleaved to Freud's own conviction in stressing "self-knowledge" and "intellectual integrity" as central to the psychoanalytic ethic. "In analysis," he suggested, man was "confronted with a more encompassing reach of 'his good' and 'his bad' than he had been aware of before." Facing up to one's "blind spots" could "give to moral awareness a depth dimension" that it would otherwise have lacked. "All great religions," Hartmann added, had "aimed at this confrontation," however they might differ with psychoanalysis in their "postulates," their "tools," and their "intent." Yet to urge acceptance of reality did "not imply . . . passive submission to a given social system."[32] On political ideology as on so much else, Hartmann held to a delicate equilibrium. Like Wittgenstein, he preferred to set the limits beyond which lay the unsayable rather than to specify what could be said within those boundaries. Further than that he would not go.

With his accustomed modesty of manner, but in full consciousness of his magisterial responsibility toward his own profession, Hartmann had tried to chart for his colleagues the future of the theory in which they had been trained. Yet his greatest contribution lay in what he had done to rescue its past. Freud had "left his followers with a terrible dilemma at the very heart of the psychoanalytic enterprise": by defining the ego as the weakest of the structural triad, he had suggested that its chances for victory in its struggles with the superego and the id were slim indeed—and implied that the outlook for successful therapy was correspondingly doubtful. Hartmann endeavored "to lead psychoanalytic

32. *Ibid.*, pp. 88–89, 94.

theory out of this dead end. . . . In the language of Freud's military metaphor," he "placed many more battalions at the disposal of the ego. . . . And he did so tactfully, painlessly, authoritatively and unobtrusively. . . . He accomplished a major piece of theoretical surgery without shedding a drop of blood."[33]

In establishing a conflict-free sphere of ego development and ego functioning, Hartmann delineated processes which were initially unconscious and yet eventually capable of contributing to rational, purposive action; he grounded his ego in the instinctual substratum of the psyche while allowing for its almost infinite elaboration at the conscious level. Those who knew him best found it "by no means accidental" that he had hit on the concept of the conflict-free: it reflected his own self-confidence and "cheerful tranquility."[34] For the run of analysts, however—particularly those tormented by doubts about themselves and the viability of their profession—the serene abstraction of his prose raised unexpected and highly sophisticated difficulties in the very course of dealing with basic and familiar ones. Moreover, it merely hinted at the promised alliance between social science and a psychoanalytic theory which had become "general" in scope. And within the terms of that theory it stubbornly adhered to a vocabulary that had already been stretched far beyond its original context.

Thus despite the precision of Hartmann's mind and the care with which he chiseled his phrases, it was often difficult to determine how his lofty formulations could be applied to the realities of clinical or social research. Or perhaps better, his intellectual refinement itself entrapped him in the delicate web of theory. He lacked the temperament of the ruthless innovator who cuts through a welter of complexities and emerges with a startling new formulation. He hated to let go any precious strand of reasoning in his theoretical patrimony. He loved to demonstrate how two lines of thought that apparently contradicted each other could be woven together in a way which gave each its due. Like the immediate predecessors of Copernicus, he "expended . . . tremendous energy . . . in 'adding epicycles' " to the metapsychology he had inherited.[35]

This metapsychology, of course, consisted of figures of speech and heuristic devices. And as a collection of metaphors it presented the further difficulty of attempting to describe a set of activities—the mind—that by its very nature defied exact delineation. If all scientific language of necessity explains phenomena in terms of something else, more tangible and closer to home, the elucidation of mental events is obliged to operate at a level and in a vocabulary even more remote from verifiable reality than is true of ordinary investigation into the natural or the social world. The figures of speech in which it is couched—whether spatial or energetic—suggest a concreteness utterly foreign to the material at hand.

It would be quite wrong to imply that Hartmann was unaware of these pitfalls. His own mind was far too scrupulous to entertain for a moment the thought that matters "really" went on as Freud had described them. But he wrote as though they did: in his prose, the four classic metapsychological modes figured as near-actualities. And from there it was only a step to relapse once more into dogmatic certainty, a step which simplified life for Hartmann's unphilosophical American admirers. He had correctly seen that Freud's concept of drives ranked along with the distinction between the conscious and the unconscious, and between the ego and the id, among the essentials whose abandonment would reduce psychoanalytic interpretation to a flat meaninglessness. Without it, the inner drama would lack an initial thrust to set it in motion. But there was no such imperative to try to explain what the drives were; as Hartmann himself recognized, this sort of explanation lay in the realm of biology—or possibly of metaphysics.[36] More particularly, retaining as he did the notion of psychic energy—or even units of energy—as their basic characteristic encumbered the theory of drives and severely reduced its plausibility.

35. Yankelovich and Barrett, *Ego and Instinct*, p. 113.
36. Kardiner, Karush, Ovesey, "A Methodological Study of Freudian Theory: II. The Libido Theory," *The Journal of Nervous and Mental Disease*, CXXIX (Aug. 1959), 136.

Hartmann had rescued the human ego and made welcoming gestures to his colleagues in the social sciences. He had notably enhanced the range and the internal consistency of psychoanalytic theory. But he had not solved the problems of vocabulary and epistemology that Freud had left to his heirs. And this was what sympathizers outside the psychoanalytic fraternity were demanding with ever greater insistence as Hartmann's life drew to a close.

III. *Erik H. Erikson and the Sense of "Identity"*

In comparing the career of Hartmann to that of Erik H. Erikson, one starts almost inevitably with a set of contrasts: a clear and early-defined sense of direction as against decades of groping; a quiet, orderly existence with only one major change of scene as opposed to a life of frequent moves and a taste for adventure; theoretical tidiness versus imprecision of method; the self-effacement of one secure in his status and his talents as against a prolonged uncertainty on both these scores that manifested itself in a curious alternation of shy and dramatic behavior. In Hartmann the young man it was already possible to discern the future mentor of the psychoanalytic movement; in Erikson's case a tall, strong, ruddy young "Viking" was only gradually metamorphosed into a dignified, white-haired figure who quite literally exuded charisma and looked "the part of the sage."[37] The one guarded his privacy while working easily and closely with collaborators his own age; the other's unusual life history set him apart from his age mates and steered him toward the public arena and the discipleship of his juniors. Hartmann's influence by imperceptible stages suffused and transformed the theory and practice of psychoanalysis; Erikson's labors remained on the margin of the movement until they suddenly and for the most part unexpectedly became the center of a cult.

Although only eight years younger than Hartmann, Erikson seemed a half-generation behind him. He waited until he was forty before publishing his first significant article. The European phase

37. Robert Coles, *Erik H. Erikson: The Growth of His Work* (Boston, 1970), p. 266.

of his life ranked in retrospect as preparation; his entire mature career was passed in an American setting, Still more, the period of Erikson's most intense activity began just as Hartmann was putting the finishing touches on his own theoretical corpus. Hence it was natural that the references to each other in their work should appear more often in the writings of the younger man. Hartmann took note of Erikson only in passing; Erikson, while recognizing a primary debt to Anna Freud, tried to specify what he owed to the co-founder of ego psychology. In his Freud centennial lectures in 1956, he credited Hartmann with having built a "bridge to a psychoanalytic theory of the environment," while characterizing as "theoretically undeveloped" his own empirical investigations along corresponding lines. Twelve years later, with the publication of a second volume of his lectures and miscellaneous papers, Erikson felt ready at last to set down more precisely what he and Hartmann had in common: in a "Theoretical Interlude"—a rare occurrence in writings which were almost exclusively clinical, historical, or discursive—he aligned himself with the older man's contention that the technical term "ego" should be sharply discriminated from the sense of one's own selfhood.[38] This emphasis on the self—or more usually, of identity—was the core of what Erikson for more than a quarter-century had been struggling to express.

From the day of his birth in 1902, Erikson's existence had unfolded in unconventional fashion. His very name gave evidence of his mixed origin and puzzling family relations. The child of Danish parents, he "grew up in Karlsruhe in Baden as the son of a pediatrician, Dr. Theodor Homburger." With the best intentions, Dr. Homburger and his wife "kept secret" from the little boy the fact that his "mother had been married previously" and that he was actually "the son of a Dane who had abandoned her" before his birth. And as though this national and paternal confusion were not enough, he had to contend with the further question of his religious identification. "Blond and blue-eyed," young Erik "acquired the nickname 'goy'" in his "stepfather's temple." To his schoolmates he "was a 'Jew.'"

38. "Trieb und Umwelt in der Kindheit," *Freud in der Gegenwart*, ed. by Theodor W. Adorno and Walter Dirks (Frankfurt, 1957), pp. 48–49; *Identity: Youth and Crisis* (New York, 1968), pp. 217–218.

Eventually, of course, the boy found out the truth. But the result was not an unequivocal turning against his stepfather. He kept the latter's transparently Jewish name as his own middle name "out of gratitude . . . but also to avoid the semblance of evasion." And he "came as close to the role of a children's doctor as one could possibly come without going to medical school." In so doing, he "mixed" what he called "an ambivalent identification" with his "stepfather, the pediatrician," with "a search" for his "own mythical father." This resolution of internal strain, however, did not emerge until years later when his "truly astounding adoption by the Freudian circle" provided him a surrogate father in "the then already mythical founder" of psychoanalysis while letting him know that the status of stepson carried advantages as well as liabilities. It made him "take for granted" that he "should be accepted where" he "did not quite belong"; it gave him the confidence to work "between the established fields" and "in institutional contexts for which" he "did not have the usual credentials."

From the very start his mother and his stepfather had had the "fortitude" to let him find his way "unhurriedly." They had not objected to his decision to forgo university studies and to "set out . . . to be a wandering artist." It was thus through rich personal experience that he stumbled upon what later became one of his key concepts—a social and emotional "moratorium" before buckling down to one's life task. After seven years of this free and "romantic" existence, he at last found a regular job that appealed to him: he signed up as a teacher in a small experimental school in Vienna. And here by fortunate coincidence he met Anna Freud, whose psychoanalytic studies of children were then in their own infancy. A training analysis with the founder's daughter followed, along with formal instruction in clinical procedure by such rising luminaries as Hartmann himself. Erikson had arrived in Vienna in 1927 as a young man uncertain of his course; he left in 1933 as a full-fledged lay analyst, married, with two small sons and an ample fund of observation of other people's children.

Thus he was not driven from the Austrian capital, as in the case of the Freuds and Hartmann, by the Nazi takeover. He left five years earlier of his own accord. "After . . . intense training under

. . . complex conditions, the idea of moving on and working independently seemed . . . invigorating." Erikson evidently sensed that in a Vienna teeming with psychoanalytic talent where the founder's heirs were already staking out their advanced positions, an untheoretical mind such as his would feel hemmed in. First, and very briefly, he tried to establish himself in his native Denmark; subsequently, and definitively, he moved to the United States, his way smoothed by his wife's American birth and the fact that child analysis was a new field which aroused interest wherever he went. From 1934 to 1935 he was at the Harvard Medical School and for the next three years at Yale. In the year of Freud's death and the outbreak of the Second World War, he moved once more, this time to the University of California at Berkeley, where he was to spend the decisive decade of his life.

Indeed, the major phase of Erikson's residence in America divided itself neatly by decades: the 1940's in California, the 1950's in the Berkshires, the 1960's at Harvard. Each had its distinctive character and focus. Throughout, however, the base point of his clinical work and writing remained the study of children: in child's play (like Wittgenstein!) he had found the royal road to understanding that Freud had discovered in the world of dreams.[39] Erikson was always at his most convincing when he spoke of children; the farther he got away from them, the more his thought wavered and blurred.

Erikson's move to California—to San Francisco Bay, that is, and not to the Los Angeles area, where so many German-speaking émigrés were to congregate—gave him a feel for American life that he might never have acquired if he had stayed in the East. As opposed to Hartmann's transplantation to a cosmopolitan and Europe-oriented New York, Erikson's decision to go West entailed a far sharper break with the cultural tradition in which they had both grown up. Associating mostly with the native-born, Erikson became fascinated by a people in which he discerned "a strangely adolescent style of adulthood." Tentatively, cautiously he

39. For all the foregoing, see Coles, *Erikson*, pp. 13–25, 30–36, 43, 180–181, and Erikson's own "Autobiographic Notes on the Identity Crisis," *Daedalus*, XCIX (Fall 1970), 735, 739–746.

began to explore the American "national character." At the same time, by another series of lucky coincidences, he found opportunities to observe at first hand the customs and beliefs of two utterly different tribes of American Indians. While he was still at Yale, an anthropologist friend had taken him to a Sioux reservation in South Dakota. At Berkeley he met the senior figure in American anthropology, Alfred L. Kroeber, who introduced him to the Yurok of the north California coast. Once again in contrast to Hartmann, "Erikson did not at first speculate on the conceptual relationship between psychoanalysis and anthropology or history. Instead he made a series of . . . direct observations of specific people living under particular and varying circumstances."[40]

During the early 1940's Erikson's provisional conclusions about both the aboriginal and the white inhabitants of the United States began to take form in a series of papers and drafts that only gradually developed into a book. This book was also to contain a reworking of the first article with which he came to general attention, "Hitler's Imagery and German Youth," published at the height of the war in 1942, and which Hartmann's collaborator Rudolph M. Loewenstein called "a unique and memorable contribution." Four years later, Erikson stopped his incidental publications: rigorously taking off one day a week from his clinical research and private practice, he settled down to complete the book that appeared in 1950 as *Childhood and Society*.[41]

Disarmingly amorphous in structure, *Childhood and Society* was in fact a much more ambitious work than it seemed. Starting with case histories, it progressed through the Sioux and the Yurok to the author's central reflections on the ego and identity until it came at last to contemporary America and Hitler's childhood. Behind this loose essay-type organization, however, lay a fixed and dramatic purpose. His conviction, Erikson explained, was that psychoanalytic method was "essentially a historical method" and that "the history of humanity" was "a gigantic metabolism of individual life cycles"; his aim, then, was to write "a psychoanalytic book on the relation of the ego to society"—something

---

40. Erikson, "Autobiographic Notes," pp. 747–748; Coles, *Erikson*, pp. 48, 61.

41. *Ibid.*, pp. 85, 113.

that Hartmann never attempted on this scale and with this wealth of clinical detail.[42]

Embedded among Erikson's case histories there now appeared the formulations for which he would later become famous—the "basic trust" that the child learned at its mother's breast, the "source of both primal hope and of doom throughout life"; the "life cycle" or "ages of man," fully spelled out with an "epigenetic diagram" attached; above all, the matter of identity. Erikson's cycle was intended to demonstrate that at each stage of life, from the infant's trust to the old person's "ego integrity," there was a hurdle over which the ego had to jump, a characteristic emotional set which the ego had to acquire in order to fulfill its potentialities; and for every stage there was a corresponding negative term—as, in early maturity (stage six), the "isolation" that made "intimacy" impossible—which marked the risk inherent in each successive turn of the cycle. For youth (stage five) identity versus "role confusion" stood as the polar opposites.[43] Indeed throughout Erikson's account, the maintenance of identity ranked as the ego's crucial and overriding task.

It was typical of him that in this, his first grapple with his most celebrated concept, he should have defined it elusively and for the most part in historical terms. Identity, he explained, could be condensed into a formula of sociopsychological change:

> The patient of today suffers most under the problem of what he should believe in and who he should—or . . . might—be or become; while the patient of early psychoanalysis suffered most under inhibitions which prevented him from being what and who he thought he knew he was.

Who one might be or become: the riddle of identity, Erikson had discovered, thrust itself in particularly bewildering form on the children of an advanced urban society. "Mechanisms of adjustment which once made for evolutionary adaptation, tribal integration, caste coherence, national uniformity" were "at loose ends in an industrial civilization." Having lost the possibility of sharing social rhythms inherited from the past—of a clearly understood

42. *Childhood and Society*, 2d ed. (New York, 1963), p. 16.
43. *Ibid.*, p. 80, Chapter 7.

step-by-step initiation into adult existence—closed off in a special-ized environment and separated from "real life," the children Erikson had encountered were obliged to grope their way toward self-awareness with little guidance from any usable tradition. In contemporary America, as opposed to the Europe Erikson had left behind him, the boy was less likely to fear and hate his father, in the classic "Freudian" mold; he was more inclined to suffer from the harshness of a mother who had "abandoned" him, who had pushed him out into a world for which he felt unprepared. And in the same breath—as though to balance his strictures against his host country—Erikson noted with approval the quasi-fraternal relations between fathers and sons that American conditions fos-tered and the "democratic" aspects of a family life in which paternal authority had long been on the wane.[44]

Childhood and Society was an immediate success. It seemed to fill a need of which the younger psychoanalysts and the more imaginative social scientists had become acutely aware. Erikson now emerged as a recognized figure on the American intellectual scene. Yet ironically enough, just a few months before his first great achievement, he had become involved in a crisis that was both public and personal and that was to deflect his career once more.

When *Childhood and Society* appeared, Erikson had just turned forty-eight. He had reached the stage of life (number seven) in which according to his own schema "stagnation" threat-ened the "generativity"—the work of "establishing and guiding the next generation"—appropriate to full and late maturity. His biographer has suggested that at this point in his life he began to traverse a second "identity crisis": in common with so many men more ordinary than he, Erikson experienced his late forties as a period of emotional peril. What occasioned his change of scene, however, was no inner upheaval but rather the turmoil which shook the University of California over the non-Communist oath which the Regents had required of the faculty. While quite willing to declare for himself that he was no Communist, Erikson

44. *Ibid.*, pp. 238, 279, 296, 312–318.

could not stomach the firing of colleagues who had refused to do
so. In June 1950 he resigned the professorship of psychology to
which he had only recently been appointed.

Although the author of *Childhood and Society* was welcome at
a number of other universities, Erikson chose once more to
become a full-time clinician. He evidently felt the need of peace, a
rural setting, and a situation conducive to sustained thought.
Joining the staff of the Austen Riggs Center in the Berkshires, he
settled down in an "ideal place" whose "ideal patients" were
young men and women with "severe but not intractable" emotional problems.[45] And in this extraordinary environment where
patients and therapists mingled with an ease impossible in a
conventional institution, Erikson began to ponder the career of a
deeply troubled young man who had set off an epoch-making
explosion in human history—Martin Luther.

Seven years after Erikson's move back East, his second book,
Young Man Luther, was published. As influential as its predecessor, it reached an even wider audience, since the author's focus
had now shifted to historical biography, or more precisely to an
"ideological" study of the "life history" of a young man destined
for greatness. Erikson's sweeping definition of ideology added a
new term to the roster of concepts he had spelled out in *Childhood and Society*; so too did his stress on the crucial need for a
"moratorium"; finally his delineation of the historical role of a
"great young man" both explained his concentration on an individual figure and sanctioned the daring extrapolations that his
study of Luther inaugurated in his work.

Ideology, Erikson specified, for his purposes meant "an unconscious tendency underlying religious and scientific as well as political thought: the tendency at a given time to make facts amenable
to ideas, and ideas to facts, in order to create a world image
convincing enough to support the collective and the individual
sense of identity." What Luther had done was to forge in the fire
of his own tribulation a new ideology suited to a new era. But he
had been able to do so only after "marking time" in a monastery:

45. *Ibid.*, p. 267; Erikson, "Autobiographic Notes," p. 747; Coles, *Erikson*,
pp. 156–159, 181.

We will therefore concentrate on this process: how young Martin, at the end of a somber and harsh childhood, was precipitated into a severe identity crisis for which he sought delay and cure in the silence of the monastery; how being silent, he became "possessed"; how being possessed, he gradually learned to speak a new language, *his* language; how being able to speak, he not only talked himself out of the monastery, and much of his country out of the Roman Church, but also formulated for himself and for all of mankind a new . . . ethical and psychological awareness. . . .

A man of this sort, "in the years before he" became "a great young man," could be conceived as "inwardly" harboring "a quite inarticulate stubbornness, a secret furious inviolacy." "Allness or nothingness, then," was the implicit "motto of such men." They truly and totally *meant* what they said.

Ideological leaders, so it seems, are subject to excessive fears which they can master only by reshaping the thoughts of their contemporaries; while those contemporaries are always glad to have their thoughts shaped by those who so desperately care to do so. Born leaders seem to fear only more consciously what in some form everybody fears in the depths of his inner life; and they convincingly claim to have an answer.[46]

This last was only the most extraordinary of the historical extrapolations with which Erikson had widened the range of his account. Along the way he had felt "obliged to accept . . . as half-history" the "half-legend" of Luther's "fit in the choir," of the young monk's having roared out during a reading from the Gospel, like an ox or a bull, his denial of some suspected transgression. Similarly Erikson had conjectured on the scantiest of evidence, or rather as his "clinician's judgment," that "nobody could speak and sing as Luther . . . did if his mother's voice had not sung to him of some heaven." Assertions such as these were bound to raise doubts in the minds of scrupulous historians. The nub, however, of the protracted controversy which Erikson's book aroused lay in its claim to have established a conceptual bridge from the indi-

46. *Young Man Luther: A Study in Psychoanalysis and History* (New York, 1958), pp. 22, 43, 47–48, 83, 109–110, 176.

vidual conscience to that of the masses, to have delineated the process whereby a man "with the sensitivity and the power-drive of a Luther" could "sow ideological seeds into fresh furrows of historical change."[47]

Thus while open-minded historians and historically inclined psychoanalysts derived immense profit from the intellectual vistas that *Young Man Luther* opened up—indeed, it was around this work that the "Erikson cult" first gathered—as the years passed they began to recognize that the presumed bridge from the individual to the mass was not so secure as Erikson's admirers had initially supposed. They remained grateful to him for having dealt with history and social milieu in an incomparably richer and subtler fashion than had been true of a neo-Freudian like Erich Fromm. They were particularly happy that Erikson's stress on the stage of life in which men discovered their ideological allegiances —from the midteens to about the age of thirty—facilitated the researcher's task by shifting the emotional weight from the classic Freudian period of half-forgotten childhood, on which data were usually sparse, to the better-documented years of late adolescence and early maturity.[48] But when those who had been stimulated by Erikson's example tried their hand at what came to be called "psychohistory," they almost invariably produced an individual biography; their efforts to project their interpretations onto a wider group remained tentative and unconvincing. Most of the time, in addressing themselves to mass behavior, they "simply and mistakenly inferred . . . the motivation for this behavior . . . from the motivation of the leader." A methodological "model based on the development of the individual in the family" proved inadequate for explaining the origins of major historical change.[49]

In 1960, after his decade of withdrawal, Erikson returned to a university setting. His appointment at Harvard carried the un-

47. *Ibid.*, pp. 23, 37, 72, 221; Coles, *Erikson*, p. 207.
48. See my *History as Art and as Science* (New York, 1964), p. 59.
49. Fred Weinstein and Gerald M. Platt, *Psychoanalytic Sociology: An Essay on the Interpretation of Historical Data and the Phenomena of Collective Behavior* (Baltimore, 1973), pp. 13, 68. This judicious review of the problem includes (pp. 12–13 n.) a roster of psychoanalytic biographies directly or indirectly inspired by Erikson's example.

precedented title Professor of Human Development, and it was understood from the start that he would not be expected to behave like an ordinary member of the faculty. His teaching load was light: from the time of his arrival to his retirement ten years later, he gave only two regular courses, a lecture course for under-graduates on "The Human Life Cycle" and a seminar for advanced students on the writing of psychoanalytic biography. In Cambridge Erikson quickly became a celebrity: having received all the intellectual recognition a man might desire, he could now afford to point with pride to his total lack of academic credentials.

The Harvard years completed the gradual shift in Erikson's interest from childhood to youth and from occasional moral commentary to explicit ethical assertion. The two miscellaneous volumes he published in this period document his overriding concern with the search for identity by the young; as a consequence and much to Erikson's chagrin, the term "identity crisis" was soon circulating among the undergraduates as a catch-all for emotional distress, however banal its origin. Here he could correctly claim to have been misunderstood. In the matter of ethics, however, there was no room for mistake: Erikson had quite consciously assumed the role of moral preceptor that Hartmann (and Freud before him) had rejected as incompatible with the profession of psychoanalysis. Whereas in *Luther* he had confined himself to characterizing in passing "the mutilation of a child's spirit" as the deadliest "of all possible sins," in the lectures which appeared six years later such ethical statements had advanced to the foreground. Erikson was now ready to employ so familiar and reassuring a word as "fidelity" or even "virtue," while reformulating each to accord with his own category of "ego strength." And "in the light of new insight" he returned to the "Golden Rule" of Christianity. As Erikson understood it, "the Rule would say that it" was "best to do to another what" would "strengthen you even as it" would "strengthen him—that is, what" would "develop his best potentials even as it" developed "your own."[50]

50. *Young Man Luther*, p. 70; *Insight and Responsibility: Lectures on the Ethical Implications of Psychoanalytic Insight* (New York, 1964), pp. 174–175, 233.

The culmination and synthesis of Erikson's new emphases came with the publication of his third major book, *Gandhi's Truth*, in 1969, the year before his retirement from teaching. Another "life history" on the scale of his *Luther*, it marked a striking departure from the model of his earlier work. Most obviously the personal references, which had never been absent in his writings, had vastly proliferated. Erikson's book on Gandhi not only recounted in detail the frustrations and intellectual breakthroughs he had himself experienced on his journeys of orientation to India; it included, halfway along, "a personal word" in which the author wrestled with his own ambivalence toward his protagonist and obliquely took the Mahatma to task for inflicting on others, more particularly on his immediate family, the violence he claimed to have eschewed. Beyond this exercise in self-revelation, Erikson was now prepared to go much further than in *Luther* in attributing to emotional suffering a positive force in the careers of earth-shaking figures:

> This, then, is the difference between a case history and a life-history: patients, great or small, are increasingly debilitated by their inner conflicts, but in historical actuality inner conflict only adds an indispensable momentum to all superhuman effort.[51]

In thus distinguishing between the ordinary victims of emotional misery and the world-historical titans destined for leadership, Erikson seemed to be delimiting, as he had not done before, the sphere of the therapeutic from the sphere of the psychohistorical. But the distinction he drew was coupled with a further change in approach which canceled out whatever clarification might have ensued. In pondering the role of the Mahatma, the author of *Childhood and Society* and of *Young Man Luther* had come to a fresh understanding of his own profession; he had "sensed an affinity between Gandhi's truth and the insights of modern psychology." Subsequently he had hit on a "convergence" between Freud's psychoanalysis and the ideological technique that the Mahatma called Satyagraha or "truth force": "in both encounters

51. *Gandhi's Truth: On the Origins of Militant Nonviolence* (New York, 1969), pp. 252–253, 363.

only the militant probing of a vital issue by a nonviolent confrontation" could "bring to light what insight" was "ready on both sides." Such a convergence, Erikson added, beyond its historical significance, might well have "evolutionary" implications. Based as it was on a "pervasive faith in the brotherhood of man," it pointed "to the next step in man's realization of man as one all-human species, and thus to our only chance to transcend what we are."[52]

Social scientists were quick to spot "in this analogy a rather serious defect." The "enormous force" of "the therapeutic situation" derived from "the stripping away of everything but a common concentration on emotional exploration. . . . With politics it" was "just the reverse: the wider the range of divergent concerns with which it" could "manage to cope the deeper it" cut.[53] Quite apart from their doubts about the notion of congruence between Satyagraha and psychoanalysis, Erikson's more expert readers were taken aback by the transmutation that *Gandhi's Truth* revealed in the author himself. The therapist had become humanity's prophet; diagnosis had yielded to exhortation. In the same period in which Marcuse belatedly won his fame, Erikson too was taken up as an idol by the young. And for reasons that were not totally dissimilar. In contrast to the more fastidious and "private" Adorno and Hartmann, Marcuse and Erikson accepted the perils of the public arena and in so doing risked the vulgarization of their thought and its celebration for propagandist ends.

In the volume of essays and papers he published in 1968, Erikson had defined, but by forecast rather than retrospect, the program he had tried to carry out:

> Psychoanalysis first studied, as if it could be isolated, man's enslavement by the id. . . . Next the focus of study shifted to man's enslavement by seemingly autonomous ego (and superego) strivings—defensive mechanisms which, in order to "contain" an upset libido economy, impoverish the ego's power of experiencing and planning. Perhaps psychoanalysis

52. *Ibid.*, pp. 245, 413, 439–440.
53. Clifford Geertz in *The New York Review of Books*, XIII (Nov. 20, 1969), 4.

will complete its basic studies . . . by investigating more
explicitly man's enslavement by historical conditions which
. . . exploit archaic mechanisms within him, to deny him
physical vitality and ego strength.[54]

The phraseology suggests Erikson's conviction that he was engaged
in "completing" the ego psychology which Hartmann and his own
therapist Anna Freud had launched. Unquestionably he had deepened and enriched the historical component in their common
enterprise. But he had done so with an admixture of extrapolation,
ethical obiter dicta, and conjecture which left reservations in the
minds of all except his most devoted followers. Moreover, his
ventures in the direction of theory, as he himself granted, often
produced clumsy and ambiguous results. This was particularly
apparent in the two new terms or schemata associated with his
name—identity and the life cycle.

Why, Erikson's readers wondered, did he have to specify so
concretely the stages of human existence? Though nearly everyone
agreed that the course of life fell naturally into a perceptible
emotional progression, it was by no means equally clear that each
life divided into the same stages and that these must be eight, no
more, no less. Why did Erikson insist on reiterating a tight
formula so much at variance with his usual discursive method?
Even his close adherents provided no convincing answer. To his
loyal biographer, the Erikson of the eight stages was "a man struggling to make his case," resorting to the expedient of an "epigenetic" chart and persisting in "developing" that chart, in order
to "highlight" views he felt to be peculiarly his own. More
detached critics, who had learned a great deal from Erikson along
the way, found in his schema an element of the culture-bound.
They surmised that a "preindustrial psychoanalyst" might describe
the stages of life less in terms of tasks to be accomplished and that
he might put his stress on puberty rather than on the protracted
adolescence so characteristic of contemporary Western society.[55]

In the matter of identity, Erikson compounded his readers'
difficulties by continually coining new definitions which were not

54. *Identity: Youth and Crisis*, p. 74.
55. Coles, *Erikson*, p. 138; Weinstein and Platt, *Psychoanalytic Sociology*,
p. 58 n.

always compatible with their predecessors. Here his biographer has offered the helpful suggestion that Erikson was not really interested in defining the concept, that he wanted to let it gradually affirm itself "by using it over and over again and working for years to give it a particular kind of meaning." Indeed the simplest formulation he ever produced he borrowed from William James: "*This* is the real me!"[56] The sense of identity—or lack of it—unquestionably ranked among the basic human experiences. But its status in psychoanalytic theory, as in historical or anthropological interpretation, remained obscure. It was a slippery term which glided back and forth somewhere between the classic ego and an individual's social role; it also came close to such a homespun and traditional word as "character." Perhaps its greatest difficulty derived from Erikson's failure to clarify its relationship to the fundamental Freudian category of the unconscious; one might hazard the guess that in his usage a person's identity became securely established when it finally emerged into the full light of consciousness.

These conceptual difficulties were inherent in Erikson's idiosyncratic style. Whereas the writing in *Childhood and Society* had had the plain, direct quality of a man still uncertain of his command of the English language, Erikson's later work bespoke an author confident that he had won his linguistic struggle and even fancying himself a stylist. From *Luther* on, his prose became increasingly elaborate, evasive, and even coy. In its pretentious and self-consciously "literary" phraseology, it was a far cry from the elegant simplicity of Freud.

Toward the memory of Freud himself Erikson invariably maintained an attitude of respect. Although he had known the founder only at a distance and had never actually "addressed him," he recalled with lively sympathy the uncomplaining fashion in which the old man had borne his suffering. For his own part, Erikson took pains to minimize his departures from standard Freudian practice. What seemed important to him was to "advance" his teaching "by small steps without abandoning" the "unique ideological foundations" he had inherited. His "primary interest," he

56. Coles, *Erikson*, pp. 82, 165; Erikson, *Identity: Youth and Crisis*, p. 19.

explained, "in the flux of phenomena precluded any attempt to find safety in orthodoxy or escape in heresy." Rather than challenging the legacy of the master, he preferred to alter the contours of psychoanalysis through hints and insinuations. Thus he afforded "the curious picture of a prominent . . . theorist who" ignored "four-fifths of Freud's metapsychology" and applied the rest in his own highly personal fashion. To a profession not yet released from an outmoded mechanistic vocabulary, he reintroduced still older words which evoked a prescientific intellectual universe; while all the time protesting his lineal fidelity, he accomplished the unparalleled feat of smuggling "the concept of the human spirit through the back door" of psychoanalytic method.[57]

iv. *The Paths Not Taken*

Hartmann and Erikson shared a reluctance to underline their points of divergence from Freud. In both cases affection reinforced the awe the founder's life and work inspired in them. Moreover, from the strictly professional standpoint, one could view certain aspects of their writings as complementary: both assumed in human beings "an inborn coordination to an average expectable environment"; both traced the unfolding of a "social character" which they took to be part of man's genetic endowment. From this standpoint, Erikson could be seen as extending or particularizing what Hartmann had enunciated in general terms. Yet in the way they went about their task of integrating ego and social milieu—as in their relationship to Freud himself—their procedures contrasted as strongly as their life styles. Hartmann tried "to maintain and repair" the founder's metapsychology. Erikson for the most part disregarded it, while holding to the "biological thrust" that was at the root of Freud's thought. While Hartmann treated the primal drives as springboards for his theoretical elaborations, Erikson returned "again and again to early sexual origins as the grounds of human development"—witness his insistence on

57. Erikson, "Autobiographic Notes," pp. 735–736, 751; *Identity: Youth and Crisis*, p. 228; Yankelovich and Barrett, *Ego and Instinct*, pp. 140, 151–153.

the suckling's "basic trust" (or disappointment therein) as the elemental life experience. In this sense their solutions to the metapsychological problem Freud had left them appeared "exactly opposite."[58]

Both, then, contended with the same dilemma of reconciling loyalty to their common master with what they had discovered on their own. Their perplexities might have been fewer—and their reasoning less tortured—if they had pursued paths which lay open to them but on which they refused to venture, paths taken with apparent ease by native-born American or British clinicians who still regarded themselves as within the psychoanalytic mainstream. One can only speculate on why it was possible for men like Abram Kardiner and W. Ronald D. Fairbairn to redefine more radically than Hartmann or Erikson the concepts which inspired the labors of all of them. Perhaps it was that acceptance in the original Viennese circle around Freud forged links of devotion which a half-lifetime's residence across the Atlantic could not shake; perhaps it was that having English rather than German as a native language afforded greater freedom in employing terms which had passed through the loose meshes of the translator's net. Whatever the reason, simultaneously with the work of Hartmann and Erikson, certain of their contemporaries were proving it possible to delete in explicit terms vast segments of the Freudian metapsychology while faithfully adhering to fundamental psychoanalytic convictions about sexuality and the unconscious.

One of the few native-born Americans to have trained directly with Freud, Kardiner has been characterized as the "broadest" and the "deepest" of the "neos."[59] More properly, however, in the emphasis he placed on the earliest discoveries of psychoanalysis and the infrequency of his ethical affirmations, he belonged with the mainstream or "Center." A decade before Hartmann died— and when his theoretical writings were virtually complete— Kardiner undertook to assess the adjustments that Hartmann had

58. David Rapaport, "A Historical Survey of Psychoanalytic Ego Psychology," *Psychological Issues*, I, No. 1 (1959), 14–16; Yankelovich and Barrett, *Ego and Instinct*, pp. 153–154.

59. Birnbach, *Neo-Freudian Social Philosophy*, p. 127. See also Kardiner's "Freud: The Man I Knew, the Scientist, and His Influence," *Freud and the 20th Century*, ed. by Benjamin Nelson (New York, 1957), pp. 46–58.

made in the Freudian corpus. Hartmann's major mistake, Kardiner argued, was to have "attempted a synthesis of the new concept of ego functions with Freud's instinctual and energic hypotheses"; the attempt was bound to fail—the delicate balance between ego autonomy and psychic "motor power" rested on precarious constructs constantly threatened with collapse. Still more, Kardiner questioned whether it was advisable to distinguish ego from superego as sharply as the structural model dictated. Instead, he suggested that psychoanalysis would do better to scrap this model and go back to the Freud of *The Interpretation of Dreams*—the Freud whose original view of the dynamics of unconscious mental operations had "demonstrated its vitality and usefulness over and over again."[60]

Did Kardiner mean to deny the force of the basic drives along with the vocabulary of psychic energy in which Freud had described them? Not necessarily: one might plausibly interpret Kardiner's critique of ego psychology as a venture in conceptual clarification that kept the drives as "givens" but discarded as excess baggage the greater part of the theory which had grown up above and around them. In Freud's mind the task of taming the drives had exceeded the strength of the unaided ego; in order to gain mastery the ego had required as an ally a ruthless tyrant—the superego—which proved just as overbearing as the amorphous and amoral id. If the emphasis was now to be shifted to ego autonomy and ego strength, was it not logical to renounce the attempt to make fine (or mechanistic) discriminations both among the drives associated with the id and between the two presumed agencies at odds with them? To translate Kardiner's terminology into common parlance: the notion of a "superagency" was required to explain neither the animal in man nor what the moralists called the voice of conscience.

It was here that Fairbairn's writings intersected with Kardiner's. A Scot working in almost total isolation from his psychoanalytic peers, Fairbairn drew attention as Kardiner did to the "most re-

60. Kardiner, Karush, Ovesey, "A Methodological Study of Freudian Theory: IV. The Structural Hypothesis, the Problem of Anxiety, and Post-Freudian Ego Psychology," *The Journal of Nervous and Mental Disease,* CXXIX (Oct. 1959), 351–355.

grettable" fact that "a developing psychology of the ego" had come "to be superimposed upon an already established psychology of impulse." (With his characteristic independence, Fairbairn translated Freud's *Trieb* as "impulse"—which in fact served better than either of the two English words ordinarily used, the misleading term "instinct" and the literally accurate but clumsy "drive.") Again like Kardiner, Fairbairn returned to the early Freud, scrutinizing once more the structural triad of the later period. To Fairbairn the id rather than the superego appeared the concept most in need of criticism and correction. If, as he suspected, no "impulses" could "be regarded as existing in the absence of an ego structure," it would "no longer be possible to preserve any psychological distinction between the id and the ego." It would be better to "split . . . ego-structure . . . into three separate egos— . . . a central ego (the 'I'), . . . a libidinal ego, and . . . an aggressive, persecutory ego" designated "the internal saboteur."

Whatever one might think of Fairbairn's new trinity of terms— and he was frank to recognize their "general correspondence" with what Freud had proposed—it had the advantage of suggesting continuity rather than unrelieved antagonism among the three and to be closer than the old triad to the way in which people actually viewed their own inner processes.[61] Moreover, Fairbairn had undergirded his hypothesis with a theory of personality that put the whole matter of drives in a new framework. It was pointless, Fairbairn maintained, to discuss impulse in the abstract: the crucial question was the "object"—that is, the person—toward whom the impulse was originally directed. And with this theory of "object relation," Fairbairn was back in the world of children's earliest emotions—more particularly their feelings toward their mothers—the realm in which Freud had arrived at his first great discoveries and in which his daughter and her pupil Erikson had made their most important theoretical contributions. He was back to the bedrock of psychoanalysis.

Regarded in this fashion, the whole vast, overelaborated corpus of theory took on new and simpler contours. If "impulse" invariably had an object, then it was "to be regarded as inseparably

61. *Psychoanalytic Studies of the Personality* (London, 1952), pp. 59, 88, 101, 106.

associated with an ego structure from the beginning." By the same token, the dynamic and the structural ways of looking at the mind became one. "Both structure divorced from energy and energy divorced from structure" were "meaningless concepts." Fairbairn's "principle of dynamic structure" conceived all emotional change as "inherently directional." It did away with "conceptions of hypothetical 'impulses'" which bombarded "passive structures, much as if an air-raid were in progress." It dealt with "impulse" not as "a kick in the pants administered out of the blue to a surprised, and perhaps somewhat pained, ego," but as "a psychical structure in action—a psychical structure doing something to . . . somebody."[62]

In short, Fairbairn's set of redefinitions abolished the distinctions among the four classic metapsychological modes. Within the old metapsychology, the "topographical" boundary between consciousness and the unconscious alone stood unaltered. Some such recasting was implicit in Erikson's careful avoidance of the issue— but he refrained from saying so. Hartmann never ventured even that far. Fairbairn's blunt, down-to-earth vocabulary accomplished something that eluded both Hartmann's refined precision and Erikson's multifaceted, shifting insights: it translated psychoanalytic theory into a language which investigators in neighboring fields could understand and further recast for their own purposes. While avoiding the methodological crudity of the neo-Freudians, it marked off what was basic and necessary from what had come perilously close to turning into a dignified intellectual game. By the 1970's Fairbairn had found few imitators—Kardiner had picked up rather more—but he had at least shown his professional colleagues, and social scientists at large, that it was possible to spill gallons of theoretical bath water and still keep the baby intact.

When it came to the application of psychoanalytic theory to the social sphere, it was perhaps natural that someone as permissive in the realm of theory as Kardiner should have been particularly successful in working with anthropologists. Like Hartmann and the Erikson of *Childhood and Society*, Kardiner believed that it was with these that collaboration would prove most fruitful. But

62. *Ibid.*, pp. 89, 149–150.

whereas Hartmann had merely outlined what might be done and Erikson had confined himself to trying his hand in his two early studies of American Indians, Kardiner went on to specify the method of such labors in common. In close partnership with a group of well-established anthropologists, he developed the concept of "basic personality" as the focus of research. In every society, past or present, Kardiner and his co-workers surmised, the early conditioning of children produced emotional "constellations" —constellations which tended "to become fixed and integrative," in the sense that "subsequent reactions" were "based upon them and compounded." This conditioning, this molding of the psyche through "practices and customs," could be viewed as operating on two levels, a "primary" level of "childhood disciplines" and a "secondary" one of "religion and folklore." In psychoanalytic vocabulary, Kardiner explained, what was secondary could be described as a "projective system." As such it came close to the meaning Erikson gave to ideology.

Kardiner and his colleagues were quick to add that "basic personality" did not imply that all "reaction types" were "precisely alike"; they were merely "uniform and consistent within a given range."[63] The concept combined concreteness and flexibility in a way which might have been expected to appeal to Kardiner's émigré contemporaries who were trying to integrate psychoanalytic theory with the study of society. But neither Hartmann nor Erikson chose to do much with it. Hartmann limited himself to a passing reference to its possible usefulness "in some respects."[64] Erikson simply disregarded it.

In Erikson's case this neglect of Kardiner's work doubtless derived from the fact that he had settled—as Hartmann never did—on an alternative path to the understanding of social behavior. Erikson's method of extrapolating from the ideological evolution of great men to the mentality of their followers—or even of their era as a whole—debarred him from pursuing a course which

63. Abram Kardiner (with the collaboration of Ralph Linton, Cora Du Bois, and James West), *The Psychological Frontiers of Society* (New York, 1945), pp. 4–5, 21, 23–25.
64. "The Application of Psychoanalytic Concepts to Social Science" (originally published in 1950), *Essays on Ego Psychology*, p. 97.

began with human aggregates rather than a single individual. It also inclined him away from anthropology and toward collaboration with historians. But to maintain sympathetic relations with history and its practitioners did not necessarily entail a concentration on individual biography or on groups of related life histories. In the 1960's historians, like psychoanalysts, were reaching out to anthropology as possibly offering the long-sought bridge from the individual to the mass. More particularly, they were impressed by the cultural anthropologists' stress on the symbols with which a society defined itself, on shared meanings expressed in verbal or institutional form, and on the ways in which human beings internalized what was expected of them—in Kardiner's words, the "secondary" processes of a "projective system."[65] In this respect, Kardiner's pioneering efforts were bringing results even when—as was true most of the time—he himself received little or no credit.

At the same time, the social scientists or historians who worked most comfortably with psychoanalysts were coming to the conclusion that there was no royal road to collaboration between their two spheres. There was little or no possibility of reaching a consensus on the systematic use of psychoanalytic theory in the study of society. It was rather a matter, as Hartmann had once suggested, of a gradual and cumulative "mutual penetration."[66] Understood thus, the *application* of Freudian theory was not the proper expression at all. Hartmann realized this, but, characteristically, he left his injunction to his colleagues on a level of abstraction too rarefied to be of much use to someone investigating a concrete topic. As for Erikson, his tendency to collect disciples produced a bevy of "Eriksonians" more concerned with following where the master had pointed the way than with questioning or refining on his method.

Perhaps this impossibility of establishing any one-to-one relationship between psychoanalytic theory and social research would

65. See my "The Historian and the Social Scientist" (originally published in *The American Historical Review*, LXVI [Oct. 1960]), *Generalizations in Historical Writing*, ed. by Alexander V. Riasanovsky and Barnes Riznik (Philadelphia, 1963), pp. 54–55; Weinstein and Platt, *Psychoanalytic Sociology*, pp. 16, 88–89.

66. "Application of Psychoanalytic Concepts," *Essays on Ego Psychology*, p. 98.

have been more apparent if people had spent less time and emotional effort in trying to trace their own descent from Freud. The spirit of the founder continued to brood over psychoanalysis —and perhaps even more over enthusiasts outside the profession who were pathetically eager to be accepted as equals by those with impeccable credentials. In both cases, the generation-old question of whether the ego psychologists should be reckoned among Freud's subverters or among his heirs continued to burn on with its accustomed intensity. In the light, however, of the broader possibilities that lay open to psychoanalysis as it little by little suffused and "informed" the entire range of social thought, the question ceased to be of particular interest. If it was advisable, even essential, to rephrase much of Freud's vocabulary and to scrap his more dubious concepts—if one further envisaged a series of different vocabularies roughly translatable one into another— then the problem of lineal fidelity lost its urgency.

Yet such a prospect did not constitute a license to pick and choose among psychoanalytic concepts in an arbitrary or grab-bag fashion. Here Hartmann was correct in criticizing the neo-Freudians for so doing and in insisting on theoretical consistency. Had he lived longer and been more polemically inclined, he might have directed a similar critique against Erikson's later writings. For Erikson—whatever his protests to the contrary—had indeed subverted the Freudian legacy: he had used the founder's terminology in so eccentric and elusive a fashion as to rob it of clear or readily communicable meaning.

Hartmann, in contrast, was not mistaken in putting a claim on Freud's inheritance. He was also unduly cautious in specifying where he had diverged from his master's example. Still more, in his filial piety, he refrained from going as far afield as he might have done while remaining loyal to the half-mythical figure whom he honored quite appropriately as the progenitor not only of his own discipline but of twentieth-century thought in its widest sense. The final irony of Hartmann's ego psychology lies in the fact that its defects derived less from an imagined apostasy than from an inability to take full advantage of the intellectual latitude which *The Interpretation of Dreams* had first revealed.

CHAPTER
6

Conclusion: The Sea Change

1. The Emigration and the Cold War

By the early 1950's, with living and working conditions in Europe restored to something approaching their prewar level, the intellectual émigrés faced the question of "going home." But after a decade or more of residence in the United States, it was often far from clear where home was. In certain cases the choice was apparent: for younger people who had found a secure position in American society and whose English-speaking children felt and behaved like Americans, it made sense to stay on; for the more elderly—particularly for writers who had experienced the agony of being cut off from their native language—the emotional pull of the old country might be irresistible. In between came those who hesitated, who made frequent trips back and forth across the Atlantic before reaching a final decision; and among these were some of the most eminent. Each case was distinct; each individual tried to sort out a different mix of considerations, whether sentimental or practical. In the end, Salvemini and Borgese, Horkheimer and Adorno, returned to Europe; Neumann and Marcuse, Hartmann and Erikson, remained in the United States.

Besides the usual and predictable arguments of cultural loyalty or economic well-being, there was a further and more special situation which impinged on the émigrés at the midcentury—the cold war and the accompanying wave of "McCarthyism." Those who have written on the emigration have had little to say about this concatenation of events: perhaps the subject has proved too delicate and embarrassing for full exploration.[1] Moreover there is no statistical method of determining how heavily ideological considerations weighed in tipping personal decisions in one or the other direction. Yet it is unquestionable that fear of an American brand of fascism gave the final push to a number who had hesitated to go back and that at a time when most native-born intellectuals either supported their government or fell silent, leading figures among the émigrés who stayed on protested vigorously against the course of American policy, both at home and abroad.

After the American declaration of war against Germany and Italy in 1941, the newcomers had shared with their hosts an attitude of solidarity in the antifascist effort; no more than a tiny minority of either group had taken a pacifist stand. In the late 1940's, this alignment began to fall apart: the émigrés were less prepared than the native-born to mobilize their energies once more for an ideological engagement. With a few notable exceptions such as Hannah Arendt, they refused to equate Communism with Nazism as alike "totalitarian" or to view Stalin as Hitler's counterpart. And for this reluctance there were compelling psychological reasons. Fascism, after all, had served as the precipitating force that had dissolved the attitude of ethical relativism or suspended judgment so many of them had entertained in the 1920's; in presenting them with an image of evil, it had led them to acknowledge their own sense of what was good. Thus while they viewed the Nazi record as totally negative, they tended to concede to Communism—even as deformed by Stalin—some glimmer or memory of the Enlightenment in its origins and potentialities for the future.

More broadly, the fifteen years from 1930 to 1945 had given the émigrés a moral base-point. The threefold combat which those years had witnessed—against economic depression, internal tyranny, and "racial" conquest—remained with them for the rest of their lives as their central ideological experience. Hence their

1. See, however, the brief comments by Laura Fermi in *Illustrious Immigrants: The Intellectual Migration from Europe 1930–41* (Chicago, 1968), p. 388.

inability to react as sharply to the new threat from the East—frequently accompanied by the conviction that the Western remobilization, this time against Stalinism, lacked the admirable qualities of its predecessor. "Hitler," Thomas Mann wrote, "had the great merit of producing a simplification of the emotions, of calling forth a wholly unequivocal No, a clear and deadly hatred. The years of struggle against him had been morally a good era"—an era followed by a fall in ethical level.[2] By 1947 or 1948 an émigré, whatever his sufferings had been, might recall his immediate past with a peculiar kind of nostalgia. How different the verdict of a native-born critic who could speak of the 1930's as a "low dishonest" time and dismiss such nostalgia as "a sentiment possible only to the very young or the very old!"[3]

Two examples out of many, one of a man who stayed in America, the other of the most famous of those who returned, may suggest the anxieties of the émigrés during the McCarthy years. In 1950, Erik H. Erikson, in throwing his support to colleagues at the University of California unwilling to take the anti-Communist oath—whose roster, incidentally, included a high proportion of Central Europeans—gave moral rather than strictly ideological reasons for his act. While alert like others of German birth to the menacing parallel with familiar events in his original home, he chose to stress the repercussions of compliance on the professors' own students. To "acquiesce in an empty gesture," he conceded, might save "the faces of very important personages." But it would "hurt people"—the students—who were "much more important." "Young people," he added, were "rightfully suspicious and embarrassingly discerning." What older people could "laugh . . . off," he noted, in a striking prediction of the temper of the 1960's, could bring about "a dangerous rift" between the generations—a rift "between the 'official truth' and

2. *Die Entstehung des Doktor Faustus* (Amsterdam, 1949), trans. by Richard and Clara Winston as *The Story of a Novel* (New York, 1961), p. 163.
3. Irving Howe, "The New York Intellectuals" (originally published in *Commentary*, XLVI [Oct. 1968]), *Decline of the New* (New York, 1970), p. 221.

those deep and often radical doubts" which were "the necessary condition for the development of thought."[4]

Thomas Mann's struggles of conscience were better-known and more prolonged. Secure like Erikson in a California where he enjoyed acceptance and respect, Mann reluctantly decided to return to Europe two years after the Berkeley oath controversy. The beginnings of his doubts about the United States dated from President Roosevelt's death. He had been happy, he recalled, to have become an American citizen—with Max Horkheimer serving as one of his witnesses—while the leader he revered was still in command. In this period, the unfavorable remarks he directed at his hosts had been limited to the ironic, veiled references in *Joseph the Provider* and to an occasional witticism about "good-natured barbarians." But by 1946 his mood had grown more somber. He felt it his "task" to oppose the coming of a third world war; and in so doing he lent his name to a number of "front organizations," a stand which in the inflamed atmosphere of the times led to the suspicion that he was pro-Communist. He received abusive mail and phone calls; he feared that his passport would be withdrawn or that he might be summoned before a congressional investigating committee. "Why can't they let me sit in peace in my garden," he lamented, "doing the work for which I am equipped, instead of throwing stones at me and . . . forcing me to interrupt my work and defend myself?" At the midcentury he was close to despair. The cold war, he wrote, was "destroying democracy and leading to general madness." And his "depression" had been "intensified by all the final partings in a single year"—by the suicide of his son Klaus and by the deaths both of his older brother Heinrich and of his youngest brother who had remained in Germany.[5] The variegated circle of talented countrymen in southern California that had earlier sustained his spirits was shrinking: some had died; others had gone home.

4. Statement of June 1, 1950, quoted in Robert Coles, *Erik H. Erikson: The Growth of His Work* (Boston, 1970) p. 157.
5. *Story of a Novel*, p. 82; to Klaus Mann, March 9, 1943, to Agnes E. Meyer, January 7, 1944, March 27, 1950, *Letters of Thomas Mann 1889–1955*, selected and trans. by Richard and Clara Winston (New York, 1971), pp. 416, 433, 597; Klaus H. Pringsheim, "Thomas Mann in Amerika," *Neue deutsche Hefte*, XIII (1966), 28, 32, 36–39.

Among the latter, of course, was Adorno. Mann found it "significant" that the philosopher turned sociologist was "feeling so energetic back . . . in our alien homeland." For precisely here was the rub; Mann was convinced that the Germans had become estranged from him. "An abysmal gulf," he wrote, lay between his "experience and that of the people who remained behind in Germany." His wartime "political" writings he recognized—with a touch of exaggeration—had been "felt as comforting and strengthening only outside" the Reich. How then, he asked, could he "make much of a contribution toward raising up out of their deep abasement" those who had reviled him? By 1947 he was ready to visit Europe: he spent the late spring and summer in Britain and Switzerland and the Netherlands without ever entering his native country. Not until two years later did he venture inside Germany; and by this time the hostile demonstrations he had dreaded were totally absent. The chief criticism he incurred was for having crossed the demarcation line to the Eastern Zone and participated in a Goethe bicentennial celebration at Weimar.[6]

But to return to Germany as a traveler was quite another matter from moving there permanently. This was a prospect which Mann still could not entertain. At the same time, with each successive postwar journey to the Old World—he went back again for long stays in both 1950 and 1951—he felt his early ties to Europe gripping him ever more firmly. In 1952 he took the plunge: the prospect of Eisenhower's election as president, incongruously enough, seems to have tipped the balance.[7] Characteristically Mann left the United States with only his light baggage and with most of his acquaintance unaware that it was a final goodbye.

In Europe the resolution of his dilemma came to him at last. He found a way of living outside Germany in a place where his own language was spoken and whose citizens combined cosmopolitanism with respect for German civilization. For the last three years of his life he made his home near Zürich—the city he loved the best and of which he had written with a sympathy that was

6. To Walter von Molo, September 7, 1945, to Manfred George, March 11, 1947, to Paul Olberg, August 27, 1949, to Theodor W. Adorno, January 9, 1950, *Letters of Thomas Mann*, pp. 479, 522, 582–583, 590.
    7. Pringsheim, "Mann in Amerika," pp. 42–43.

amply returned. A year before his death he enjoyed a final reunion with Hermann Hesse in Nietzsche's celebrated retreat of Sils Maria in the Engadine. Despite Mann's disillusionment after 1945, he had learned in Roosevelt's America, in common with Adorno and Neumann and so many others, to experience democracy as an everyday reality, and in the end, by settling in Switzerland, he discovered how he could combine his democratic loyalty with his abiding attachment to the cultural tradition of the Europe in which he had grown to manhood.[8]

ii. *From the Demonic to the Banal: Faustus and Eichmann*

Three months before embarking on his first postwar trip to Europe, Mann had completed the novel that was to embody his final retrospective judgment on his own country. Sixteen years later another émigré, a full generation younger than he, was to offer an equally stark indictment of the nation which had driven them both into exile. In style and content Mann's *Doctor Faustus* and Hannah Arendt's *Eichmann in Jerusalem* may appear totally unrelated. Yet to juxtapose them is to suggest the urgency of coming to terms with their native land that so many of the émigrés felt without quite knowing how to formulate it and the startling difference that a decade and a half made in the way such an assessment might be drawn up.

The fourth and last of Mann's major novels, *Doctor Faustus* marked the closest he ever came to a literary and intellectual summa. He aimed to compose "nothing less than the novel of" his "era, disguised as the story of an artist's life, a terribly imperiled and sinful artist." This "kind of ideal figure" would emerge as "a 'hero of our time,' a person who bore the suffering of the epoch." The novel's "central idea" combined in a single tormented existence "the flight from the difficulties of the cultural crisis into the pact with the devil, the craving of a proud mind, threatened by

8. Henry Hatfield, "Thomas Mann and America," *The Legacy of the German Refugee Intellectuals* (special no. of the review *Salmagundi*) (Fall 1969–Winter 1970), pp. 184–185.

sterility, for an unblocking of inhibitions at any cost, and the parallel between pernicious euphoria ending in collapse with the nationalistic frenzy of Fascism."[9] The vehicle Mann chose for conveying this overwhelming message was a contemporary reworking of the Faustian legend which Oswald Spengler had not been alone in setting up as the archetype of the insatiable striving in the Western soul.

Begun in May 1943 and completed just short of four years later, *Doctor Faustus* consumed its author's creative powers during a period of thunderous world events—the antifascist victory and Germany's fall, the opening of the cold war and the political reaction in America—and, as he said of his imaginary narrator, his pen must often have trembled at the task. For from the leisurely, far-off, sunlit serenity of *Joseph the Provider*, Mann had returned to the darkness and cold of his native land. "The only major work that he wrote entirely outside . . . Germany proved to be the most German of all." Time and again, to convey the "demonic" in his theme, Mann resorted to the archaic language of Luther; demonology seeped through the crevices of his account, in his struggle to fathom the centuries-old evil in his own people. Two-thirds through his writing, Mann himself fell dangerously ill and was obliged to undergo major surgery. His "wildest" book, he noted, was taking shape as he was turning seventy; "never before" had "any work so agitated and moved" him. No longer—or only at rare intervals—could he find his accustomed refuge in the emotional distance of irony: he was now at grips with material that plumbed the depths of what he had himself experienced, "a reality that threatened to overwhelm him."[10]

In contriving his protagonist, Mann drew most obviously on the biography of Nietzsche. His Adrian Leverkühn went through Nietzsche's life span—transposed to forty years later—as he re-enacted key episodes or aspects of the philosopher's story: the half-intentional contraction of syphilis in a reckless attempt to extend

9. *Story of a Novel*, pp. 30, 38, 88.
10. Gunilla Bergsten, *Thomas Manns Doktor Faustus* (Stockholm, 1963), trans. by Krishna Winston under the same title (Chicago, 1969), pp. 9, 133–134; *Story of a Novel*, p. 221.

his artistic reach, the inability to love another human being, the end in a decade of gentle, uncomprehending madness under his mother's care. Nietzsche had of course been a musician among philosophers, and behind him in Mann's account there also lurked the memory of another heaven-defying figure who had teetered on the edge of insanity, Ludwig van Beethoven. Mann's "hero of his time" almost of necessity had to be a composer. For in the novelist's mind music had invariably ranked as both the highest and the most dangerous of the arts—the one most characteristic of his fellow Germans and in which their acknowledged superiority over other nations carried the most disturbing implications. All his life Mann had alternately combated and succumbed to his infatuation with Wagner, whose *Ring* remained "at bottom" his musical "homeland."[11] A composer it must be, then, and a *German* composer, as the novel's subtitle insisted, who bore upon his shoulders the heavy ambiguity of his country's cultural tradition.

Yet to cast in the form of a novel the life of a creator of music meant to make that music real—possibly even audible—to the expert reader. This tour de force Mann carried off with his customary blend of meticulousness and literary piracy—borrowing without giving credit, picking other people's brains, exploiting scraps of information from whatever source came his way. On Adorno, a recent acquaintance, he relied for technical competence in close musical analysis; indeed, without Adorno's help Mann could scarcely have written the elaborate descriptions of imaginary cantatas that marked an innovation in the craft of fiction.[12] From Arnold Schönberg he pilfered the invention of the twelve-tone scale—much to the former's annoyance, which Mann answered with "astonished and grieved" respect.[13] Whatever complaints the composer himself might lodge, it was quite apparent that the Faustian Leverkühn was not Schönberg: he was rather a cold, remote, indefinable figure whose works were molded in a style of deceptive simplicity, of "dynamic archaism," incurring at one and

11. *Ibid.*, p. 95.
12. See the repeated grateful references in *ibid.*, pp. 42–48, 72, 103, 117, 150–156.
13. To *The Saturday Review of Literature*, December 10, 1948, *Letters of Thomas Mann*, pp. 567–569.

the same time "the reproach both of bloody barbarism and of
bloodless intellectuality."[14]

To catch so elusive a protagonist, Mann called upon a narrator—a friend of the composer from childhood, transparently his
inferior, whom Leverkühn treated most of the time with impatience or condescension. Yet to put down the good Serenus
Zeitblom as nothing more than a mildly foolish "humanist of the
old school," moved by his friend's music to "a mixture of excite-
ment, enthusiasm, admiration and deepest distrust," would be to
mistake the subtlety of the novelist's intent. By confiding the
recital to "a harmless and simple soul, well meaning and timid,
. . . who could only wring his hands and shake his head," Mann
escaped "the turbulence of everything direct . . . and confes-
sional." And in the process he managed to express his own inner
division: by splitting himself into two related but contrasting
characters, he found a dialectical means of conveying his deep
ambivalence about his country's culture and its national fate. If
Leverkühn spoke for Mann the artist, Zeitblom voiced the author's sentiments as a responsible citizen of Germany and the
world. It was to the latter that Mann assigned the task of tracing
the dismal course by which the national qualities that had once
aroused the admiration of mankind had succumbed to exaggeration and the demonic. Zeitblom's utterances were in the style of
Mann the publicist or propagandist, doing his wartime duty in a
more optimistic tone and at a lower intellectual level than when
he marshaled his full creative power. In the narrator of *Faustus*—
where parody figured prominently as an artistic device—the novelist performed the virtuoso feat of mimicking the aspect of his own
personality best known to his American acquaintance.[15]

14. *Doktor Faustus: Das Leben des deutschen Tonsetzers Adrian Leverkühn, erzählt von einem Freunde* (Stockholm, 1947), trans. by H. T. Lowe-
Porter as *Doctor Faustus: The Life of the German Composer Adrian Leverkühn as Told by a Friend* (New York, 1948), pp. 374, 377. I have altered
the translation slightly.
15. Georg Lukács, *Thomas Mann*, 5th ed. (Berlin, 1957), trans. and abr.
by Stanley Mitchell as *Essays on Thomas Mann* (New York, 1965), p. 85;
Story of a Novel, p. 31; Bergsten, *Mann's Faustus*, p. 163; Hatfield, "Mann
and America," p. 182. For examples of this self-mimicry, see *Doctor Faustus*
(Eng. trans.), pp. 175, 505.

Beyond what it might do for Mann himself, his narrative technique enabled him to write as he intended a book that "itself would . . . become the thing it dealt with: . . . a musical composition." Just as superimposing Zeitblom's account upon the life of Leverkühn made it possible for the author to introduce his own reflections on contemporary events, so this method of storytelling gave *Faustus* a musical quality in its structure and its organization of themes. Like a complex series of chords, it resounded simultaneously on all the levels of its conception.[16] In temporal terms, the novel recalled or portrayed at least three different epochs. Remotely and through linguistic or atmospheric evocation, the era of the Reformation loomed in the background: in common with Erich Fromm, Mann had discovered in Luther's time the spawning ground of his country's subsequent arrogance and misery. On its second and more ostensible level, *Faustus* recounted the life of Leverkühn himself—born in the mid-1880's, initiating his pact with the devil twenty years later and sealing it shortly before the outbreak of war, producing his finest work in the late 1920's, gone insane in 1930, dead a decade later. Finally, in the narrator's constant asides to his readers, the novel reflected the tragedy of Germany in Hitler's grasp: beginning to write, as Mann himself did, when the bombardment of the Reich was mounting and eventual defeat was becoming a near-certainty, the imaginary Zeitblom finished his account nearly two years earlier than the actual author—at the supreme moment in the spring of 1945 when Allied tanks were rumbling unopposed through the countryside and the Second World War was crashing to its close.

Within these three time dimensions, the alert reader could discern how the sequences of Leverkühn's life corresponded precisely with the vicissitudes of his nation's twentieth-century history. His pact with the devil coincided with the point at which Germany's leaders succumbed to the self-assertion that was to lead to the desperate gamble of the First World War. His years of

16. *Story of a Novel*, p. 64. On this simultaneity, see Bergsten, *Mann's Faustus*, pp. 44, 135–136, and Erich Kahler, "The Devil Secularized: Thomas Mann's Faust" (originally published in *Commentary*, VII [April 1949]), *Thomas Mann: A Collection of Critical Essays*, ed. by Henry Hatfield (Englewood Cliffs, N.J., 1964), p. 116.

most intense creativity were those of the zenith of Weimar culture just prior to its extinction. "How strangely the times," Zeitblom commented, "these very times in which I write, are linked with the period that forms the frame of this biography! For the last years of my hero's rational existence . . . were part and parcel of the mounting and spreading harms which then overwhelmed the country and now are being blotted out in blood and flames."[17]

The interweaving of the composer Leverkühn's fate with that of his people could scarcely have been expressed in more explicit terms. In the course of the narrative this theme appeared as early as 1914, when the word "breakthrough" figured in the double sense of military aggression and the perilous quest of the artist facing late in time—as the Germans had come belatedly to world power—the problem of bursting the bonds of mere imitation. ("You will break through time itself . . .," the devil had promised Leverkühn, "and dare to be barbaric, twice barbaric indeed, because of coming after the humane, after . . . bourgeois raffinement.")[18] As the story unfolded, its dual themes gradually merged into one: Leverkühn's collapse anticipated the total defeat of his nation; the "sinful" pride of the artist was mirrored in the behavior of the Nazi chieftains. In the end, German culture itself was called into question by the very novelist who had so often spoken in its behalf. "The nation whose power of abstraction" was "the highest, whose spirituality" was "the most perfectly and perilously detached, the nation of Kant . . .," plunged "ahead of the rest into a subanimal condition."[19] The "good" and the "bad" German proved inseparable.

The final device to which Mann resorted in bringing together all the elements mingled in his account—the "chorus of voices from German intellectual history" that had thundered through it—was to "take back" Beethoven's Ninth Symphony and more particularly the "Ode to Joy" of Schiller which constituted its last movement. It was with these words that Leverkühn cried out his woe at learning of the death of a little nephew—the "marvelous child" who at the very end had lifted the curse of lovelessness which

17. *Doctor Faustus* (Eng. trans.), p. 482.
18. *Ibid.*, pp. 243, 307–308.
19. Kahler, "The Devil Secularized," p. 121.

weighed upon the composer. And it was the same words that
Mann made his own in voicing his agonized doubts about the
literary and philosophical tradition which had nourished him.
What he and his imaginary composer together "took back" was
not merely the lofty strains of Beethoven and Schiller; the example
of Goethe too became dubious—the Goethe whose succession
Mann was proud to claim and with whom he had identified more
than once in his own creative endeavors. The last of the sym-
phonic cantatas Mann ascribed to his Leverkühn—"The Lamentation of Dr. Faustus"—like the title of the novel itself, transparently recalled Goethe's masterpiece. Just as its wild grief
mocked Schiller's joy and love for mankind, so its "deep diabolic
jest" canceled out the salvation which the Faust of German classic
literature had at length attained.[20] In recapturing an earlier, more
authentic Faustus than that of Goethe, Mann undercut the entire
humanist current in his nation's thought over the past century and
a half. The demonic had triumphed: the disembodied dreams, the
elaborately cultivated *Geist* of the "good" Germans in the end
stood revealed as a dangerous illusion.

But not quite. Mann recoiled from the notion of leaving his
protagonist and his people in total abandonment. Although
Adorno had insisted that he harden his account of the "Lamentation"—that he had been "too kindly, . . . too lavish" in consoling his readers—Mann succeeded in rewriting his conclusion in a
tone which still admitted a glimmer of light: a "hope beyond
hopelessness," a "transcendence of despair." "God be merciful to
thy poor soul," were the narrator's and the novelist's last words,
"my friend, my Fatherland!"[21]

The Germans and the Jews, one of Mann's minor characters
had observed, could not "help perceiving . . . a striking analogy"
between them. "In just the same way" they were "both hated,
despised, feared, envied; in the same measure" they alienated

20. *Doctor Faustus* (Eng. trans.), pp. 478, 487–490; Bergsten, *Mann's
Faustus*, pp. 91, 186, 191.
21. *Story of a Novel*, pp. 222–223; *Doctor Faustus* (Eng. trans.), pp.
491, 510.

others and felt alienated themselves.[22] The novelist was fully aware of the outrageousness of his comparison. Yet as a cosmopolitan and someone whose German-speaking acquaintance in California was preponderantly of Jewish origin, Mann was in a position to understand, as his countrymen who had remained at home failed to appreciate, that his own nation's tragedy and the tragedy of the Jews were two faces of the same reality. The destruction of European Jewry ranked as the most monstrous of Germany's crimes—the macabre chain of events in which whatever had once figured as life-giving in the demonic aspect of the national tradition had been exposed as irredeemably fraudulent. If the Allied military who devastated the Reich from end to end often did not know or care why they were inflicting such punishment, the literary elite in exile never doubted where the supreme sinfulness of their country lay.

But to reenact on the postwar German stage the evil of the immediate past—to demonstrate to the Germans themselves the full inhumanity of their conduct—seemed beyond the capacity of both victors and vanquished. While the Bonn government made financial restitution to the Jews, the trials of the major criminals did not succeed in teaching a lesson. Within Germany, this was perhaps only to be expected: indifference and moral numbness were the predictable reactions to a horror too vast for the ordinary mind to admit. What was more surprising was that even in the new state of Israel—which owed its existence to Hitler's legacy—it proved impossible to recall demonic history in a fashion that would carry conviction to an observer predisposed to believe the worst.

In 1960, a decade and a half after the war's end, Israeli agents abducted from his refuge in Argentina Adolf Eichmann, who was reputed to have been the architect of the Nazi extermination policy. Flown secretly across the Atlantic, Eichmann was duly tried in Jerusalem the following year and executed in 1962. Among those in the courtroom sat Hannah Arendt—the now celebrated author of *The Origins of Totalitarianism*—whose report of the trial stirred up even more of a furor than had greeted her first

22. *Ibid.*, pp. 407–408. I have altered the translation slightly.

book. For with a new directness of style, she bluntly argued that the key to the evil of the Nazi period was to be found not in the cosmic barbarism which Mann had lamented but in the "banality" of procedures to which apparently normal human beings had given their assent.

In Hannah Arendt's view Eichmann presented his accusers and his judges the insuperable problem of dealing—whether on a legal, a moral, or an intellectual plane—with a man unable to understand his own past deeds. If he could have been depicted as a "monster," his trial would have been immensely simplified. But this he transparently was not. What was one to do with a person to whom thought was alien and who "had at his disposal a different . . . cliché"—every one of which, however it might contradict another, gave him a sense of "elation"—"for each period of his life and each of his activities?"[23]

Beyond that, the nature and extent of Eichmann's guilt—for guilty he certainly was—emerged as less clear-cut than had been anticipated. For one thing, "his role in the Final Solution, it now turned out, had been wildly exaggerated—partly because of his own boasting, partly because the defendants at Nuremberg and in other postwar trials had tried to exculpate themselves at his expense, and chiefly because he . . . was the one German official who was an 'expert in Jewish affairs' and in nothing else." Yet even in this capacity Eichmann's guilt proved to be enmeshed with that of others. And among the latter could be counted not merely the top Nazis but "gentlemen" and ostensibly "unpolitical" figures below Hitler or Himmler but above Eichmann in the chain of command: "the elite of the good old Civil Service" had been "vying and fighting with each other for the honor of taking the lead" in these dreadful doings. When Eichmann had discovered the bureaucratic lay of the land, he had "sensed a kind of Pontius Pilate feeling"; he had "felt free of all guilt." Who was he "to have [his] own thoughts in this matter"?[24]

Together Eichmann and his colleagues had resorted to a bizarre reversal of moral scruple. They had succeeded in overcoming their

23. *Eichmann in Jerusalem: A Report on the Banality of Evil*, rev. and enl. ed. (New York, 1965), pp. 49, 53–54.
24. *Ibid.*, pp. 114, 210.

"animal pity . . . in the presence of physical suffering" by "turning these instincts around. . . . Instead of saying: What horrible
things I did to people!" they were "able to say: What horrible
things I had to watch in the pursuance of my duties, how heavily
the task weighed upon my shoulders!" On the rare occasions on
which he had witnessed atrocities, Eichmann had in fact been
affected by what he saw. But in place of the "normal" reaction of
pity for the victims, he—in common with hundreds of others—
had managed to convince himself that it was rather those in *his*
position who deserved commiseration for the dreadful responsibility they had been obliged to bear.[25]

Whatever their stupefaction at this line of reasoning, Eichmann's judges had to decide to whom such crimes should ultimately be ascribed. And theirs was no simple task. As Arendt
explained in elaborate detail, within the tangled, overlapping
structure of the agencies which had handled the Final Solution, it
was often impossible to determine with precision the source of
orders phrased in euphemisms decipherable by the initiated alone.
Moreover, in the death camps themselves "it was usually the
inmates and the victims" who had actually manipulated the
instruments of extermination. Thus, in Eichmann's case, the
Israeli court found itself trying "a mass murderer who had never
killed (and who in this particular instance probably did not even
have the guts to kill)." To its credit the court met the difficulty
head-on: in its final judgment it laid down the principle that
within the unprecedented series of events it had passed in review,
"the degree of responsibility" increased as one drew "further away
from the man who" had used "the fatal instrument with his own
hands." Those who maintained—quite correctly—that they had
never committed murder were infinitely more guilty than the
wrecks of humanity who had performed the role of killers.[26]

If all this was true—and the major controversy Arendt aroused
raged not over the Final Solution as such but over how the Jews
themselves had faced their own destruction—where did it leave
the question of the evil in Germany's immediate past? If the

25. *Ibid.*, p. 106.
26. *Ibid.*, pp. 215, 246–247.

crimes of the Nazis could be characterized as a vast "banality" in which millions had shared and very few had understood exactly what they had done, did that make the German people more or less guilty than had earlier been supposed? Within the emigration opinions varied almost as widely as within the American intellectual community at large. But as the postwar years had passed, one change of sentiment at least paradoxically bore out a part of Arendt's contention. Back in Germany the banal had come fully into its own. When *Doctor Faustus* was published, an émigré could still feel frightened by Germany and the Germans—this was a further reason for hesitating to return. Fifteen years later the same individual was far less likely to be afraid: anti-Semitism, as Horkheimer and Adorno had predicted, had perceptibly waned; right-wing nationalist movements had again and again failed to win a substantial following. Bonn, a bevy of commentators insisted, was not the same as Weimar. If the new Federal Republic provided a less exciting cultural atmosphere than its predecessor in German democracy, by the same token it was less troubled and precarious. If the men of Bonn seemed almost to give preference to the banal, was this necessarily a cause for regret?

In the decade and a half which had elapsed between the appearance of *Faustus* and that of *Eichmann*, the new Germany of Adenauer and his heirs had taken shape—down-to-earth, complacent, and unpolitical—a Germany in which the middle-class philistine set the tone. The Bonn regime might appear stuffier than that of Weimar, but it was nowhere near so disquieting. It lacked the intellectual and ideological militancy which had pulsated through the years from 1918 to 1933, but it provided a more solid assurance that the worst would not occur. Somewhere along the way the demonic had been exorcised from German culture. Had it expired in the apocalypse of 1945 or from the sheer boredom that had followed?

III. *Centennial Celebrations*

The émigrés who chose to go back to their native lands, whatever their fears that their countrymen might no longer understand them, could at least be confident that they would not be ignored. Germany and Austria and Italy needed all available talent: educational levels had fallen everywhere, and with the majority of intellectuals in their middle years heavily compromised by association with fascism, the young people had no recourse but to turn for guidance to the elders who had preserved a moral equilibrium through the era of tyranny. This special—and temporary—prestige of the prefascist generation was understandably greater in the German-speaking world than in Italy; the latter offered no parallel to Horkheimer and Adorno's triumphant return to Frankfurt.

Intellectually as well as physically, Italy was far less devastated than what had only yesterday been called the Greater German Reich. If both peoples undertook a work of restoration, it was more the Germans who thought of themselves as building upon the rubble of their cultural life; the Italians were inclined rather to speak of a return to normal after the "parenthesis" of Mussolini's rule. The fact that most Italian intellectuals had adopted an attitude of prudent indifference toward Fascism persuaded them that there was little to be changed after its fall. Croce and the Croceans had traversed the authoritarian decades unscathed. What needed to be done, then, beyond giving public endorsement to those who already wielded an unofficial sway over the social thought of the peninsula?

This euphoria of picking up where Italy had dropped its cultural baggage twenty years earlier could not last long. Too much had happened in the meantime beneath the surface of Fascist orthodoxy and Crocean complacency. Since the early 1930's, younger intellectuals throughout the country had quietly but persistently been seeking new models and new styles of thought. In literature the search led them to the stripped prose of the American novel. In social thought it led to Marxism—the subtle, quasi-idealist Marxism of Antonio Gramsci. The publication of Gramsci's prison writings in 1947 ranked as the decisive intellectual event of the immediate postwar era; it inspired a school of historians and social investigators who for the better part of a decade preempted the field.[27] Thus Gramsci after his death accomplished from within

27. See my *Consciousness and Society* (New York, 1958), pp. 102–104, and *The United States and Italy*, rev. ed. (Cambridge, Mass., 1965), pp. 237–

the country what the émigré critics of Fascism such as Salvemini and Borgese had been unable to effect—a thoroughgoing reevaluation of Italian culture. In this sense the "inner emigration" of Gramsci and his heirs—something more desperate and perilous than what the Germans meant by the term—can be reckoned as the functional equivalent of the work of an Adorno outside his native land.

If neo-Marxism reached Italy with the rush and the enthusiasm of a late arrival, the same was true to a lesser extent of psychoanalysis. Here the vacuum after 1938 left virtually nothing with which to make a new start. In 1945 the whole country counted only seven analysts. Two decades later the number had increased nearly tenfold. Once again aided by an American example, the Italians had done in twenty years what elsewhere had taken two or three generations. But in terms of the educated population at large, psychoanalysis had still not penetrated Italian styles of thought. Its influence remained restricted to a sophisticated urban minority. And its diffusion had come less through writings by members of the profession than through works of fiction—the novels of Alberto Moravia and Elsa Morante, and above all the enormously popular *The Leopard* (1958), the posthumous masterpiece of the Sicilian Prince Giuseppe Tomasi di Lampedusa, whose wife was one of Italy's senior practicing analysts. In novels such as these, the psychoanalytic element was usually veiled and allusive: while sexuality was ever present, the vocabulary retained a classic simplicity uncontaminated by technical terms and neologisms.[28]

Italian postwar writers of fiction took pride in the fact that the origins of the antirhetorical honesty with which they depicted the social universe went back deep into the Fascist years—Moravia's youthful success, *The Time of Indifference*, had appeared as early as 1929—and they correctly saw themselves as constituting for the first time in their country's history a self-confident galaxy of

<hr>

240, 243; also Mario Sansone, "La cultura," *Dieci anni dopo 1945–1955: Saggi sulla vita democratica italiana* (Bari, 1955), pp. 519–522, 533–536, 541–544, 566–573.

28. Michel David, *La psicoanalisi nella cultura italiana* (Turin, 1966), pp. 224, 241, 482–510, 528–529, 539–544.

The Sea Change

novelists. In the German-speaking lands the situation was the reverse. Here the twentieth century's major generation was passing from the scene: those who had finally devised a type of novel appropriate to the recalcitrant German language—Mann and Hesse among the Germans, Musil and Broch among the Austrians —were in exile or dead. Moreover, the ultrarefined, ultrapsychological example they offered appeared remote from the demands of a literature that was struggling to rise from the ruins of defeat. The young Germans who first gathered in 1947 to read and discuss their attempts to put on paper what might be said after the catastrophe could find little in the immediate past to serve as a guide.

Gruppe 47, the loose association of younger writers whose annual or semiannual meetings marked the stages of Germany's post-Nazi literary revival, refused to accept Adorno's dictum that after Auschwitz it was barbaric to write poetry at all. But like the Italians they demanded an honesty—both among themselves and with their public—which could be almost barbaric in its brutality. This was a new kind of literary movement: a group that was not a group, an avant-garde only in the sense of "good will," a "shadow government" of culture which was "more shadow than government" and which issued no programs or manifestoes—a group whose goals were "so simple and self-evident" that it seemed "superfluous . . . to formulate them." Its gatherings featured reading and unsparing criticism of its members' own works. This critical ruthlessness drew a sharp line between the younger generation and the established writers, even those with unimpeachable anti-Nazi credentials. The "angry young men" felt at ease among themselves; their delicate-tempered elders could not have endured what the group jocularly called a grilling on the electric chair. Thus although Mann more than once gave encouragement to Gruppe 47, it would have been hard to imagine him undergoing its ministrations.[29] Those who in the 1950's emerged as the younger novelists with reputations extending beyond Germany's frontiers, Heinrich Böll and Günter Grass, were robust figures

29. Reinhard Lettau, ed., *Die Gruppe 47: Bericht, Kritik, Polemik: Ein Handbuch* (Neuwied and Berlin, 1967), pp. 11, 31–32, 261, 279, 282, 315, 355, 379.

who had found a new idiom, with an irony that cut deeper than Mann's, to express what they had learned as adolescents of the cruelty of their countrymen and their subsequent exasperation at the philistinism they saw around them.

In social thought it likewise took a decade for a new generation of German writers to emerge; here, however, the link with the great figures of the past was closer than in imaginative literature. Sociologists such as Hans Albert and Ralf Dahrendorf revived the liberal or Weberian tradition; in Jürgen Habermas, Horkheimer and Adorno found a successor. The reknitting of the younger Germans' ties with the generation of their intellectual grandfathers became fully visible in the centennial celebrations in which the German-born, among whom former or present émigrés played a leading part, joined with eminent foreigners in honoring the memory of Sigmund Freud and Max Weber.

The centenary of Freud's birth came too early to exert a maximum influence. In 1956 Germany and Austria were still in the initial stages of their intellectual revival. Thus it was logical that Horkheimer and Adorno should have given a didactic and even an elementary cast to the proceedings they organized in Frankfurt. As their own brief remarks suggested, they saw their main task as one of refamiliarizing the German-speaking world with a body of thought that had migrated en masse to Britain and America. The same was true of the introductory lecture which had been assigned to Erikson. Quite simply Erikson strove to tell his new and unfamiliar German audience who Freud was and what he had done—to reacquaint the Germans, in his original language and that of the founder of psychoanalysis, with the achievement and self-doubt of a figure who had remained hidden from their view for nearly a quarter-century. And in so doing Erikson stressed Freud's own comparison of his work with Darwin's—it had "turned out to be . . . a true vision and a blueprint for a science" —while defending him from the charge that he had "detracted from the 'dignity' of sexuality."[30]

30. "Sigmund Freuds psychoanalytische Krise," *Freud in der Gegenwart,* ed. by Theodor W. Adorno and Walter Dirks (Frankfurt, 1957), Eng. ver-

The passage of a further decade and a half might perhaps have been expected to suffice for the German-speaking countries to catch up with their Freudian inheritance. But when the International Psychoanalytic Congress met in Vienna in 1971, the Americans and Americans-by-adoption still dominated the scene. If the Congress had been held in Germany rather than in Austria, the difference in weight between the old and the new homes of psychoanalysis would have been less overwhelming; but in the native city which Freud had alternately loved and hated it was painfully apparent that the birthplace of his movement had become a backwater. The Viennese, however astonished to discover that the founder of psychoanalysis might rank even higher than Mozart among the sons of Austria, did their best to be hospitable. Anna Freud danced a waltz in the late-nineteenth-century splendor of the Rathaus: the childless matriarch of psychoanalysis who had worked with children throughout her life reigned for a few days as an intellectual sovereign in the city from which she and her father had fled thirty-three years earlier.

With Hartmann recently deceased, the founder's daughter ranked without question as the greatest of the handful of returning Viennese. But there was also Erikson, who had trained with her in Vienna and who, at the insistence of the younger analysts he had inspired, had been added to the program as originally announced. Protesting against the heavily theoretical tone of the proceedings, Erikson called for a return to clinical evidence—an emphasis which, ironically enough, had not always been apparent in his own recent writings.[31] Freud's heritage, one might conclude, had returned to the lands of German speech, but it had come back in English translation and indelibly altered by its change of residence.

The Weber centennial of 1964, held at Heidelberg, in which Adorno once again played an organizing role, cast its net more

sion, "The First Psychoanalyst," in Erikson's *Insight and Responsibility: Lectures on the Ethical Implications of Psychoanalytic Insight* (New York, 1964), pp. 21–27, 33, 35.

31. Edith Kurzweil, "The (Freudian) Congress of Vienna," *Commentary*, LII (Nov. 1971), 80–83.

widely than either of the celebrations in honor of Freud. A greater number of fields of study was represented, and the major participants came from a more varied assortment of nations. The host was the German Sociological Association, and the ostensible aim of the gathering, as the title of its proceedings announced, was to assess the contemporary relevance of Weber's example for the discipline of which he ranked as the most influential founding figure and which was currently experiencing a boom in his native land. Eventually, as could have been anticipated, the discussion veered toward politics. In view of Weber's own polemical involvement—despite his struggle to keep this sort of utterance distinct from his "scientific" work—such a turn of events was not entirely inappropriate. Yet it took on added acerbity from the fact that some of the government officials present could not resist the temptation to enroll Weber among the spiritual progenitors of German democracy and from the choice of a militant non-Weberian—Herbert Marcuse—to give the closing address.[32]

With Adorno content to figure in a minor capacity—he had, after all, already said what he needed to say about Weber—the chief responsibility devolved on visitors from abroad. On each of three successive days in late April, a distinguished foreigner or émigré discussed a key aspect of Weberian sociology, followed by an array of commentators, of whom a bare majority were German. On the first day the man who had done the most to introduce Weber's method to the United States, Talcott Parsons, treated the congenial theme of "value-neutrality" and objectivity. The following day it was the turn of Raymond Aron, who had performed a similar function in France, to speak of Weber's relation to power politics. In the climactic final session Marcuse, presumably picked to balance the favorable presentations of the other two, dealt in astringent terms with the association of rationality and capitalism which had been a cardinal principle of Weber's teaching.[33]

Marcuse argued that Weberian sociology was neither so rational

32. Guenther Roth, " 'Value-Neutrality' in Germany and the United States," *Scholarship and Partisanship: Essays on Max Weber* (with Reinhard Bendix) (Berkeley and Los Angeles, 1971), p. 46.
33. These papers and the discussions following them are published in *Max Weber und die Soziologie heute: Verhandlungen des 15. deutschen Soziologentages*, ed. by Otto Stammer (Tübingen, 1965).

nor so value-free as its creator had imagined. The notion of "formal rationality," he maintained, had "changed imperceptibly in the course of . . . Weber's analysis." It had been transformed into "a question of domination, of control"—the control exercised by capitalism through the dynamic of industrialization. This domination Weber had conceived as the "fate" of Western man. But society, Marcuse replied, was not "nature." To the world of economics and human relations, the word "fate," with its connotations of a law "largely independent of individuals," did not apply. Who, he demanded, decreed such a fate? If it was men themselves—and there could be no other answer—then they could abolish the domination they had themselves imposed.

Marcuse aimed his most telling observations at Weber's linkage of bureaucracy with charismatic leadership. If bureaucracy could be reckoned the administrative form of "modern economic rationality," the same could not be said for the character of domination at the very top. If the bureaucracy subjected itself "to an extra- and suprabureaucratic power"—to the power of charisma—then "the Weberian conception of reason" ended in irrationality. Thus "Weber's analysis of bureaucracy" broke "through the ideological camouflage. Far ahead of his time, he showed the illusory character of modern mass democracy." While his analysis of capitalism betrayed the insufficiency of his own value-neutrality—while he had taken into his " 'pure' definitions of formal rationality valuations peculiar" to the phenomenon he was discussing—by the same process he had inadvertently exposed the irrational in modern society. Was there perhaps, Marcuse concluded, "in Max Weber's concept of reason the irony that understands but disavows? Does he by any chance mean to say: And this you call 'reason'?"[34]

Grudgingly, obliquely, Marcuse gave Weber his due. Like Adorno a few years earlier, he recognized in the sociologist's writings ambiguities and nuances which made him something more than the patron saint of value-neutrality. Such a critique, at once hard-hitting and respectful, was what most of the younger

34. "Industrialisierung und Kapitalismus," *ibid.* (pp. 161–180), trans. in revised form by Jeremy J. Shapiro for Marcuse's *Negations: Essays in Critical Theory* (Boston, 1968), pp. 213–217, 219, 223, 226.

6. *Conclusion: The Sea Change* 263

generation wanted to hear. But not all. Wolfgang J. Mommsen, who himself had written unsparingly of Weber's successive political stands, refused to accept Marcuse's interpretation of his own work as implying that Weber had ever envisaged an alliance with the German right.[35] And it was left to a young Italian philosopher steeped in German social thought to attempt a sophisticated restatement of value-neutrality in contemporary terms. Weber's formulation, Pietro Rossi maintained, was no longer "tenable." It would be wrong to restrict the value aspect of sociological method, in classic Weberian fashion, to "the preliminary stages," of an investigation or to "the delimitation of the sphere of research. . . . On the contrary, reference to value assumptions" found a place "in all the succeeding steps of the inquiry," whether as "working hypotheses" or as "explanatory models."

Yet this modification and correction, Rossi insisted, did not entail abandoning Weberian fundamentals. One should hold fast to the conviction that the social sciences had "the task neither . . . of proposing norms of conduct nor of pronouncing the values related to these norms; . . . the social scientist—like every other scientist"—had no right "to offer his personal opinion as his research results." The problem was rather one of establishing "from case to case . . . what valuations" were "legitimate for a particular discipline. . . . The exclusion of value judgments" meant banning "only . . . a specific kind of valuation" that was "scientifically illegitimate"; it constituted "no general prohibition of every sort of value statement." Within this new formulation, Weber's teaching still applied: despite its "insufficiencies," the "relationship between value-neutrality and objectivity" he had enunciated remained "a basic principle of social-science method."[36]

Rossi's brief remarks rescued Weber from both his detractors and his uncritical apologists. And in so doing they reflected the experience of nearly a half-century of post-Weberian research and theory: while it had proved impossible, as Horkheimer and Adorno and Marcuse had repeatedly argued, to protect the "purity" of social thought from value-entanglement, it was a far cry from such a recognition to the sort of categorical moral dicta in

35. Stammer, *Weber und die Soziologie*, pp. 215–216.
36. *Ibid.*, pp. 91–94.

which the neo-Hegelians indulged. Objectivity had proved even more difficult of attainment than Weber, for all his scruple and self-torment, had supposed; but as an intellectual ideal it had not been superseded.

iv. *Paul Tillich as Paradigm: Fusion, Misunderstanding, Transmutation*

When Marcuse and Erikson went back to their native land to speak in honor or in criticism of the masters of twentieth-century social thought, they figured at least as much in their new capacity as Americans as they did in their old guise as Central Europeans. Survivors of a generation that for the most part had either died or returned across the Atlantic, they came to Frankfurt or Heidelberg or Vienna surrounded by the aura of a popularity which had eluded their German-speaking contemporaries. Moreover—and partly in consequence of this public acclaim—they had become enmeshed in the bitterest controversy their new country had traversed since the Second World War.

A few months after the Weber centennial, the endemic conflict in Southeast Asia erupted into full American involvement. These two events of 1964–1965 marked an intellectual and moral watershed. Both Erikson and Marcuse, who shared an ethical goal of "pacification," opposed the Vietnam war—Erikson indirectly through his work on Gandhi's nonviolence, Marcuse in vehement denunciation of "neo-colonial" inhumanity. In both, the war intensified and accelerated a basic change in orientation: after the mid-1960's Marcuse and Erikson alike declared their own values more explicitly and to larger audiences than they had before; they figured less as social theorists and more as polemicists or sages. While this change betokened the extent of their "Americanization"—they no longer hesitated, as an émigré might, to attack the policy of their adopted country—it masked the ways in which their thought and action remained in a German mold. The timeliness of their utterances concealed what was Romantic or nostalgic in the assumptions from which they spoke.

This rootedness in the values of a rural society—this tug back

toward the spiritual universe of early-nineteenth-century Germany
—also characterized a thinker a half-generation older who died in
that same year 1965 when the violence of the Vietnam war began
to dominate the public consciousness. Paul Tillich had been
Marcuse's friend; Erikson delivered a eulogy at the memorial
service for him at Harvard University. Of all the intellectual émigrés to the United States, Tillich was perhaps the one who
embraced America most whole-heartedly and received most affection in return. Yet in his case also an ambiguity lurked in the
background: he too remained more German than his American
admirers suspected. Tillich's experience in the country he came to
love may serve as a final paradigm for what was assimilable in the
emigration and what held stubbornly true to the values of an Old
World childhood.

> My attachment to my native land in terms of landscape,
> language, tradition . . . has always been so instinctive that I
> could never understand why it should have to be made an
> object of special attention. . . .
> I have always felt so thoroughly German by nature that I
> could not dwell on the fact at length. . . .

Thus Tillich wrote of himself in his autobiographical reflections.
"Nearly all the great memories and longings" of his life, he
recalled, were "interwoven with landscapes, soil, weather, the
fields of grain and the smell of the potato plant in autumn, the
shapes of clouds, and with wind, flowers and woods."[37] The
passage served to explain why the quasi-pantheist nature mysticism
of German Romantic religiosity—the example of Schelling and
Schleiermacher—remained the base point from which he never
strayed. An unlikely figure, one might conclude, to take the path
of emigration and to find acceptance in a new home. Yet there
were in Tillich other *Wahlverwandtschaften*—elective affinities he
discovered in the United States and that struck a responsive chord
among listeners who knew nothing of his intellectual origins.
   If the American fancied himself the eternal frontiersman, Tillich regarded his own life as passed forever "on the boundary." For

37. *On the Boundary: An Autobiographical Sketch* (New York, 1966),
pp. 17, 93.

a man so constituted, emigration was only an outward manifestation of what had always been a spiritual tendency to roam.
Profoundly attached to rural life, but irresistibly attracted to the
social and cultural tumult of cities—his thought suspended between philosophy and theology, Marxism and political conformity,
theism and disbelief—Tillich conceived the boundary experience
as his destiny. Born in 1886 the son of a rural Lutheran pastor, he
had managed to combine the teaching of theology with a personal
life untrammeled by convention and in sympathy with an artistic
bohemia. In the early 1930's, as a professor at Frankfurt, he had
maintained congenial relations with left-oriented colleagues of
Jewish origin such as Mannheim and Horkheimer, and it was
along with them that the Nazis deprived him of his university
chair in April 1933. In Frankfurt, he had fitted naturally into the
cosmopolitan *esprit frondeur* of the Weimar avant-garde: "Paulus
among the Jews," his friends quipped, using the Latin form of his
name by which he was invariably called.[38] And it was also natural
that that other eminent "Aryan" who accompanied the Jews into
exile, Thomas Mann, should have turned to Tillich for the information on theological study he needed for his *Doctor Faustus*—a
request with which the latter gladly complied, only to find to his
chagrin that the novelist had transformed into parody the reminiscences he had offered.

In another sense, such a twist was justified. Tillich was never
really comfortable as a professor of theology. Although he taught
for two decades at the Union Theological Seminary in New York,
he preferred the secular atmosphere of Harvard, where he came as
an elderly man in 1954. His basic aim, as he explained it shortly
before his death, was to interpret traditional religious symbols in
such a way that secular men—and he included himself among
them—could understand and be moved. In this respect, he was
the German and Protestant counterpart of Jacques Maritain and
Gabriel Marcel in France, who similarly tried to give Catholicism
a fresh meaning for the irreligious.[39] Far more than the founder

38. For Tillich's Frankfurt years, see the reminiscences of his widow Hannah: *From Time to Time* (New York, 1973), pp. 143–153.
39. See my analysis in *The Obstructed Path* (New York, 1968), Chapter 3.

of Protestant neoorthodoxy, Karl Barth, Tillich reckoned with
what was non-Christian or alien to the Christian style of thought.
Had Barth, with his fundamentalist austerity, left Germany for
the United States rather than Switzerland, he would scarcely have
found across the Atlantic the welcome and understanding that
greeted Tillich almost from the start.

The substance of Tillich's thought falls outside the scope of the
present inquiry.[40] From the theological standpoint, debate over
his novel, permissive formulations raged during his lifetime and
continued after his death. For some it was "impossible to see . . .
the God of revelation" in his redefinition of faith as "ultimate
concern." For others such a transcending of "the theistic idea"
provided exactly the assurance they required to keep them within
the Christian fold. More broadly, it was Tillich's philosophical
stance that gave him a central relevance for the emigration. As the
only existentialist to thrive on American soil, he suggested what
was assimilable in an intellectual current which for the most part
met resistance or misunderstanding in the United States. Tillich
was so robustly and unashamedly himself that he could afford, as
others could not, to disregard the predominant empirical tradition
of his new country and the neopositivism or analytic tendency
which seemed to be sweeping all before it. Instead of combating
the reigning style of thought, he settled for coexistence: "he once
asked a logical positivist to listen to him lecture and hold up a
finger every time he heard something he could not understand; the
logical positivist replied that he would have to hold his finger up
from beginning to end."

The explanation for this extraordinary state of affairs lay on the
"boundary that Tillich bridged most significantly," the one "between the . . . German idealist tradition of the 19th century and
the alienation and anxiety of 20th-century experience. In a peculiarly haunting, improbable fusion, it was Tillich's genius to wed
his beloved Schelling to Kierkegaard."[41] In similar fashion he
succeeded in linking the disquieting and utterly alien Nietzsche to

40. For a sympathetic and comprehensive treatment, see James Luther
Adams, *Paul Tillich's Philosophy of Culture, Science, and Religion* (New
York, 1965).
41. Michael Novak, "The Religion of Paul Tillich," *Commentary*, XLIII
(April 1967), 53–55, 62.

an authentic American tradition. Those who had been brought up on the New England Transcendentalists could hear comforting echoes in the words of the new arrival from across the sea:

> Philosophical idealism in America had had a definitely Protestant tinge, and the many theologians and the few philosophers who still looked back nostalgically to . . . idealism were not ready to take the leap to Barth or Kierkegaard. Tillich met their needs perfectly. He did not propose a renaissance of idealism; he combined Schelling . . . with the most modern movements, spoke approvingly of everything that was avant garde, and, while acclaimed as an existentialist . . . , excelled in the art of obviating any either-or.[42]

Thus if Tillich's theological formulations frequently jarred his public, his ethics gave hope to people awash in a sea of relativism. His respect for what he named "the courage of despair," his search for "meaning beyond meaninglessness," won the attention of skeptics who would have scorned the reasoning of a conventional theologian. For in effect what Tillich did was to press unbelievers to give an answer to the question why they were not total ethical nihilists and to recognize in their own conduct the grounds of *their* ultimate concern.[43] And he did it in a way that was so liberated from asceticism, so overflowing with vitality and endorsement of the process of living in all its contradictory aspects, that he conquered the hearts of those who could find nothing beyond poetic meaning in his vocabulary. Misunderstanding or half-understanding sufficed for Americans athirst for affirmations and who were only too happy to take the leap beyond the verifiable which Tillich asked of them.

The other intellectual émigrés with concerns extending beyond the boundary of a single discipline had encountered a similar half-understanding in the lands of English speech. Readers thinking exclusively in the English language almost never succeeded in

---

42. Walter Kaufmann, "The Reception of Existentialism in the United States," special no. of *Salmagundi*, p. 88.
43. More particularly in *The Courage To Be* (New Haven, Conn., 1952), pp. 140, 142, 175, 178.

entering fully into the idea world of men whose deepest reflections continued to go on in the other language they had spoken as children. Even Wittgenstein, whose influence had been the greatest of the German- or Austrian-born of his generation and whose writings were unique in being published in parallel German and English texts—whose experiments with two languages in which he was almost equally fluent might have been expected to bridge, if any human being could do so, the gap between these universes of discourse—even Wittgenstein suffered the fate of transmutation by his adherents into far more of an Anglo-American analytic philosopher than he actually had been or had become.

This matter of language suggests an initial discrimination to be made in assessing the profit and loss to Central European thought from its sojourn across the Channel or the Atlantic. In spheres in which nuance of expression was not crucial—where the major terms employed were conventional or international, and meanings direct and unambiguous—exposure to Anglo-American intellectual life brought almost pure gain. For the natural sciences or for disciplines that approached them in precision of method, it is appropriate to speak of a fusion or symbiosis of thought. And the same is true of particular and empirical studies within a clearly defined range. The critics of fascism, for example, suffered no serious diminution of meaning in finding themselves obliged to publish their works in English. On the contrary, what they wrote became even more biting and specific from being cast in a language that lent itself to plain speaking.

In the speculative type of thinking, however, which the Germans had always considered their peculiar province, the fusion remained incomplete or aborted. When Neumann turned from the study of fascism to a broader investigation of the nature of authoritarian rule, he bogged down in conceptual difficulties consequent on his transitional situation between two incompatible styles of thought. When Erikson discovered his own newly won facility at writing English, the result was a hybrid style that was too elaborate for what he had to say. In contrast, by limiting himself to an austere and meticulous prose, Hartmann overcame more successfully than any of his generation mates the problem of writing in an unfamiliar tongue. At his hands, ego psychology—even in its farther reaches—came close to a precision of diction which rendered the shift from German to English harmless and possibly benign.

Hartmann was a shining exception. In general the Central Europeans who aimed at the speculative heights were well advised—as in the case of Horkheimer and Adorno—to stick to their native language. This is not to say that they derived no benefit from their stay in America. Far from it—Adorno went home a wiser person, more persuaded of the value of empirical research, more inclined to respect his intellectual adversaries. In common with many lesser men, his understanding had been enriched by an experience he had temperamentally resisted. And unlike the more pliant of the émigrés, he had taken to himself what his hosts had to offer without relinquishing his own philosophical patrimony.

It would be incorrect, then, to say that the sea change of Central European social thought, in widening its audience, had made it more superficial. But in altering its tone and its vocabulary, the transmutation did not develop that thought as much as might have been imagined. At a level of abstraction above the specific empirical study, it was difficult to detect how and where the émigré generation had surpassed the generation of their intellectual fathers. Of the major expatriates from Central Europe, Wittgenstein alone unmistakably "went beyond" the work of Freud and Weber.

The critics of fascism had never claimed to do so. Salvemini remained throughout his life untouched by the teachings of Germans and Austrians a half-generation older than he. Neumann at the time of his death had just come abreast of Freud. Mannheim and Marcuse and Fromm and a number of others conceived of themselves as having fused the Marxian and the Freudian traditions, but the product of such an admixture invariably proved to be fragmentary or elusive, eccentric or sentimental. Of all the synthesizers, Adorno put on the most dazzling performance, but his highest flights were forever being dragged to earth by the Hegelian ballast he refused to jettison. With a similar devotion, Hartmann and Erikson hung on to more of the strict Freudian inheritance than they required: in their sharply contrasting fashions, both oscillated between self-confident independence and fidelity to the founder of psychoanalysis. Their hesitation in this respect goes far to explain their failure to establish a viable canon for the psychoanalytic study of society. Ironically enough, ego psychology was at its best when it returned to early Freudian fundamentals. This was the baffling difficulty that a conscientious theoretician such as Hartmann faced: how was one to refine on a body of teaching whose most persuasive features were at the same time its most elemental?

If not in the elaboration of theory, then possibly in their speculations on language and value, the émigré generation saw farther than their predecessors. By the midcentury it was no longer intellectually feasible to treat human discourse in the summary fashion which had earlier seemed to suffice. The development in the meantime of two new social studies—linguistics and anthropology—had forced the more perceptive workers in other fields to subject their own notions of language to critical scrutiny. An intense focus on the forms of communication linked the achievement of Wittgenstein and Adorno to that of younger figures in France such as Merleau-Ponty and the structuralists. And in this reexamination it became apparent that words did not invariably offer—as in the "talking cure" of psychoanalysis—the path to understanding: music emerged as an alternative or even privileged mode of discourse.

Yet if one had resort to music, one evoked a realm in which meanings were never unambiguous. In such a perspective, the social thinker's aspiration to direct, one-to-one communicability dissolved; he found himself obliged to abandon Weber's conviction that in theory at least he could devise a sociological proof which a different investigator, raised in an alien culture, would acknowledge as correct. And through the same process of self-questioning, he was led to inquire more deeply into value systems at variance with the one he took for granted; he felt the urgency of an unremitting assessment of value—whether his own or another's—pressing against him from all sides. No longer, with Freud, could he dismiss morality as "self-evident" and get on with his "scientific" work; no longer, with Weber, could he entertain the hope of fully isolating such work from contamination by value judgments. His personal experience as an antifascist and an exile had thrust upon him the task of making values explicit in unfamiliar contexts where the methodological precepts of the immediate past provided uncertain guidance. Not the least of the accomplishments of the émigré generation was to have demonstrated to themselves and their successors how to discuss human affairs in a way that combined scholarly scruple with passionate ethical commitment. Intellectual honesty remained the social theorist's supreme ideal; but it was now coupled with the realization that its attainment depended on a self-awareness even more complex and ramifying than the masters of twentieth-century thought had imagined.

Index

ABOUT THE AUTHOR

H. Stuart Hughes was born in 1916 in New York City. He received his A.B. from Amherst College and his A.M. and Ph.D. from Harvard. In 1967 he was awarded an honorary L.H.D. by Amherst.

Mr. Hughes taught history at Brown University before he enlisted in the Army as a private in 1941. By 1944 he was Chief of the Research and Analysis Branch of the Office of Strategic Services in the Mediterranean theater; later he held the same post in Germany. He was relieved from active duty as a lieutenant colonel in 1946.

Since then he has been Chief of the State Department's Division of Research for Europe; Assistant Professor of History at Harvard; Associate Professor and Professor and head of the Department of History at Stanford; and, since 1957, Professor of History at Harvard, where in 1969 he was named Gurney Professor of History and Political Science. He also has been a Visiting Member of the Institute for Advanced Study at Princeton, a Fellow of the Center for Advanced Study in the Behavioral Sciences at Stanford, a Fellow of the American Academy of Arts and Sciences, and the holder of a Guggenheim Fellowship. He has twice been decorated by the Italian government, first for his war service, subsequently for his work in Italian historical studies. In 1967 he was Bacon Exchange Professor at the University of Paris (Nanterre).

Mr. Hughes is the author of eight previous books: three in the field of intellectual history: *Oswald Spengler: A Critical Estimate*, *Consciousness and Society*, and *The Obstructed Path*; two general histories: *The United*

States and Italy and *Contemporary Europe: A History;* and three volumes of essays: *An Essay for Our Times, An Approach to Peace,* and *History as Art and as Science.*

Mr. Hughes's public activities outside the university have included an Independent candidacy for the United States Senate from Massachusetts in 1962, and serving first as co-chairman and from 1967 to 1970 as sole chairman of SANE: A Citizens' Organization for a Sane World. He is married and has three children.